Children of Imprisoned Parents

ALSO OF INTEREST AND FROM MCFARLAND

African American Women with Incarcerated Mates:
The Psychological and Social Impacts of Mass Imprisonment
(Avon Hart-Johnson, 2017)

Children of Imprisoned Parents

A Workbook for Holistic Caregiver and Child Well-Being

AVON HART-JOHNSON *with*
GEOFFREY JOHNSON *and*
RENATA A. HEDRINGTON-JONES

McFarland & Company, Inc., Publishers
Jefferson, North Carolina

ISBN (print) 978-1-4766-8717-9
ISBN (ebook) 978-1-4766-5350-1

LIBRARY OF CONGRESS CATALOGING DATA ARE AVAILABLE

Front cover image: © Inna Reznik/Shutterstock

Printed in the United States of America

*McFarland & Company, Inc., Publishers
Box 611, Jefferson, North Carolina 28640
www.mcfarlandpub.com*

We dedicate this book to the many caregivers around the world who rearrange their lives and devote their energies to ensuring that children with incarcerated parents have the opportunity to grow, excel, and have a fair chance at succeeding in life. Supportive caregivers cultivate faith and hope in their children rather than seeing the world as a dark and painful experience. With this optimism, caregivers establish the template for their children to follow. Through positive experiences, children learn to dream big and find the silver lining in their lives. Attuned caregivers are the superheroes who stand in the gap and serve on the front lines of parenting.

Table of Contents

Part II. Tackling the Big Topics

Part III. Storybooks and Bibliotherapy

Preface

This workbook is designed to raise awareness about parental incarceration. Our goal is to promote holistic care and well-being for caregivers and children affected by incarceration. This book, *Children of Imprisoned Parents: A Workbook for Holistic Caregiver and Child Well-Being*, provides tailored interventions and activities. The workbook is a derivative of and companion to *Children of Imprisoned Parents: A Guide to Holistic Caregiver and Child Well-Being*, a textbook that explains in detail how children and families are impacted by family member imprisonment.

We created this workbook because we believe in the power of self-determination and resilience. We all may find, at some point in our lives, that we need a superhero to help find the silver lining. The parents or caregivers we refer to in this book are the superheroes, the adults who protect children from harm and shield them from danger. Caregivers range from parents, grandparents, siblings, aunts, uncles, and fictive kin to a host of others who provide guardianship to children.

Foundational Research

The guidebook and workbook are an outgrowth of a research study we conducted, titled *Children of Incarcerated Parents: Caregivers' Family Relations and Communication Strategies* [C-FRACS] (Hart-Johnson & Johnson, 2022) and documented in "*Mommy, I Want to Talk to My Dad*": *Exploring Parental Incarceration, Bibliotherapy, and Storybooks* (Hart-Johnson, et al., 2022). In this study, we, as the co-principal researchers and authors, explored caregiver-child communication and family dynamics related to parental incarceration using semi-structured interviews and grounded theory data analysis. The study was conducted in the Washington, D.C., metropolitan area (Maryland, Virginia, and all of Washington, D.C.). We share insights and themes gained from our primary research through the tailored workbook activities, which are designed to respond to the challenges faced by caregivers and their children (Hart-Johnson & Johnson, 2022). In this workbook, any reference to "Focus Group Caregiver" refers to the aforementioned study. See Appendix A for more detail.

Note to Audience | Users

Ultimately, the content will integrate nicely into academic domains and course-work where interest in children of incarcerated parents might intersect, including in areas of criminal justice, crisis intervention, family systems intervention, early childhood development, psychology, human and social services, law, and public policy.

Users of this workbook include but are not limited to

- caregivers, non-incarcerated parents, grandparents, siblings, guardians, relatives, non-kinship parents, and justice-aligned parents seeking to enhance communication skills and build secure bonds with children affected by parental incarceration;
- practitioners who provide direct and indirect services for caregivers and their families (e.g., mental health professionals, human services workers, social workers, counselors);
- educators and early childhood development students/specialists who contribute to shaping the minds of young children across the globe;
- facilitators, students, educators, and community advocates who work with families impacted by incarceration;
- corrections-based/justice-aligned facilitator-led parenting programs in jails, prisons, and detention facilities; and
- researchers who want to better understand and advance the literature in this domain.

Language and Comprehension: For the Adult Learner

- This workbook emphasizes and honors *andragogy*, the idea that adult learners have the ability to be self-directed and motivated in their own learning endeavors as well as the ability to engage in facilitated instruction using strength-based modalities (Lopez, 2023).
- We hope that all learners are invested in continuous growth and development. With that in mind, this curriculum was written to reach multiple audiences. The content offers learners of all backgrounds opportunities to learn new skills, advance comprehension, and deepen their knowledge related to the presented subjects.
- The content in this book is flexible and advances problem-solving, critical thinking, and self-paced reflection.
- Facilitators are encouraged to use this book and its prompts to advance

individual learning and/or to encourage a collaborative learning environment in group settings. *Caution is offered, when introducing personal analogies, metaphors, and individual testimonies to pair with and to advance learning through examples. Please ensure that facilitator examples align with the provided content to avoid inadvertent misinterpretation of the materials. Thank you for your understanding.*

Features of This Book

Each module is "self-contained" and each focuses on a specific topic, challenge, or phenomenon. The modules provide reference material: *additional resources* containing reading material, media sources, and relevant websites to enrich the learner's knowledge of the course content. These modules contain four sections comprising *section focus|case examples* to orient the reader on the topic; *section objectives*, which call out the goals of each section; overview, which is a brief summary of the section focus; and *foundational learning*, which gives background, applicable theory, supporting material, and/or insights. The *activities* are knowledge checks to reinforce foundational learning. The activities are designed to encourage engagement in role-play, critical thinking, and reflections of parent-child dynamics. Activity keys are provided for all exercises except where the learner is asked to use *critical thinking* or *critical reflection*. These reflective activities help learners to relate ideas and experience (theory and practice), understand and interpret the content, and formulate or apply presented material. Ultimately, the exercises give readers, caregivers, and their children a safe space to practice life skills.

Introduction

The test of the morality of a society is what it does for its children.
—Dietrich Bonhoeffer

If you are reading this book, chances are you care about children with incarcerated parents. Perhaps you are a caregiver or a practitioner with empathy and compassion toward this young population of children. For that sensitivity, we are grateful. We have written this workbook with you in mind. As researchers, advocates, authors, and practitioners, we are reminded by our work that many children worldwide are experiencing disrupted childhoods because of parental incarceration, along with other adversities and losses. We believe that these adversities can be minimized if not omitted from the lives of young children. The authors also acknowledge that there are many caregivers across the nation who are responding to these challenges, using strength-based practices, love and nurturing, and creating safe homes for children to thrive. We draw upon their knowledge and wisdom along with empirical literature to form the basis for this workbook.

This problem is significant. Approximately 22 million children worldwide have incarcerated parents (Sevenants & Wang, 2021). In the United States alone, one in 28 children experiences a mom or dad serving a sentence in jail, prison, or detention facilities (Prison Fellowship Ministries, 2018–2022). More than five million children have a parent on community corrections–based supervision (e.g., parole or probation, home detention). These statistics convey that 5.2 percent of America's children experience social conditions related to this phenomenon. One in five children with an incarcerated parent is under age five. Of the 2.7 million confined parents, approximately 40 percent have a child under ten years old (The National Institute of Corrections, 2020). Non-incarcerated parents or family members usually care for the children who are left behind. We refer to these individuals as *caregivers* throughout this text. Without intervention, affected children face the risk of adverse childhood experiences influencing, if not altering, their futures.

We believe in the power of hope and self-determination. However, hope without action is not effective in changing the trajectory of children's lives. Yet, the human spirit tends to look for good in seemingly deleterious conditions. This workbook exemplifies finding ways through strength-based interventions to build upon the grit and fortitude of the human spirit.

Familial Impacts

Incarceration of a parent is often only one of the multitude of challenges children and their caregivers face. Loss tends to bring about cascading impacts that affect the lives of families. These can be heartbreaking and are often not quantifiable—the loss of hopes, dreams, and shared experiences with loved ones. The confined parent likely will miss birthdays, milestone achievements, and important "firsts" and "lasts," like a child's first steps, graduations, funerals, and other significant events.

While remaining optimistic, the literature affirms that incarcerating one or more parents can set in motion events that can destabilize the family and the children. Protective actions can counteract or soften the impacts of these encounters.

The way incarceration affects one family may not affect another family in the same way. While it is understood that each family is unique in its structure and behavior, it is also recognized that the incarceration of a mother, father, or significant family member may disrupt the stability and functioning of the household. Financial strains associated with incarceration, such as attorney and court costs, bail, or the loss of a secondary income may pose burdens on household resources, adversely affecting the whole family.

Holistic Focus

Our strategies for effective caregiving are holistic. We combine knowledge of developmental, psychological, social, and environmental factors, while considering the uniqueness of each child. With this focus, caregivers and supportive adults can help steer a child's life course toward a healthy adulthood by providing constructive outlets for children. To safeguard children, adults must implement preventative measures to protect children's minds, bodies, and their futures. Therefore, a holistic approach to child well-being is necessary because these elements are all connected.

This workbook provides activities designed to help support caregiver-child well-being. We focus on the caregiver and the child because the child will likely endure adversity if the adult caretakers themselves are not emotionally, physically, or socially well. The workbook provides exercises to build resilience, improve communication, and create opportunities to enhance parenting strategies and family bonding.

Transitions and Stress on the Family System

Transition and change can be positive and/or disruptive. When incarceration separates families (e.g., for distances greater than 50 or so miles), families may wish to move to be closer to the prison. This geographic change might enhance connections. Other families may need to move to a less expensive dwelling due to a loss of income when a financially contributing member is incarcerated. These types of change may be disruptive since it can set in motion the need for the primary caregiver to take on extra responsibilities. For example, the caregiver may need to register children for different schools, change childcare providers, or move to unfamiliar neighborhoods. Just the stress of moving, for a child, can be significant. These transitions can contribute to disrupting the family normative routines (short- or long-term). Meanwhile, the children are often the last to know about forthcoming changes. Therefore, we designed modules to help plan for transitions with a focus on caregiver self-care and communication (Module 1 through 7), given that these changes can be stressful. The modules also place emphasis on parenting styles and provide considerations for developing social support and family networks to assist the family during times of need.

Young people require routine and stability to feel secure and safe. When lots of change and multiple transitions occur, this can be upsetting and stressful, depending on a child's age. Furthermore, for a child with an incarcerated parent, to face multiple losses and change can be destabilizing. Suddenly losing other significant relationships such as peers and friends, favorite teachers, the familiarity of the previous home, and persons, places, or things that offer security can be overwhelming. Each of these transitions represents a particular kind of loss, possibly resulting in grief (Module 2). Yet, there are ways to mitigate and perhaps minimize the potential harmful impacts. The thought-provoking activities in this workbook may help with these transitions.

Grief

Children tend to love unconditionally. Children with close bonds and attachments to their confined parents may grieve the parent when they are absent. Moreover, a child's grief may be difficult to recognize or identify unless the caregiver looks for the signs. Grief can be tricky to observe in children because they may not always appear to be grieving. This workbook provides examples of grief and activities for caregivers to explore with their children (Module 2).

Stress

Because excessive amounts of stress due to trauma (e.g., unrelenting change, having multiple caregivers, and unstable living conditions) can overburden and put children's mental and physical systems in overdrive. We provide insights on the body-brain connections during childhood development (Modules 3 to 5).

Young children may need caregivers or parents to help them regulate since they often lack the maturity to overcome these particular challenges. Life events eventually may provide children with the experience and subsequent confidence to survive all the various forms of disruption and transitions, thereby building resilience. However, children need the parents/caregivers to provide essential reassurance and assistance with developing coping strategies.

Child Development

Caregivers can help children build resilience and coping skills, based on their knowledge and understanding of child development trajectories and their understanding of expected milestones related to infancy, toddlerhood, preschooler years, and middle childhood. This workbook focuses on the important knowledge that can help users better understand the expected development of each age group (Module 3, Module 4, Module 5, and Module 6, respectively). Child development advances simultaneously in the areas of emotional, physical, cognitive, and social development. Each of the aforementioned modules provide foundational knowledge about the alignment between emotional (attachment, concepts of self, self-esteem, emotional intelligence, fear, mindfulness, trust-building, separation anxiety, and other constructs), physical (play, fine and gross motor skills), cognitive (brain), and social (life skills) development.

Caregiver-Child Communication

It may not be easy to tackle difficult topics with young children. A caregiver's communication with the affected child about their parent's incarceration may lag for many reasons. In our research, we found that when caregivers did not discuss the absence of parents, it was because (1) they lacked the resources or tools to facilitate communication or prompt discussion; (2) they were afraid that informing the children would influence emotional burdens; and (3) they did not feel confident about how much information to share aligned with age-appropriate language. Module 7 offers information and activities to respond to these communication challenges.

Our research also revealed four types of caregiver communication methods (see Module 7, Appendix C). The first approach is *Direct communication*. This mode of communication entails sharing information with the children but not giving granular detail about alleged parental crimes. *Indirect communication* entails avoiding the truth or creating alternative truths or stories about the parents. *Abstention* entails saying nothing at all. Finally, *Reflection* includes reviewing the shared information and determining if a "redo" or a "do-over" is necessary. Perhaps caregivers needed to provide clarification or to sequence the discussion of importance with the child, based on the child's maturity level.

Finally, communication and trust are the foundation of healthy family systems. Given that miscommunication could result in unintended consequences such as children developing trust issues, we offer interventions related to communication. Caregivers can use these strategies to help with discussions, based on their parenting style. We also offer a family planning tool that empowers families to develop privacy codes of conduct. This practice of establishing family guidelines might help set boundaries and delimiters for public discussion (Module 7).

All Hands on Deck

Support can be instrumental when families experience crisis. Incarceration of a parent generally disrupts the family system. This disruption can also affect children, typically the most vulnerable members of the family unit. By definition, minor children are children under 18 years of age. Given the potential vacuum that the absent parent creates in the family system, at times, the family roles become blurred, and, unintentionally, boundaries are crossed. At times, children may be expected to perform chores and responsibilities generally completed by parents or adults. Sometimes, children become the emotional confidant and sounding board. When this type of role juxtaposition infringes upon a child's capacity and ability to perform the tasks, it is called *parentification* (and/or boundary disturbances). The ambiguity of roles and blurred boundaries of responsibilities are covered, and we offer suggestions for seeking support networks (Module 8). In other words, an all-hands-on-deck approach is recommended to integrate internal and external support that balances roles, responsibilities and healthy boundaries.

The Importance of Play

All children deserve a chance at having a childhood that affords them love, safety, guidance, and education. Parents bear the responsibility of caring for the young children under their care. Play is an integral role in how children interpret, adjust to, and process their world (Module 9).

Play activities can promote social connections and opportunities where children build critical life skills. According to Lev Vygotsky, a child development psychologist, a child's social and cultural environment can influence their development. Children's social skills and development are generally integrated in play activities that foster engagement with others.

Risks and Protective Factors

While parental incarceration is fraught with risks detrimental to children, caregivers can introduce protective factors that offset these risks and build resilience with a keen focus on emotional intelligence (Module 10).

Because incarceration is considered one of the Adverse Childhood Experiences (ACEs) that a child might encounter, parents and caregivers are introduced to activities aligned with preventing or mitigating the associated risks. These exercises are designed to instill their children with resilience and coping strategies (Module 11).

Incarceration is widespread, yet some people do not understand its impact on families and children. Therefore, some children are at risk for feeling stigmatized, some experience bullying, and unfortunately, while rare, some children are at risk for suicide ideation. It is, therefore, important to share this understanding of the potential risks as well as prevention methods aligned with each phenomenon related to suicide (Module 12). Caregivers are advised to take all threats of external bullying and self-harm seriously. Resources are provided in the module for emergencies and preventative measures.

Anger

Children may experience a wide range of emotions related to a parent's absence and confinement. They may at the least become confused and concerned about the parent's status. Depending on a child's age, they may experience many different emotions that align with growing up. For instance, children may experience an array of new emotions, including anger (Module 13). They may feel frustrated one minute, afraid the next. Many of these emotions are normal. However, we highlight deviations from the norm to inform caregivers when behaviors may require intervention.

A Cause for Hope

Finally, as researchers and advocates, we understand how incarceration can leave adverse impacts on families and children who may already face life challenges. This work is critical; now is the time for all hands on deck. We can change the trajectory that researchers warn about, with everyone doing their part. In the past, scholars warned that children of incarcerated parents were at risk for antisocial behaviors, future mental health problems, academic challenges, and even criminal behaviors (Dallaire et al., 2010; Johnston et al., 1995; Christian, 2009). While these children face such risks as fractured family systems, limited engagement with their confined parents, and stigma, recent literature counters past thinking by instilling hope (e.g., Ashmitha 2020; Kahler, 2021). Advanced research strongly argues that children can overcome adverse risks and odds with caregivers' protective measures. There is reason for optimism and finding silver linings in perceivably dire circumstances (Module 15). This workbook provides assistance to accomplish this quest.

Bibliotherapy-Based Children's Books

Literary stories using bibliotherapeutic tools (using storybooks for problem-solving, analogizing life circumstances, and promoting well-being) can have multiple benefits for caregivers and children. Tailored and specific storybooks can provide parents with the tools to navigate these feelings and help children to learn about emotions. Notably, this modality is aligned with answering our second research interest regarding how children's books could support caregivers' discussion about parental incarceration.

The ancillary storybooks offered here describe relatable characters, allowing children to draw upon their own imaginations and feelings to identify the characters in the books with circumstances similar to their own lives. In these storybooks, literary devices (e.g., suspense and foreshadowing) lead the readers on a journey of events unfolding in stories related to family-member imprisonment. The plots are realistic, logical, sometimes humorous, and they elicit empathy, sadness, happiness, and joy. Sensory elements bring each story to life, enhanced by metaphor and illustrations. These books can be paired with this workbook or used as stand-alone resources.

Storybooks can help children find hope. Through tailored stories, children learn they are not alone in their circumstances. The name of the modality aligned with using storybooks for problem-solving, promoting healing, and advancing well-being is *bibliotherapy*. Using bibliotherapy principles, readers and their children pair the storybooks with interactive workbook activities to enhance communication, increase socio-emotional competencies, and build comprehension skills (Modules 16 through 20). Each storybook focuses on parental incarceration, using age-appropriate scenarios. Each of these books is available through Amazon.com.

The children's books are:

Hart-Johnson, A. (2021). *Baby Star Finds Happy*. A Story About Parental Incarceration. Finding a silver lining when a parent goes to prison or jail. Extant-One Publishing. ISBN 9798775914110.

Hart-Johnson, A. (2017). *Jamie's Big Visit*. Grownup Timeout. Prison Visits and Parent's Incarceration. Extant-One Publishing. ISBN 9798702126258

Hedrington-Jones, R.A. (2021). *Truth and The Big Dinner*. A Story About Parental Incarceration. Finding a silver lining when a parent goes to prison or jail. Extant-One Publishing. ISBN 9780996741026.

Johnson, G. (2021). *Rocko's Guitar*. A Story About Parental Incarceration. Finding a silver lining when a parent goes to prison or jail. Extant-One Publishing. ISBN 9798732160369.

Story Summaries

Baby Star Finds "Happy," by Dr. Avon Hart-Johnson [ideal for children ages 0 through 5]: *Baby Star Finds "Happy"* is a story about a child's journey embracing friendship, family, and forgiveness when a mother goes to jail. Baby Star learns that sadness is a normal response when a person who is loved leaves the family. She also learns that she is not at fault for her mother's absence.

Rocko's Guitar, by Dr. Geoff Johnson [ideal for children ages 7 and under*]: *Rocko's Guitar* is a story about a young boy who adores his dad, a budding musician. Rocko's bond with his father strengthens when his dad gives him a cherished guitar for his birthday. However, their relationship must withstand an unexpected separation due to Dad's incarceration.

Truth and the Big Dinner, By Dr. Renata Hedrington-Jones [ideal for children ages 10 and under]: *Truth and the Big Dinner* is a story about "Truth," a little girl who is just beginning to explore her self-identity and self-image. To her, the big dinner is a day that she can show off her new hairdo and rekindle her affectionate relationship with her mom. She loves her big family. However, the family has concealed a big secret: Mommy is incarcerated and not coming home for the big dinner.

*Jamie's Big Visit*** By Dr. Avon Hart-Johnson [ideal for children ages 10 and under]: This book chronicles Jamie the Bear's experience as he learns about grown-up time-out (incarceration). This guide helps a parent or caregiver to explain and minimize the possible challenges associated with a child's first prison visit.

*We overlap the age groups for these stories to indicate that these books can be used for multiple age groups in most cases.
**The book *Jamie's Big Visit* publication predates the associated research study.

References

Ashmitha, P., & Annalakshmi, N. (2020). Understanding pathways to resilience among children of incarcerated parents. *Indian Journal of Positive Psychology, 11*(2), 75–87.

Bailey, B.A. (2021). *Conscious discipline: Building resilient classrooms.* Oviedo, FL: *Loving Guidance.*

Christian, S.M. (2009, March). *Children of incarcerated parents. Washington, D.C.:* National Conference of State Legislatures.

Dallaire, D.H., Ciccone, A., & Wilson, L.C. (2010). Teachers' experiences with and expectations of children with incarcerated parents. *Journal of Applied Developmental Psychology, 31*(4), 281–290.

Hart-Johnson, A., & Johnson, G. (2022). Caregivers' family relations assessment and communication strategies. *Science Publishing Group, 11*(5), 157–168. https://www.sciencepublishinggroup.com/article/10.11648/j.pbs.20221105.12.

Hart-Johnson, A., & Johnson, G. (2025). *Children of imprisoned parents: A holistic guide to caregiver and child well-being.* McFarland.

Hart-Johnson, A., Johnson, G., & Hedrington-Jones, R. (2022). "Mommy, I want to talk to my dad": Exploring parental incarceration, bibliotherapy, and storybooks. *Open Journal of Social Sciences, 10*(11), 391–418.

Johnston, D., & Gabel, K. (1995). Incarcerated parents. In Johnston, D., & Gabel, K., *Children of incarcerated parents,* 3–20. New York: Lexington.

Kahler, M.M. (2021). *Identifying resiliency and protective factors that lead to successful life outcomes after experiencing parental incarceration: A phenomenological study* (Doctoral dissertation, Northcentral University).

Lopez, A. (2023). *Sunday morning coffee: Pedagogy vs. andragogy.* https://www.pasttheedges consulting.com/blog/pedagogy-vs-andragogy?ss_source=sscampaigns&ss_campaign_id=650 6f8c5bfa2ee0835d09022&ss_email_id=6506f91125c7990d3ae0d71f&ss_campaign_name= Pedagogy+vs+Andragogy&ss_campaign_sent_date=2023-09-17T13%3A03%3A21Z.

The National Institute of Corrections. (2020). *Communicating with families and children in correctional facilities; Part 2.* https://nicic.gov/communicating-families-and-children-correctional-facilities-part-2.

Prison Fellowship Ministries. (2018–2022). Prison fellowship ministries. https://solutionsbank.candid.org/solutions/prison-fellowship-addressing-over-incarceration-by-transforming-the-justice-system.

Sevenants, K.M., & Wang, H. (2021). (2019–2021). Global estimate of the number of children with incarcerated parents (Version 1). [Dataset]. https://inccip.org/resources/.

Caregiving and Children's Holistic Well-Being

Understanding Caregiving and Children's Essential Needs

MODULE FOCUS

- Section 1.0. Putting on the Caregiver's Oxygen Mask, First. Understanding caregiving and self-care in the context of parental incarceration.
- Section 1.1. Caregiving with Mindfulness. Explore caregiver self-care through mindful focus and self-compassion.
- Section 1.2. Parenting Styles. Analyze parenting styles and grandparent kindship care.
- Section 1.3. Caregiving and Managing Change. Examine the caregiver role related to facilitating change and transition.

Resources

Read Guidebook: Hart-Johnson and Johnson (2025) | Chapter 1, "Caregivers, Put on Your Oxygen Mask, First."

Additional Resources

The Centers for Disease Control and Prevention. (2020). *Activity Page*. Retrieved from https://www.cdc.gov/childrenindisasters/pdf/coping_activity_page_english-p.pdf.

The Centers for Disease Control and Prevention. (2020). *Helping Children Cope with Emergencies*. Retrieved from https://www.cdc.gov/childrenindisasters/helping-children-cope.html?msclkid=0b95b3c5c63311ec9065dc56be7b339f.

Moran, D.J., & Ming, S. (2020). The mindful action plan: Using the MAP to apply acceptance and commitment therapy to productivity and self-compassion for behavior analysts. *Behavior Analysis in Practice*, 1–9.

Play-it-through-UK. (2019). Retrieved from https://play-it-through.co.uk/2019/09/12/emotional-first-aid-trauma-tapping-technique.

Introduction

Caregivers could change the world one life at a time, starting with the children under their care. These guardians have the potential to nurture, teach, and shape children into wonderful human beings. Providing care for children with incarcerated parents can be challenging for various reasons. However, understanding these challenges provides a platform to mitigate potential adversities, especially when informed about potential interventions.

While caregiving can be demanding, it can be managed using tools and resources that contribute to caregivers managing stress through self-care practices. In this section, we present exercises that address self-care and highlight self-awareness. Mindfulness and self-awareness not only benefit the caregivers but also may have a positive impact on the children. This section also delves into different parenting styles and raises awareness of how parenting practices can be enhanced through strength-based parenting approaches. A focus on grandparenting, raises the awareness of the instrumental role they are playing in the lives of affected children. Finally, the module considers change management—an essential aspect of minimizing the adverse impacts of change and transitions related to the incarceration of a family member.

Section 1.0. Putting on the Caregiver Oxygen Mask, First

Section Focus | Case Example

Caregiver Self-Care

The mind, body, and emotions are affected by stress. Significant changes in the family system can bring on stress associated with unknowns, lack of control, and general anxiety of not having enough information to make an informed decision. These are typical scenarios associated with stressors of everyday life, complicated by family-member incarceration. Caring for children under these circumstances can be challenging. Caregivers may find that they put the needs of others before their own. Self-care can be the antidote to these dilemmas.

Section Objectives

- ☐ Learn about the importance of caregiver self-awareness and self-care
- ☐ Understand the importance of prioritizing personal health
- ☐ Critically reflect on rituals and routines to support well-being
- ☐ Critically reflect and identify ways that caregivers can help children to de-stress

Overview

Les Brown, a prominent motivational speaker from the United States, once said, "Ask for help, not because you are weak, but because you wish to remain strong." Remaining strong for others requires attunement toward personal health and well-being. Caring for young children can bring both joy and challenges—all requiring energy. As many caregivers are aware, this role comes with a significant responsibility for the well-being of children. Caregivers often make substantial sacrifices, adjusting their home environments, budgets, and schedules, and even revising retirement plans to meet their children's needs. These adjustments can become the primary focus of caregivers' priorities. As a result, they may overlook the need to care for themselves—the very vessel needed to support others. Using the analogy of flight attendants, "put your oxygen mask on first, before helping others."

Foundational Learning

Prioritizing personal health is essential for overall well-being. Self-care is more than grooming and exercise. It also entails managing arising difficulties. Stress management and self-care go hand in hand. Moreover, monitoring and understanding personal health require cultivating self-awareness. A daily check-in routine can enhance self-awareness, involving emotional status, physical assessment, and an overall well-being evaluation. Practicing self-awareness might involve starting each morning by asking yourself, "How do I feel?" Tuning into your emotional, physical, and spiritual well-being can provide opportunities to address issues before they escalate. A mindfulness practice could include affirmations like, "I am present, accepting my feelings with self-love and self-compassion, ready to embrace each day anew." Moran and Ming (2020) propose self-directed activities through a mindful action plan (MAP). The steps involve: (1) being present; (2) affirming personal values; (3) committed action; (4) recognizing oneself in the present moment; (5) diffusion [observing thoughts without being controlled by them]; and (6) acceptance.

Scientific studies remind us that stress can contribute to negative health outcomes (Kivimäki & Steptoe, 2018). Stress may lead to conditions like high blood pressure, diabetes, and heart disease (Rainforth et al., 2007). Self-awareness practices empower individuals to focus on preventive strategies, taking intentional steps toward achieving physical, mental, spiritual, and social wellness. Establishing self-care routines can promote a healthy lifestyle that leads to optimism. These routines might involve responding to concerns identified during self-awareness check-ins.

As suggested, seeking support is not a sign of weakness, but rather a means of sustaining one's strength and wherewithal. Informal support, such as social engagement, can serve as another outlet for healing. This form of connection may involve trusted confidants and provide the benefits of interpersonal engagement. Trusted friends and family can offer comfort during high-stress times and share ideas to alleviate concerns.

Additionally, spiritual or mindfulness routines might include intentional moments of stillness and silence. Carving out time in daily routines may help individuals to appreciate the present beauty of life (e.g., cultivate gratitude and find new meaning in current circumstances that offer caregivers and their families stress relief bolstered by a sense of purpose).

Finally, here are some general tips for self-care and de-stressing:

Be kind to yourself • Give yourself a pep talk • Encourage yourself • Name your talents and gifts • Forgive yourself • Honor yourself • Mother and nurture yourself • Be empathetic when reflecting on your journey • Give yourself permission for a fresh start every day.

ACTIVITY 1

Caregiving & Children's Essential Needs

Sometimes, situations arise that are beyond the control of family members. Lack of control sometimes feels uncomfortable, stressful, and even bewildering. Establishing routines can provide stability. Predictability can help reduce the stress of the unknown and the ongoing changes for caregivers and children. For example, family members cannot control court outcomes for a parent facing incarceration. However, the family can develop a regimen of responding to the crisis by managing their sphere of influence and recognizing what is outside of their purview to change. Self-care regimens can help minimize stress related to negative news and feeling hopeless. By focusing on what is possible, family members can develop a sense of agency or empowerment.

For this activity, consider the previously mentioned self-care practices.

☐ Critically reflect upon self-care rituals for each of the following categories [Domains] listed in the Table 1.0 Caregiver Self-Care Rituals.

☐ Note at least one ritual and/or practice that might enhance self-care for each category in the table labeled "[Rituals or Practice Ideas]." For example, self-directed morning meditation or yoga practice rituals might enhance *emotional* well-being, or a walk in the park might reduce *physical* stress. These commitments also help to establish a schedule and predictable patterns for children to model.

Please note that there is no answer key for this critical thinking exercise.

Table 1.0. Caregiver Self-Care Rituals

Domain	*Ritual or Practice Ideas*
Emotional	
Physical	
Social	

ACTIVITY 1.1.

Children need self-care too. Children learn primarily from their caregivers' behavior and tutelage about responding to stressful situations. These conditions can serve as opportunities to teach children problem-solving and self-care skills. When caregivers are having a stressful day, their children likely know. Children might be stressed, as well. While stressors in life are commonplace, continuous or extreme amounts of stress can be overwhelming for young children. Caregivers can help.

For this activity, consider ways to help children de-stress. Strategies might include engaging children's creativity. Using the arts and creative skills can offer caregivers and children emotional release and allow shared time together. The Centers for Disease Control and Prevention (2020) recommendations:

Step 1: Consider ways to introduce routine and consistency in the lives of your children and family.

Step 2: Take a moment to practice breathing exercises (breathing in through the stomach and breathing out twice as long [for this exercise, ask children to pretend they are breathing into a balloon]). Check in with yourself and your children, asking them about how they are feeling. Where do these feelings show up in the body? Make note of these emotions, differentiating when these emotions subside or escalate. What worked to make you or your children happy or feel better? These are the steps that can be repeated when feeling stressed.

Step 3: Now consider ideas to help you and your children de-stress. In Table 1.0.1., name activities that you can implement to help children de-stress, providing at least *one strategy per category*.

Table 1.0.1. Caregiver-Child Self-Care Rituals

Domain	*Ritual or Practice Ideas*
Emotional	
Physical	
Social	
Spiritual or Mindfulness	

Please note that there is no answer key for this critical thinking exercise.

Section 1.1. Caregiving with Mindfulness

Section Focus | Case Example

WHO'S CARING FOR THE CAREGIVER?

"Thank God, I have a family around me to lift me up and to support me in times of need. With something that deep, it just doesn't go away."
—Focus Group Caregiver

Section Objectives

- ☐ Learn about caregiver self-care and self-compassion alternatives
- ☐ Review and assess caregiver resources (Appendix F)

Overview

By definition, *caregiving* means looking out for others and taking care of their needs. Caregivers who have an optimistic outlook and have learned to balance their emotions may be well suited for the task of supporting others. To master the skill of achieving equilibrium (a balanced life), it takes practice. Caring for children who are experiencing challenges can be concerning. Caregivers may feel that, at times, they fully understand the needs of the children in their care and have a firm grip on the household. At other times, however, they may feel doubtful, and isolated in their role. These feelings are human, and they are normal. Remember, new conditions might be stressful because of the unknowns. These are signs that self-care and self-compassion are warranted.

When feelings of being overwhelmed dominate, it may be difficult for caregivers to realize there are multiple outlets available for support. One step involves taking a personal inventory of daily self-talk and thoughts. Mindfulness practices can help caregivers to remain focused on self-care and self-compassion.

Foundational Learning

O'Leary (2021) advises, there are a few actions that parents can take to integrate self-compassion in daily mindfulness practices. These reminders include the following self-care and self-compassion considerations:

Remember: no caregiver is perfect. Accept the notion that perfection is not possible nor sustainable. Setting the bar too high sets false expectations. Recognize that you are striving to use your skills, intuition, knowledge, and compassion to raise children who need you. There is no one grading your progress harder than you are grading yourself. Use self-compassion as you would offer compassion to a true friend.

Be kind to yourself. Each day, you have an opportunity to begin again. With this new possibility and focus, yesterday's mistakes are behind you. Focus on incremental goals for the day ahead. Expect delays or mistakes. It is human to err. Be forgiving and treat yourself with kindness. Speak to yourself with loving, forgiving self-talk and reinforce your own self-love by affirming you are worthy of self-love.

Remember you are not alone (There's an app for that). Even in a seemingly isolated world, you are not alone. There are caregiver support groups that meet in person; others are virtual connections from around the world where they meet using a virtual meeting format. A Google search, Eventbrite query, or a social media search for support groups might reveal private groups or memberships to forums of interest. These groups are usually free of charge. or they may ask for a donation or nominal fee. Support could also entail trusted friends and family. Google Play and Apple Store also offer virtual tools that are encouraging and uplifting (see Section 8.3 Support Inventory for support group evaluation criteria).

Second, third, fourth, fifth chances are all new beginnings. Give yourself as many chances as you need to get it right. You are not striving for perfection; you are striving to care for yourself so that your caregiving experience can be meaningful and optimal. If you are tired, bitter, worried, frantic, fuzzy or not fully present, chances are you will make mistakes, overlook responsibilities, and feel even worse. Remember, it is okay to start over again.

Recognize your humanness. Realize that you are human and that your worries, concerns, stressors are all a part of human nature. You will encounter stress or situations for which you do not have the answers. There will be times that you are happy and sad all in the same day. Embrace life as an opportunity to keep striving. This teaches children also how to rebound and deal with uncertainty. Parent by using optimism and logic rather than fear and unplanned strategies.

Care for yourself, kindly. There is only one you. No matter what your image, physical stature, intellect, personality, quirks, strengths, or constitution, love yourself, fully and embrace your uniqueness. In the final analysis, no one will love you the way you can love yourself, unconditionally. Self-love and self-compassion work hand in hand. Find ways to embrace your uniqueness.

See Appendix F under caregivers' resources (self-care).

ACTIVITY 2

Caregiving & Children's Essential Needs

For this activity, reflect on content covered thus far in Module 1. Recall mindfulness practices identified in the previous section. Consider the importance of personal well-being. Caregivers who take care of others need to be psychologically, physically, and socially well, themselves. First, address the questions; then think of a ritual, mindfulness routine, self-care (SC) practice, or an activity that contributes to your well-being. In Table 1.1.0 Rituals, place an "X" in the "I practice this activity or routine at least once a week" column. If you need more self-care focus in the identified area, then place an "X" in the last column. Consider those areas marked with an "X" areas for self-care goal setting.

Table 1.1.0. Rituals

Question/Statement	Briefly Name Your SC or Mindfulness Practice	I practice this activity weekly.	I need more focus in this area.
My self-care routine considers emotional, physical, and social well-being.			
My pleasurable activities are?			
My stress-reducers are?			
My mindfulness practice that helps me to relax is?			
My favorite family activity entails?			
When I am in need, I…?			
I get rid of negativity by…?			
I motivate myself by…?			
My goals/bucket list of activities are my priority?			
I ask for support or help by…?			
I am proud of my ability to…?			

Consider the placement of your "X's." If you find that the majority of placement is in the "I need more self-care focus in this area" column, then now might be an opportunity to create self-care rituals and set some small goals. These routines of personal attention can help enrich your life and contribute to self-actualization (becoming all that you believe you are capable of becoming). Take a moment to note in this section, ideas on how to increase self-care rituals. Perhaps, a gradual introduction to setting small self-care goals is a beginning. A routine as simple as a morning stretch, completing a crossword puzzle once a week, or taking a moment to enjoy the morning, afternoon, or evening outdoors atmosphere are all worthy of consideration. Remember, each day is a new beginning and an opportunity to set new goals. Setting goals should not introduce guilt, but rather invite opportunities to remain optimistic. Please note that there is no answer key for this critical thinking exercise.

Notes:

Section 1.2. Parenting Styles

Section Focus | Case Example

SALLY LEARNS TO COOK

Sally had just turned seven years old. Sally's "Granny" is 78 years old and is the primary caregiver for Sally and her two siblings (two and four years old, respectively). Sally's mother and father are both incarcerated. "Granny" tries to keep up with the young children, but it is difficult mustering the energy to care for them. Sally is a big help; she fetches Granny's cane when needed. Sally sometimes changes the two-year-old's diaper. Sally seems mature beyond her years. Sally and the children watch television as much as they like. Granny does not want to impose unnecessary rules because the children have been through tough times. The children are allowed to eat whatever and whenever, they want if it is available. Grandma and Sally get along well. Sometimes, Granny tells Sally about her worries and concerns about the incarcerated parents. Sally sometimes responds with confusion, but Granny thinks Sally is mature enough to handle the discussion. On Saturday night, Sally decided that she would make dinner for her siblings. This meal preparation was the first time Sally had cooked. The menu was popcorn and hot dogs.

Section Objectives

☐ Deepen an understanding of kinship care and grandparent caregiving
☐ Learn to differentiate between parenting styles
☐ Critically reflect on the importance of using intentional parenting practices and parenting styles

Overview

Parenting styles are considered general practices related to raising children. These styles can be applied by parents as well as grandparents. Given the growing trend of grandparents raising children impacted by incarceration, this section focuses on grandparenting.

It can be a wonderful experience taking care of grandchildren. Sometimes. these children seem mature, well beyond their years. They tend to share their youthful energy that inspires smiles and love. With all of this goodness, there may also be tasks that require caregivers who are grandparents to develop strategies that consider children's youth and maturity.

Taking in minor grandchildren with incarcerated parents may call for physically and emotionally prepared grandparents. According to the North Dakota Post Adopt Network (2020), feelings of apprehension are normal as grandparents adjust their lives to the needs of young children in the home. Some grandparents may feel unprepared for the resultant feelings aligned with parental incarceration, including anger, guilt, grief, anxiety, and frustration associated with the matter. At the same time, caregivers may feel gratitude for the opportunity to bond with grandchildren, not wanting to hinder the relationship in any way. They may fear setting rules, holding difficult discussions that might risk causing any kind of emotional pain and/or confusion. These sentiments may influence their parenting/caregiver styles.

Foundational Learning

Kinship Care and Caregiving. *Sally Learns to Cook* provides a practical framework to examine the concepts of kinship care and grandparent caregiving. In this context, these terms describe the phenomena of grandparents raising their children's children. In the case example, Sally's grandmother provides kinship care and has taken over parenting responsibilities. The grandmother assumes the primary caregiver role for all of the children since the incarceration of both parents. Sally's grandmother is not alone in her circumstances. In the United States, approximately 2.7 million grandparents are raising their grandchildren (U.S. Census Bureau, 2019). Grandparents are often at retirement age, potentially have health challenges because of their advanced years, and they may live on fixed incomes. If not managed, each of these considerations can contribute to accumulated stress.

Intentional Parenting. Grandparents and other caregivers can use intentional parenting practices to help children build coping and resilience competencies while reducing personal stress. These techniques might also ease the burden of new caregiving roles. Basic strategies include of intentional parenting and resilience building include: (Australian Christian College, 2020): (1) helping children develop strong and positive interpersonal relationships; (2) encouraging children to develop a solid sense of self and independence; (3) assisting children with strategies to build emotional regulation; and (4) allowing children trial-and-error opportunities, to take risks and learn from mistakes. Additionally, parents should, among other things ensure that children: (1) engage in physical activity, (2) receive proper medical care, (3) eat balanced meals, and (4) receive attuned parenting.

Establishing Healthy Boundaries. As the excerpt calls out, Sally is seven years of age. After several years of having an empty nest, grandparents may wonder how to care for young children. It could be challenging for grandparents to raise children at a young and inquisitive age (three to seven years). Children at this age are eager to become their caregiver's helper. Some children seem to be advanced, both cognitively and physically. Children in Sally's age range should be able to follow basic instructions and perform simple chores. Grandparents can help children advance their life skills and overall well-being by remaining committed to setting boundaries and while enhancing their abilities. Setting healthy boundaries can ensure that children take on chores aligned with their capacities. Setting boundaries can also ensure that caregivers get a little help from the children while also being attuned to what might be overwhelming for young people. Assigning age-appropriate chores can help children develop skills. Additionally, during times of stress, all family members may feel empowered with a sense of agency and that they are doing their part to help.

Parenting Styles. Parenting styles are aligned with caregiving, intentional parenting, and boundary setting. Caregivers/parents may have unique styles and methods of caregiving. Identifying one's parenting styles may reduce stress. A caregiver's parenting style may dictate how they engage with their children. There are three types of parenting styles to consider in this section: authoritative, permissive, and authoritarian. While the list provides general descriptors of parenting styles, parents are not static in their caregiving behavior. For example, there may be times when caregivers lean towards authoritative parenting and are more permissive at other times.

1. Authoritative Parenting:
   a. Sets clear rules.
   b. Uses age-appropriate language to express rules, boundaries, and expectations.
   c. Uses self-control, models appropriate behavior, manages stress.
   d. *Effective role to parent children.* Uses love, support, and positive engagement along with a strength-based parenting approach.
2. Permissive Parenting:
   e. Rules are unclear, inconsistent, confusing, or avoided.
   f. Children are dependent on the parent/caregiver, who is more of a friend than a parent.
   g. *The role is ineffective parenting,* where children might have a great deal of freedom, loose boundaries, and have little structure and security. Children may become rebellious and impulsive. Children are denied the opportunity to problem-solve through practiced positive discipline.
3. Authoritarian Parenting:
   h. "Helicopter" parents with strict rules and no in-between.
   i. Use of coercion, rude language, dictatorship, punishment and threatening children with punitive or manipulative practices.
   j. *Parenting is ineffective and is fear-based.* Children are likely to demonstrate hostility and aggression. They may model parents' negative behaviors. Children may experience a great deal of stress. The attachment style of these parents may be distant, forming disorganized attachments.

ACTIVITY 3

Caregiving & Children's Essential Needs

For this activity, reflect on Section 1.2 content covered thus far. Review *Sally Learns to Cook*. Consider Granny's condition and her new responsibilities of caring for three children. Select a parenting style or a combination of styles that best match Granny's Style of parenting from the brief information provided in the case example. Complete this activity as an individual or group activity. Note the parenting style by placing an "X" (authoritative, permissive, or authoritarian), then discuss or consider the strengths and opportunities to enhance the skill to benefit both the parent and the child in the table below. Your reflective ideas can be noted in a journal, digital notebook, or paper source. Please note that there is no answer key for this critical thinking exercise. Learners can consider *parenting styles*, noted in foundational learning. *Note: Facilitators may use this exercise for group engagement by incorporating materials such as a whiteboard or flipchart to record learners' responses.*

Action	Permissive	Authoritative	Authoritarian
Granny is a loving, supportive caregiver.			
Granny takes in the children even though she is older and relies on a cane to walk.			
Granny lets Sally change the baby's diaper.			
Granny does not want to impose unnecessary rules on the children.			
Granny allows the children to eat whatever and whenever they want.			
Granny shares her worries and concerns with seemingly mature Sally.			

Section 1.3. Caregiving and Managing Change

Section Focus | Case Example

BIG SIS

Maria had always lived with her father, never remembering or knowing her biological mother. Maria's whole world changed when her father suddenly went to prison. Moving in with Big Sis the next day was emotionally devastating for Maria. *Big Sis* was her dad's friend and Maria's godmother. Maria's familiar friends, neighborhood, and her dad were now absent from her life. Big Sis had never raised a child.

Section Objectives

- ☐ Learn about the significance of change and transition
- ☐ Gain knowledge about stress-reduction strategies for children
- ☐ Critically reflect on methods of managing change

Overview

Humans are conditioned to deal with a reasonable amount of change. However, frequent change can introduce added stress and insecurities because of the newness of transitions. Neuman (1998) indicated that individuals never grow too old for the need to feel secure. He further posited that people are naturally resistant to change because of fear of the unknown. In the case example, Big Sis, Maria likely feared the changes occurring in her life without having a say in the decision-making. This appears natural and normal. Part of Maria's fear is fear of lacking control over her future. She may also worry about her non-kinship caregiver's parenting style since the caregiver is unfamiliar with Maria's daily habits. Children like Maria generally have no control over what adults decide for their lives. Children with incarcerated parents may face new family arrangements that might alter their sense of normalness and comfort. Clarity can offer children peace of mind.

Foundational Learning

Change can introduce opportunities that feel good or are challenging (Derler & Ray, 2019). Derler and colleague posited that change is hard because our brains favor predictability. Consider how change might affect children who have formed significant attachments to persons, places, and things associated with childhood and their home dwelling (referred to as symbolic attachments). It may be difficult to leave these significant attachments behind if transition calls for moving to a new home. Many children of incarcerated parents face transition in their environments because of the complications of parental incarceration. As noted, parental incarceration may call for lifestyle modifications. Change can be overwhelming and frightening.

Planning and preparing children for change can help them gain "buy-in" and allow them to see the good in the transition. In the case example, *Big Sis*, Maria does not have a long history of being cared for by a caregiver other than her father. Maria is likely devastated to lose her father to incarceration. Additionally, she must move into a new home. Big Sis has no parenting experience and may hold concerns about understanding Maria's moods, behavior, and how to address her needs. One way to better understand Maria is to ask her how she feels. Additionally, inquire about her history (likes, dislikes, and habits). Big Sis can spend time with Maria, building interpersonal connections through communication and using activities that foster engagement and opportunities for building attunement. Big Sis might help Maria adjust by applying specific stress-reducing change management strategies.

Change Management Strategies. Neuman (1998) indicated that children might feel a sense of ease if the caregivers reinforce that

- the caregiver is there for them, and they will always have their prior family even though the incarcerated parent is not present.
- the sense of "family" means being loved and cared for no matter where the parents live. The incarcerated parent can let children know that a new caregiver arrangement is taking place.
- the absence of Dad (and/or Mom) does not define the child's worthiness.
- the caregiver can share that they may not know everything about childrearing, but they are willing to learn because they care.

Stress Reducing Strategies. Managing change amid crises helps alleviate stress. For instance, planning for transitions can include understanding children's feelings and ideas regarding a residential move and a new caregiver. Try to minimize adverse impacts when change is unavoidable. Precautions include:

- If possible, hold a meeting to discuss new living arrangements.
- Inform the child about their new caregiver.
- Learn about the child's health habits and personal history.
- Help the child to emotionally prepare for the move by giving them a heads-up.
- Understand the significance of the child's relationships and possessions (symbolic attachments).
- Invite the child to assist in the preparation of their new personal space (e.g., helping to decide the bedroom setup) in the home.

ACTIVITY 4

Caregiving & Children's Essential Needs

Reflect upon the case example, Big Sis, and review Section 1.3 to address the following questions. Provide brief answers or discuss in a group setting.

1. What stress-reducing steps can *Big Sis* take to alleviate Maria's emotional distress?

2. How can Big Sis learn about Maria's habits and history?

3. What can Big Sis do to prepare her home environment for the new relationship?

4. What, if anything, can Maria's father (who is currently incarcerated) do to support this change?

See Answer Key for Section 1.3, Activity 4, after Module 1 Reference list.

Notes:

References

Australian Christian College (2020). *Key strategies to build resilience*. Retrieved from https://www.acc.edu.au/blog/build-resilience-in-children/

The Centers for Disease Control and Prevention. (2020). *Activity Page*. Retrieved from https://www.cdc.gov/childrenindisasters/pdf/coping_activity_page_english-p.pdf.

Derler, A. & Ray, J. (2019). *Why change is so hart-and how to deal with it*. Retrieved from https://neuroleadership.co.in/2019/12/12/why-change-is-so-hard-and-how-to-deal-with-it.

Hart-Johnson, A., & Johnson, G. (2022). Caregivers' family relations assessment and communication strategies. *Science Publishing Group*, 11(5), 157–168. https://www.sciencepublishinggroup.com/article/10.11648/j.pbs.20221105.12.

Kivimäki, M., & Steptoe, A. (2018). Effects of stress on the development and progression of cardiovascular disease. *Nature Reviews Cardiology*, 15(4), 215–229.

Moran, D.J., & Ming, S. (2020). The mindful action plan: Using the MAP to apply acceptance and commitment therapy to productivity and self-compassion for behavior analysts. *Behavior Analysis in Practice*, 1–9.

Neuman, G. (1998). *Helping your kids cope with divorce the sandcastles way*. New York: Random House.

North Dakota Post Adopt Network. (2020). *Supporting adoptive and guardianship families in North Dakota*. Retrieved from www.ndpostadopt.org

O'Leary, W. (2021). *7 Self-compassion reminders for parents of kids who are struggling*. Retrieved from https://www.mindful.org/7-self-compassion-reminders-for-parents-of-kids-who-are-struggling.

Play-it-through-UK (2019). Retrieved from https://www.pasttheedgesconsulting.com/blog/pedagogy-vs-andragogy?ss_source=sscampaigns&ss_campaign_id=6506f8c5bfa2ee0835d09022&ss_email_id=6506f91125c7990d3ae0d71f&ss_campaign_name=Pedagogy+vs+Andragogy&ss_campaign_sent_date=2023-09-17T13%3A03%3A21Z

Rainforth, M.V., Schneider, R.H., Nidich, S.I., Gaylord-King, C., Salerno, J.W., & Anderson, J.W. (2007). Stress reduction programs in patients with elevated blood pressure: a systematic review and meta-analysis. *Current hypertension reports*, 9(6), 520–528.

U.S. Census Bureau. (2019). Retrieved from United States Census Bureau. https://data.census.gov/cedsci/table?q=grandparents%20raising%20grandchildren&tid=ACSDT1Y2019.B10002&hidePreview=false.

Answer Key for Section 1, Activity 4.

  1. What stress-reducing steps can Big Sis take to alleviate Maria's emotional distress?

  Reinforce that Big Sis is there to support the child. Big Sis can share that she does not know everything about Maria but is willing to learn. Understand the importance of symbolic attachments (any significant toys/stuffed animals, clothing, pictures, etc.).

  2. How can Big Sis learn about Maria's habits and history?
  Ask the child how she feels, her likes, dislikes, and habits.

  3. What can Big Sis do to prepare her home environment for the new relationship? Learn about the child's relationships, possessions, ask the child to help with planning and preparation of her bedroom.

  4. What, if anything, can Maria's father (who is currently incarcerated) do to support this change? Inform Maria about the new caregiver arrangements and support the child.

Managing Loss and the Family

MODULE FOCUS

- Section 2.0. Childhood Grief: "Does My Loss Even Matter?" Examine incarceration in the context of family system loss, grief work, and disenfranchised grief.
- Section 2.1. Grief Work for Caregivers and Families. Discuss caregiver-child emotions during a family crisis. Grief work is expanded with a specific focus on capital punishment.
- Section 2.2. Symbolic Attachment: Teddy's Gone. Analyze the influence of attachment loss.
- Section 2.3. Loss and Attachment. Expound upon attachment loss and consider the role of caregivers' facilitating grief work and coping strategies.

Resources

Read Guidebook: Hart-Johnson and Johnson (2025) | Chapter 2, "Parental Incarceration: Does My Loss Even Matter?"

Additional Resources

Optional Text: Joy, S. (2013). *Grief, loss, and treatment for death row families: Forgotten no more.* Lanham, MD: Lexington.
Review Appendix B: Do's and Don'ts

Introduction

While it is true that incarceration can restrict physical togetherness, potentially exacerbating emotional loss for affected children and families, the condition can also illuminate opportunities to build strong bonds and enhance family commitment. According to Hart-Johnson (2014), family member incarceration can feel like the grief experienced when losing a loved one through death. Grief is the emotional response to losing a significant attachment (Worden, 2002). This emotion highlights the depth of human love and capacity for caring.

The intensity of the grief reaction may vary depending on how meaningful the relationship was before the loss. Sometimes, loss can feel like losing a part of oneself because of deeply rooted connections and emotional ties. Such may be the case between children and their incarcerated parents.

Loss can be especially complicated when society doesn't understand family member incarceration. With this lack of awareness, they may frown upon the incarceration status. Yet, a child and family members may have unconditional love for the person who is now incarcerated. *When their grief is not acknowledged or supported by society, it is called disenfranchised grief* (Doka, 2002).

Children may experience disenfranchised grief more intensely than adults, especially if they fear others will leave them, too. While children are experiencing these intense emotions, their caregivers may also grieve and feel loss, compounded by other life situations. The caregivers may fear for the well-being of the incarcerated family member. They may not have the means to support the children and need to release them to foster care. There could be many scenarios that family members face. Family members may feel mixed emotions, such as anger, sadness, bewilderment, frustration, anxiety, all related to the parent's arrest, incarceration, and sentencing.

Grief Work

While individuals may express their feelings differently, there are typical signs of grief related to non-death- and death-related loss:

- Sadness and bouts of crying
- Over- or undereating
- Insomnia or sleeping outside of everyday habits and routines
- Withdrawing from socializing with friends and family members
- Anxiety and preoccupation with the loss

Managing grief is called *grief work*. This process generally requires taking active steps toward emotional adjustment and healing. When grief is acknowledged and addressed, people may learn to work through the emotional pain, make meaning of the circumstances, and learn to accept the conditions of loss.

Sometimes, people get stuck in their grief process. This state of limbo can prolong grief and ambiguity regarding closure if the person is alive. Pauline Boss (2000) defines one kind of grief associated with a lack of clarity and closure as an ambiguous loss. There tends to be lingering uncertainty about the person's current or future role in the lives of the griever. The uncertainty and lack of clarity tend to render the issue as *unfinished business*.

Children may feel *ambiguous loss*—not knowing whether the incarcerated parent will ever return. This condition might be especially true if no one informed the children about the parent's status and whereabouts. Additionally, suppose a caregiver was untruthful or not forthcoming about the parent's whereabouts (e.g., children were told their incarcerated parents are in the military, away at school, or out of the country). In those cases, children may question why the parent never said goodbye. Children may feel abandoned and confused.

There are times when the loss is more overwhelming for children of incarcerated parents. For example, a parent serving a life sentence or capital punishment (death-row) may mourn before the actual and final loss of this parent. Children can learn to manage grief and other difficult emotions. They can learn to work through difficulties with caregiver support. However, first their grief must be acknowledged (noting that at times a therapist may be needed if conditions exceed a caregiver's ability to intercede and reach resolution).

According to the Centers for Disease Control and Prevention (2020), children can also feel grief from a loss of common routines and former lifestyles and engagement. This piling on can compound the loss. The CDC advised that caregivers can help children cope by:

- Acknowledging the loss and the meaning of the relationship.
- Trying not to minimize the loss regardless of the role or significance.
- Teaching children how to relax (using breathing techniques, exercising, yoga, and meditation).
- Planning times for social activities (reinforcing that it is okay to take a break and be children).
- Letting children talk with trusted people (e.g., helping professionals such as grief counselors, therapists, or licensed clinicians) who listen and show empathy.

Additional steps include:

- Staying in the present and a focus on mindfulness (avoid worrying about future losses and stay present, finding joy in daily experiences).
- Developing rituals that memorialize fond moments and important milestones.
- Reading self-help books related to grief work.
- Finding silver linings.

In this module, we cover nuances of grief through activities related to understanding grief and doing grief work. We introduce the constructs, symbolic attachments to express the importance of children's rituals and coping related to toys and security objects. We end the section with a focus on managing family loss and attachment.

Section 2.0. Childhood Grief: "Does My Loss Even Matter?"

Section Focus | Case Example

Auntie May

Charlie spent most of the weekend in his room. However, unlike most days, today he did not play computer games. Auntie May checked in and found Charlie sitting on his bed, crying. When she approached him, he was embarrassed and looked away. Auntie May guessed Charlie was sad because of his mom's incarceration. Auntie May said to Charlie, "You're okay. It's all right. You are going to be just fine."

Section Objectives

- ☐ Learn about non-death loss
- ☐ Understand and learn to identify signs of grief in children
- ☐ Identify and understand examples of disenfranchised grief
- ☐ Learn how parental feedback can impact children's emotions

Overview

The topic of grief can be an awkward conversation to manage. Most people do not know what to offer words beyond, "I'm sorry for your loss." What do you say when the person is still alive? Caregivers such as Auntie May tend to console children using techniques they have been taught or heard over the years. Such statements as "You're okay" are meant in good will.

It is best to acknowledge children's grief to avoid inadvertent invalidation of their feelings. If children believe that their reactions are exaggerated, they may begin to suppress their feelings. Acknowledging the emotions and doing grief work might alleviate the deepness of grief.

As introduced earlier, children may feel disenfranchised grief. If they feel grief and are informed by adults that they are "okay" or that "it's all right," it may cause children to question whether their feelings are relevant. While parents mean well, these statements may produce unexpected results. An alternative to these statements is to acknowledge the child's feelings, perhaps stating, "It sounds like you are really sad, let's talk about your feelings." Or, a parent could offer, "I feel sad, too. It is normal to feel sad when you miss someone you love." In this way, the child's feelings are acknowledged and validated. These prompts may also serve as discussion starters.

Grief is the emotional response to fractured or broken attachment bonds resulting in temporary or permanent separation (Worden, 2002). Non-death loss refers to separation from someone still alive. In the context of this workbook, grief is the emotional response to experiencing the absence or removal of a parent from the household (e.g., related to confinement in jail or prison). Recall that signs of grief in children might include the following characteristics:

- Sadness; bouts of crying.
- Not wanting to eat or overeating.
- Insomnia or sleeping outside of normal habits and routines.
- Not socializing with friends and family members.
- Anxiety and preoccupation with the loss.

Self-disenfranchised grief describes an individual's sense of shame or stigma, denying their own right to grieve or minimizing the significance of its meaning (Doka, 2002). Many families of the incarcerated have felt self-disenfranchisement of grief, especially those of high-profile legal (e.g., media covered crimes) cases or families of individuals on the sex-offender registry and/or on death row.

Foundational Learning

Disenfranchised grief is a reaction to negative and judgmental interpretations of the loss. The general response to loss entails expressing emotions, seeking support or condolences, and finding ways to live without the absent person (Doka, 2002). In other words, under *enfranchised* (socially acceptable) conditions, people learn adaptive coping methods, aided by supports. For example, during a funeral, affected people are surrounded by a host of significant family and friends. However, the challenge associated with the negative connotation of incarceration is that people tend to shy away from accepting widespread support. This is largely due to the stigma associated with incarceration (which may be aligned with beliefs regarding criminal justice aligned individuals). Even though the general public may relate crime and incarceration to socially unacceptable behaviors, children may still grieve the absence of their parents.

ACTIVITY 5

Managing Loss and the Family

Reflect upon 2.0 Auntie May. Consider Charlie's grief reaction. Now, consider Auntie May's response and feedback to Charlie. Circle the most appropriate responses for each question (True/False) and address any open-ended questions.

After reviewing and answering Questions 1 through 4, explain your rationale for choosing your answers. Using 50 words or less, answer in the section labeled "Rationale." Facilitators, you may use the "Rationale" section as a group discussion.

1. Charlie's habits have changed. He is feeling sad and lacks the energy to play video games. His behavior suggests that he is missing his mom and experiencing grief.   ☐ True   ☐ False

2. Auntie May's reaction to Charlie conveyed conflicting sentiments. She offered, "You're okay," "It's all right," "You are going to be just fine." Her response might invalidate Charlie's feelings.   ☐ True   ☐ False

3. Auntie May can help Charlie process his feelings related to grief by acknowledging that crying is a normal emotional response.   ☐ True   ☐ False

4. Auntie May illustrates Charlie's embarrassment and is considered an example of disenfranchised grief.   ☐ True   ☐ False

Rationale
Question 1:
Question 2:
Question 3:
Question 4:

See Answer Key for Section 2.0, Activity 5, after Module 2 Reference list.

Section 2.1. Grief Work for Caregivers and Families

Section Focus | Case Example

THE WHOLE FAMILY GRIEVES

Everyone in the family grieved differently, but they all knew they had lost someone special. The children lost their father, and their mother lost her husband. As a wife, I have experienced deep grief because my husband is serving life. He is on death row, and every time we get his "death date," we all prepare for his death, but it never happens. So, we keep cycling through this death preparation over and over, but then, the appeals come. It is like attending the funeral for the same person over and over again, but they never really die. It is "horrible" for the whole family. We are stuck in this holding pattern.

—Focus Group Caregiver

Section Objectives

☐ Understand the significance of grief related to families of loved ones on death row
☐ Deepen knowledge about disenfranchised grief in the family system
☐ Learn why it is advised to address rather than suppress grief
☐ Critically reflect on helping children learn the basic tasks of grief work (seminal work: Worden, 1991)

Overview

The case vignette is heartbreaking. Capital punishment (a.k.a., death row) cases may be the most insurmountable grief expressed in this workbook. If you are experiencing or if a family that you work with is experiencing these conditions of loss, we offer our sincere condolences for these foreboding experiences. We offer this content because neglecting this condition further disenfranchises affected families. This disenfranchisement makes this focus imperative and important to address.

Our work as advocates exposes us to these types of incredible life situations. While difficult, as individuals struggle with losses, hopefully, they discover ways to manage their unique sorrow and emotional pain. Experiencing loss is difficult enough. However, we have found that when loss is coupled with shameful circumstances shrouding the loss, the grief may deeply resonate and feel "stuck" inside, without an outlet. This condition may result in abstention from taking steps toward healing. Yet, we remain hopeful. One of our constituents found that through advocating for families with the similar conditions, she was able to honor her own loss while using self-determination to change the system.

The Whole Family Grieves expresses the sentiments of an entire family's potential trauma and disenfranchised grief. Their feelings of loss and their cycle of preparing for a death that continues without closure has left this family in limbo. Grief work generally involves seeking and/or receiving consolation from others and having a sense of connectedness. With a social network to help the affected person, they may regain a sense of identity, managing to live without the absent person. When loss is disenfranchised, social supports are largely absent. Such circumstances, for example, as when family members are on "death row" or are subjected to capital punishment, may be overwhelming for families and their social networks. Family and friends may wish to distance themselves from high-profile cases involving crimes that rise to the level of life sentences or death row. It may be too surreal for most people to comprehend.

Foundational Learning

Families with loved ones facing capital punishment generally are absent from platforms that provide benefits related to receiving social support, activism for families, and public forums offering relief from social stigma. Therefore, many of these families may feel compelled to suffer at home, alone, in silence, as if they themselves have committed a crime (Joy, 2013).

Long (2011) offers that a promising possibility for families who encounter the perpetual loss of a loved one serving capital punishment sentences. Long suggests:

- Reestablishing support networks with trusted and understanding confidants.
- Practice self-regulation techniques.
- Learn anxiety management such as deep breathing, body scans, and "thought-stopping through self-guided dialogue," and
- Practice learning to recall events without reliving the history.

One of the first steps might include processing how two things can be true at the same time. As difficult as it may be, loving a person who is serving a life sentence and/or subjected to capital punishment does not require you or the children to punish yourself. Learning affirming self-talk might help. Reminding yourself that your compassion and unconditional love makes you a supportive person rather than feeling guilty because you are *free on the outside*. Another method of reflection entails reminding yourself of your commitment to support your loved one through affirming communication, uplifting discussions, similar to those supporting individuals with terminal illnesses.

Address rather than suppress the grief. Caregivers may need to look for signs of intense grieving in their children and seek out professional help; perhaps, for the whole family. Hidden or disenfranchised grieving is not always apparent in children. Feelings of grief and loss may linger under the surface because children may think it is abnormal to grieve someone on death row (especially if others believe the crime is heinous). For instance, the sensationalism of a crime, its media coverage, and resultant public disdain may cause children to hide attachments and feelings of their loss.

Working through grief. Generally, working through grief can be thought of as the active process of making meaning of the emotional reactions to loss (for adults and children).

Worden (1991) indicated that there are tasks associated with grief work. These four tasks include: (1) accepting the loss; (2) working through the emotional pain; (3) acquiring new skills or roles; and (4) rechanneling energy in new ways or through other outlets.

Other ideas:

Invite the person serving a life sentence or on death row to help develop a coping plan with the children. This may give the children and other family members permission to actively work on healing. It may also help to relinquish the guilt of family members surviving on the outside.

Work with a grief counselor and seek to understand the nature of grief and how loss is an inevitable part of life.

Each day, grant yourself permission to engage in self-care. Teach children to do the same. Remind them to set aside personal time to engage in fitness, recreation, and other activities, acknowledging that these are pathways toward well-being.

Set family goals. Remember to establish goals and try to achieve them. Ask yourself, in five years' time, in reflection, what would I have wanted to accomplish?

Remind yourself daily that taking care of yourself (mentally, physically, and spiritually) enables you to be strong for those who need you most.

Honor your trusting relationships. Find ways to celebrate each other and your quality time together.

Look for the strength in each family member and honor their potential for developing resilience.

Activity 6

Managing Loss and the Family

Reflect upon *The Whole Family Grieves*. Now, consider the following recommendations related to helping children with grief work by Hooyman and Kramer (2006) who offer an alternative grief work process, in the following steps:

- Create rituals or ceremonies as a memorial that honors the absent person.
- Encourage children to get involved in the ritual.
- Model expressions and discuss feelings that acknowledge the loss.
- Do not try to replace the person, but rather create a memory. Consider creating memory boxes or other symbolic representations of bonds and love.

Now, consider the family circumstances in *The Whole Family Grieves*.

Record at least two ideas related to the three prompts below. Record your ideas related to seeking support, relief, and healthy coping. *Facilitators, you may use these topical areas as group discussions.* Please note that there is no answer key for this critical thinking exercise.

Prompts:

1. Seek out formal support.
2. Find relief from grief by introducing daily routines.
3. Find ways of healthy coping.

Ideas
Idea 1:
Idea 2:
Idea 3:

Section 2.2. Symbolic Attachments: Teddy's Gone

Section Focus | Case Example

Teddy's Gone

Jill's favorite toy was a teddy bear given to her by her dad. Dad no longer lived in the home. He is incarcerated. Sometimes, Jill could be heard talking with Teddy. For instance, she once said, "Stop crying, Teddy; Daddy is coming home." Everywhere Jill went, her stuffed teddy bear was with her. Eventually, however, the bear became soiled and dirty. Teddy's once fuzzy hair was tattered and worn. On the day that Jill turned five, there was so much activity. The family was moving into a different house. Once in the unfamiliar home, Jill searched the house, looking for her Teddy, hoping to find the bear tucked inside an unpacked box—no such luck! Sheila, the mom, wanted to make the day special despite the move, so she bought birthday cupcakes to celebrate. When it was time for Jill to open her gift from Mom, she discovered that the gift was a new teddy bear. Jill began to cry. She sobbed, "Teddys gone." Jill's mom, Sheila, was confused. She thought Jill would be happy to swap Teddy for a cleaner bear.

Section Objectives

☐ Identify defining features of symbolic attachments (transitional or security/comfort objects)
☐ Understand the potential stressors related to multiple losses, change, and transition
☐ Critically reflect and identify ways to help children cope with change

Overview

If each of us reflects upon our childhood, there is likely to be an object to which we are fondly attached. In *Teddy's Gone*, the missing teddy bear illustrates a symbolic attachment. Young children, like Jill, often attach meaning to objects used for comfort and symbolic play. For example, children latch on to security blankets, pacifiers, toys, and stuffed animals. These sources of comfort and security are a means of self-regulation. According to the American Academy of Pediatrics, children use security objects to help children deal with separation from a parent or loved one. These objects are also considered transitional objects in that they help children to move from a state of total dependence on caregivers to a state of autonomy or independence (Cale, 2018).

Security objects might serve as imaginary friends for young children. It is not unusual for toddlers to speak to their toys. This practice is common since children often use play experiences to process their emotions. For example, when Jill talks to the bear, her words convey that she misses her dad. Children at Jill's age possess *magical thinking*, and stuffed animals like Teddy can become a source of comfort, as if it were a living being.

Foundational Learning

Symbolic attachments describe how people attribute meaning and emotional ties to objects. Symbols may carry deep significance in some cultures and societies. Symbolic colors might represent tradition, culture, religiosity, and emotional connections. Symbolic objects may represent relationship bonds, valued memories, and potentially, deep-rooted emotional ties.

Multiple losses. In *Teddy's Gone*, Jill's scenario represents multiple losses: (1) the dad is incarcerated, (2) the teddy bear parallels the loss of father-child relationship bonds, and (3) the loss of familiarity. Parental incarceration can present situations that compound feelings of loss. Jill's message to Teddy, "Stop crying, Teddy; Daddy is coming home," may suggest that she has cried tears for her father. Additionally, telling the bear to suppress his emotions might suggest how Jill learned to deal with her feelings. Changes in living arrangements can also trigger loss of familiarity. While the move is required, it may represent losing a place Jill has known all her young life. Consequently, she may feel as though she is losing everything meaningful. Children's identities are sometimes tangentially tied to persons, places, and things.

Change and transitions. The excitement of moving to a new home or apartment can be both exhilarating and stressful. At times, moving is carried out with time constraints to transition from one home to the next. With these changes comes pressure and sometimes, chaos. Frequent and sudden change can introduce anxiety in children. While some change is good, children can become stressed from disruptions to their daily lives. Young children especially need routine to help them feel reassured that life is under control, and they are not at risk for unwanted change.

Coping. Caregivers can help children cope with change by planning for transitional activities and informing the children in advance. Also, restoring normative schedules can help with these transitions. For example, in *Teddy's Gone* the caregiver might engage Jill in a discussion about moving. As a caregiver, she might hold a discussion about what will be permitted to carry during the move and what needs to be downsized. The mom could also offer Jill a choice to select her favorite toys to carry, indicating the clear limits for the new dwelling (which might be smaller). Allowing choice offers children a sense of agency. When children are allowed to have choices, they feel included and valued. Otherwise, children may feel helpless or that their opinions do not matter.

ACTIVITY 7

Managing Loss and the Family

Reflect upon the case example, *Teddy's Gone*. Consider how symbolic attachments (i.e., comfort or transitional) describe attributed meaning and emotional ties to objects. Imagine being a parent whose priorities are to move into a new dwelling, coupled with finding ways to celebrate the young child's (Jill) birthday. Consider the following questions and answer briefly in the ideas section (1 through 4), below. First, recall any significant objects offering comfort in your own histories as a child. *Facilitators, you may use these four questions prompts for group discussion.*

1. Describe your symbolic attachment, noting why the object was important, and what it represented in your life.
2. Develop a plan/strategy for Jill to manage the transition from one home to the new dwelling. What are 3 important priorities Jill should consider?
3. What are the parallels and significant of the previous Teddy Bear?
4. Why does change produce such stress?

Ideas
Idea 1:
Idea 2:
Idea 3:
Idea 4:

Please note that there is no answer key for this critical thinking exercise.

ACTIVITY | 7.1

Optional Group Discussion:

With symbolism in mind, please address the following questions as an individual or group activity:

1. What alternatives could Sheila, the mom, use rather than replace the teddy bear?
2. What can Sheila do to console Jill?
3. What can Sheila do to better understand Jill's emotional needs?

Remember, there is no single right answer. Often, the answers to these questions are situational. Record your answers in the Notes section below. *Please note that there is no answer key for this critical thinking exercise.*

Notes:

Section 2.3. Loss and Attachments

Section Focus | Case Example

Multiple Children

Each of the following children experienced family disruptions due to parental imprisonment.

> *Jay* is a five year old, a confident, happy child, who bounces back from most adverse challenges.
> *Sarah* is three years old. She is timid, shy, and withdrawn.
> *Jamal* is eight years old. He is the most popular student in his class, loving the attention from his teacher and other adults.
> *Mitchell* is ten years old. He loves computer games and keeps his distance from his peers.
> *Ebony* is nine years old. She wants attention and love; however, when others concede, she pushes them away.

Section Objectives

☐ Learn and apply knowledge about attachment styles (secure, insecure, anxious, ambivalent, avoidant, and disorganized attachments)
☐ Gain knowledge about how loss and attachment seem to work hand in hand
☐ Understand how parental incarceration might align with social isolation

Overview

Attachment and loss are universal experiences that everyone will encounter in their lifetime. These concepts represent the degree in which humans love, care, and demonstrate affection toward persons, places, and things. To grieve or to experience significant loss suggests that there was a relationship attachment in the first place. Therefore, loss and relationship attachment might be indelibly linked.

Children with incarcerated parents experience separation and loss, and they may respond in different ways, depending on the prior strength of the relationship with the parent. Even children who do not have significant bonds with their parents may grieve a lost opportunity for that bond.

Attachment styles are the thoughts, emotions, and the ability to establish relationships and connections or disconnects with people who are a part of an inner circle. During early childhood, young infants and toddlers learn to form attachments based on parenting conditions and how well their needs are met by their primary caregiver(s).

Foundational Learning

To better understand loss, attachment styles, we focus on its theory. Recall that *Attachment theory* is the psychology of parent-child bonding (Bowlby & Ainsworth, 2013). This theory explains what occurs when a child's primary caregiver satisfies or neglects a child's need for nurturing and care. For example, children whose needs are attended to and who receive love and nurturing may develop secure bonds with their parents. Conversely, neglected children, left for long periods, may have developed insecure relationships with their primary caregivers.

Attachment styles (Table 2.3.0) explain the variations in the parent-child connection or disconnection and levels of warmth associated with the relationship. There are five descriptions of children's general behaviors towards attachment relationship bonds. They include secure, anxious, ambivalent, avoidant, and disorganized attachments.

Table 2.3.0 Attachment Styles
Secure Attachments: The individual is supported and surrounded by attuned, attentive, empathic, and loving people. They feel connectedness when with a caregiver or even when alone. Children may display connectedness and close bonds, as evidenced by hugs, engagement, sitting near the caregiver, and feeling trusted enough to venture off and play. Babies who have secure relationships are generally less stressed.
Anxious Attachments: These individuals are always hungry for more attention and love. They need people in their lives to help them feel complete; but always feel as though something is missing. Children with anxious attachment may seem to be sensitive to negative comments. They may isolate to get more attention. Anxious attachment is from fear of abandonment.
Ambivalent Attachments: These individuals are timid, suffer social anxiety, feel alone and often feel as though the parent is present at one time and then distant during others. Children may feel they cannot trust their parents because they will be disappointed. Children with ambivalent attachments tend to feel as though abandonment is imminent—that fear keeps them on edge from forming close relationships.
Avoidant Attachments: The individual keeps a distance from intimacy and avoids relationships of closeness and bonding. Children with avoidant attachment styles may suffer abandonment when they were/are children. Babies with avoidant attachment are less likely to cry during distress and may not seem to need the caregiver attending to them. However, they may have physiological stress responses such as elevated stress hormones (Hamblen & Barnett, n.d.) when left alone.
Disorganized Attachments: To these individuals, attachment is about survival. There is no consistent way to deal with stressful situations. They need attachment and connectedness to others—as a desperate measure to survive stress, distress, and fear of aloneness. Children with disorganized attachment tend to show dysregulation, where they vacillate from feeling timid and distant to wanting a relationship. As the name suggests, the behavior is disorganized. Disorganized attachment may be a result of being traumatized. These children may demand their mother's closeness, then resist or push the mother away—not wanting to be anywhere near this caregiver. This behavior describes a fearful-avoidant attachment. The behavior could be subtle or obvious.

Note: Remember the aforementioned attachment styles are generalities. No two individuals are the same. Additionally, attachment styles are not limited to one style. A person could have a dominant style and still experience factors associated with other styles. Finally, attachment styles can change. Through self-awareness and positive steps towards self-care and healing, a person can learn to overcome feelings associated with undesired attachment styles.

ACTIVITY 8

MANAGING LOSS AND THE FAMILY

Reflect upon Attachment Styles, listed in the Section 2.3 Foundational Learning section. Now, address the following critical thinking activity. Review each description of the children listed in the case example, Multiple Children. Make note that no single attachment style can fully describe children. List the attachment style in Table 2.3.1. However, with their profile, try to match the attachment style based on their behavioral descriptions. Now, ponder and make note of ideas regarding how a caregiver might respond to each child's strengths, and address their unique needs.

Table 2.3.1. Name the Attachment	
Name	*Attachment Style*
Jay	
Sarah	
Jamal	
Mitchell	
Ebony	

See Answer Key for Section 2.3, Activity 8, after Module 2 Reference list.

Ideas:

References

Boss, Pauline. (2000). *Ambiguous loss: Learning to live with unresolved grief*. Cambridge: Harvard University Press. *ProQuest eBook Central*, https://ebookcentral.proquest.com/lib/waldenu/detail.action?docID=3300190.

Bowlby, J., & Ainsworth, M. (2013). The origins of attachment theory. *Attachment theory: Social, developmental, and clinical perspectives*, 45(28), 759–775.

Cale, E. (2018). *Understanding children's security blankets*. Retrieved from https://www.hellomotherhood.com/understanding-childrens-attachment-to-security-blankets-5753301.html.

The Centers for Disease Control and Prevention (2020) Activity Page. Retrieved from https://www.cdc.gov/childrenindisasters/pdf/coping_activity_page_english-p.pdf.

Doka, K. (2002). *Disenfranchised grief*. Champaign: Research Press.

Hamblen, J., & Barnett, E. (n.d.). *PTSD in children and adolescents*. Retrieved from https://www.ptsd.va.gov/professional/treat/specific/ptsd_child_teens.asp.

Hart-Johnson, A. (2014). *Symbolic imprisonment, grief, and coping theory: African American women with incarcerated mates* (Doctoral dissertation).

Hart-Johnson, A., & Johnson, G. (2022). Caregivers' family relations assessment and communication strategies. *Science Publishing Group*, 11(5), 157–168. https://www.sciencepublishinggroup.com/article/10.11648/j.pbs.20221105.12.

Hooyman, N.R., & Kramer, B.J. (2006). *Living through loss: Interventions across the life span*. New York: Columbia University Press.

Joy, S. (2013). *Grief, loss, and treatment for death row families: Forgotten no more*. Lanham, MD: Lexington Books.

Long, W. (2011). *Trauma therapy for death row families. Journal of Trauma & Dissociation*, 12(5), 482–494. https://doi.org/10.1080/15299732.2011.593258

Worden, W.J. (2002). *Grief counseling and grief therapy: A handbook for the mental health practitioner* (3rd edition). New York: Springer.

Worden, J.W. (1991). Grieving a loss from AIDS. *The Hospice Journal*, 7(1–2), 143–150.

Answer Key for Activity 5

1. Charlie's habits have changed. He is feeling sad and lacks the energy to play video games. His behavior suggests that he is missing his mom and experiencing grief.	☑ True ☐ False
2. Auntie May's reaction to Charlie conveyed conflicting sentiments. She offered, "You're okay," "It's all right," "You are going to be just fine." Her response might invalidate Charlie's feelings.	☑ True ☐ False
3. Auntie May can help Charlie process his feelings related to grief by acknowledging that crying is a normal emotional response	☑ True ☐ False
4. The case example, Auntie May illustrates Charlie's embarrassment and is considered an example of disenfranchised grief	☑ True ☐ False

Answer Key for Activity 8

Jay displays characteristics of secure attachments. He is confident and shows that he may have had his needs met by his primary caregiver.

Sarah seems to lean towards avoidant attachment. She prefers to keep her distance from intimacy and avoids connections. Finding ways to gradually build trust is important. Games that involve touch at a respectable distance might help. Asking permission to hug as a greeting while respecting Sarah's boundaries is important. Sarah may come to embrace those of whom she loves in her own time.

Jamal shows signs of anxious attachment as he seeks out attention at all costs.

Caregivers may wish to reinforce love and point out Jamal's strengths and positive attributes. Helping Jamal to understand love and familial support might also help.

Mitchell shows signs of ambivalent attachment, where he is introverted and prefers to be isolated. Helping Mitchell to develop confidence and social interpersonal skills might be helpful.

Ebony shows disorganized attachment. While she seeks out love, she consciously or subconsciously pushes people away when they get too close. Helping Ebony understand her emotions in a manner that does not cause defensiveness is key. Ebony needs trust and secure bonds. She needs to know that if she entrusts someone with her heart, they will not abandon her. Therefore, look for ways to build a solid foundation built upon trust and commitment.

Caution—the above are only fictional scenarios used for illustration of attachment styles. More information on attachment styles can be found at: Harvard University, Attachment Styles, https://scholar.harvard.edu/sociology1152/attachment-styles-0

Infants and Parental Incarceration

MODULE FOCUS

- Section 3.0. Kangaroo Care: Infants and Reading Intervention. Consider caregiving for infant children with confined parents and implementing coping strategies.
- Section 3.1. Babies and Survival. Explore the importance of establishing routines and rituals for infants.
- Section 3.2. Attuned and Attached. Discuss strengthening caregiver attunement skills and attachment bonds.
- Section 3.3. Parental Incarceration. Expand upon infant emotional development.

Resources

Read Guidebook: Hart-Johnson and Johnson (2025) | Chapter 3, "Born in Prison."

Additional Resources

Hart-Johnson, A. (2021). *Baby Star Finds Happy*. A Story About Parental Incarceration. Finding a Silver lining when a parent goes to prison or jail. Extant-One Publishing. ISBN 9798775914110.

Hart-Johnson, A. (2017). *Jamie's Big Visit*. Grownup Timeout. Prison Visits and a Parent's Incarceration. Extant-One Publishing. ISBN 9798702126258.

Hedrington-Jones. (2021). *Truth and the Big Dinner*. A Story About Parental Incarceration. Finding a Silver lining when a parent goes to prison or jail. Extant-One Publishing. ISBN 9780996741026.

Johnson, G. (2021). *Rocko's Guitar*. A Story About Parental Incarceration. Finding a Silver lining when a parent goes to prison or jail. Extant-One Publishing. ISBN 9798732160369.

Introduction

Generally, caregiving offers opportunities for young children, especially babies, to receive love, affection, and close-knit bonds. However, parental incarceration can sometimes pose challenges to these opportunities. A young infant separated from the mother at birth may experience emotional and physical distress. A mother is generally the child's first attachment. If this bond is broken, it may cause the child to feel physical and emotional withdrawal. If the child was born under corrections supervision (e.g., medical ward at a prison hospital) and subsequently separated, building secure attachment bonds to avoid or minimize separation anxiety is critical.

This module focuses on the importance of understanding developmental milestones and attuned caregiving methods and offers recommendations on effective parenting.

Section 3.0. Kangaroo Care: Infants and Reading Intervention

Section Focus | Case Example

THE MAGIC OF STORIES

The mother left her baby with her younger 29-year-old sibling named Arial just before she voluntarily turned herself in at the jail because of a warrant for her arrest. That morning, Arial wondered how she, without prior parenting experience, would care for an infant who was not her own while the mother served time in jail.

Section Objectives

- ☐ Learn about the potential impacts of parental incarceration on infants
- ☐ Understand how storybooks can serve as a tool to enhance child development
- ☐ Learn and apply the concepts of "Kangaroo Care" how it pairs with reading to children.

Overview

Reading is a powerful tool to enhance the lives of babies. Caregivers can use this tool to bond with children, enhance literacy, and show attuned parenting. Reading can be used to help infants through their grieving experience through the act of parent-child connectedness. This activity may be especially helpful for children who have lost their maternal bond due to incarceration.

There appears to be a myth that infants are oblivious to the perils of parental incarceration. Some people believe that children simply need a place to live, with proper nutrition, and the rest will take care of itself. Researchers convey that this sentiment is untrue (Trout, 2018; Weller & Shaver, 2010). Most children separated from their confined mothers lived with them before arrest. Infants separated from their incarcerated mothers may need extra care and tailored support because of the potential for trauma and prolonged adverse effects of disrupted mother-child bonds (Weller & Shaver, 2010).

After separation from their mothers, children tend to live with grandmothers (50%), and approximately 20 percent live with their biological fathers, with about 10 percent going into foster care (Weller & Shaver, 2010). The remainder of affected children may live with siblings, godparents, stepparents, relatives, or fictive kin.

Foundational Learning

"A child who reads will be an adult who thinks."
—Unknown

Infants of incarcerated parents who are cared for and nurtured by one caring adult can thwart adverse outcomes (Center for Developing Child Harvard [CDCH], 2015).

Giving a child love, no matter if the bond is for a short or long time, can provide nurturing care and support.

Reading storybooks to children is a means of promoting attachment bonds with infants even if they do not understand the words. Holding an infant and reading to them using soft and inviting tones while also engaging in the storyline builds connections (Iuele, 2018). Reading to a young child generally involves close proximity between the child and reader; engaging in eye contact, showing deliberate attention and purposeful discussion, while exercising the types of behaviors that show affection. The act of reading complements teaching related to kangaroo care. This term describes bonding through touch and making skin-to-skin contact (holding the baby on the chest, upper shoulder, or lap). When paired with reading, the benefits include (Iuele, 2018; Walker 2013):

- Aids the baby's physiological systems.
- Makes the engagement meaningful and hopeful for the parents.
- Infants are soothed and relaxed.
- The caregiver feels rewarded as they contribute to the child's care.
- This process of bonding is enhanced by singing to the child, as well.

What if the parent is incarcerated? Parents who are separated from their children and are confined may feel that all hope is lost. However, there are interventions used to promote connectedness between infants and their incarcerated parents. This programming involves using reading programs along with paired video visits. A parent can read a book to the child during the video visit. Infants between the age of two-to- seven months can make eye contact and smile at the video camera lens, resulting in interaction with the incarcerated parent. Reading to an infant improves speech and brain development even though young children initially cannot understand language. Reading can be a fun activity, especially as children reach the six-month stage. They may come to enjoy the reading time and point at objects and pictures in the books. The most important part of this intervention is that the parent remains connected to the child through voice, engagement, and visual contact. Advocates who wish to promote programs such as reading to children during live video visits or prerecording may wish to research implementing standing programs that might offer these options at the jail or prison.

Building comprehension and cognitive development. Even for nonincarcerated parents, reading to children is essential to help children advance skills building. By the time a child reaches a year old, if the caregiver continues to engage in reading activities, the child may have accumulated the knowledge of all the sounds to learn their native language. By 19 months, children generally understand up to 10 or more words.

A child's cognitive development describes how children learn and reason. Reading supports social, emotional, and cognitive development. A baby's social development includes interaction with the engaging caregiver (e.g., the caregiver's expressions, voice, and the reciprocal response of the child). Emotional development includes responding with joy and positive engagement with the caregiver. Between about six to nine months, children demonstrate responsive smiling and focus their attention on their caregivers when they are reading to the child. They also recognize feelings and expressions. Therefore, caregivers reading to children should use expressive words and tones. Closer to nine months of age, infants also recognize that other people have feelings. By the time a child nears 12 months of age, they should have the sensory development to be aware of sights, sounds, taste, touch, and smell. Storybooks generally contain these sensory characteristics.

Additionally,

Use events and play activities to stimulate and hold children's interest.

Explore ways to learn about children's interests and likes/dislikes through games and engagement such as reading storybooks.

Preserve parent-child contact if possible, so that the child does not grow up to think the caregiver caused the separation.

Respond based on the uniqueness and needs of the child.

PUTTING IT ALL TOGETHER:

- Using the Kangaroo Care theory, children benefit from caregiver-child physical contact.
- Reading, eye contact, and responsive smiling: Eye contact and responsive smiling are modes of communication between child and caregiver. When the caregiver reads to the child, uses loving tones, smiles, and enthusiasm, this shared experience becomes reciprocal. Infants increasingly will use their body language to express their feelings. Verbally, they may make happy cooing sounds or laughter to express joyful emotions.
- Storybooks with sensory elements help children to understand concepts.

As Walker (2013) indicated, children can benefit from caregivers reading to them early in life. This process of reading can help bolster emotional regulation while also increasing bonds.

Finally, children's books are essential elements for child development. They contribute to learning and play experiences between caregiver and child. Books can introduce children to a beautiful new world. Caregivers should read to their children every day, if possible. Infants are generally fond of books that include the following:

BOOK FEATURES

- Colorful and bright illustrations
- Rhymes and vivid phrasing
- Repetition
- Soft materials
- Pop-ups or cutouts
- Different shapes, colors, and sizes

Consider the Children's Books listed under Module 3, Additional Resources, as an aid to discuss parental incarceration. Remember to blend other fun books into the child's reading list. It is important for children to learn from a variety of books.

Activity 9

Infants and Parental Incarceration

Review Section 3.0 Kangaroo Care and pay particular attention to the benefits of reading to infants. If you have infants, plan a reading activity with your child. Select a book that includes many of the "Book Features" listed above. Consider a book that is age- appropriate and interesting. You may choose one of the books from the Module 3 *Additional Resources*, optional reading list. Using one of the books or a selection of your choice, follow the preparation and engagement steps below. Please note that there is no answer key for this critical thinking exercise. Note your reflections under "Notes."

Preparation

1. Select a children's book (draw from our learning resources or any digital or hard-copy children's book).

2. Read the book at least two times to become familiar with the content (before reading to your child).

3. Get acquainted with the storybook characters and identify the sensory elements (sight, sound, taste, touch, and smell) used in the story. Note any emotions and critical takeaways to share with the child.

4. Practice using expressions and pointing out essential elements of the book in preparation for the reading activity with your child.

Engagement

If possible, cuddle or hold the child as close as comfortably possible when reading.

1. Read with expression (high and low tones, with excitement); comment and ask questions and point out important parts of the book.

2. Read the same story more than once (the same story can be read multiple times a day or during the week; you decide).

3. If the book is one from the optional reading list regarding incarceration, use the book as a means of explaining to the infant where mom or dad is (e.g., "Mom is in a place like the storybook"). Children may not have the language to communicate back, but they are indeed learning communication through this engagement.

4. Do not feel silly reading to your infant. Just the act of being next to them shows affection and that you care. (Browse Part III of this workbook for more ideas on reading activities).

Notes:

Section 3.1. Babies and Survival

Section Focus | Case Example

RITUALS OF STABILITY

Babies have one goal in mind: Survival. All methods of communication originating from infants are a means to get their needs met. Crying, cooing, and kicking can get the job done!

Section Objectives

- ☐ Learn about the importance of routine and rituals
- ☐ Identify with ways to build the healthy cornerstones of child development
- ☐ Advance critical understanding of caregivers' need to create stability and a safe space for infants and children of all ages

Overview

A baby's primary goal is to survive. To achieve that goal, baby's use their rudimentary communication skills. A baby's earliest form of language is crying, cooing, and kicking. This communication helps a baby inform their caregiver that they need food, attention, proximity, and warmth. Routines and rituals introduce predictability, familiarity, and safety. Additionally, when the caregiver addresses a baby's needs, this increases trust.

Foundational Learning

Caregivers of infant children have the benefit of watching these young human minds shape into thriving independent and unique beings. Their infancy years are critical foundations to their future engagement and interaction with the world. During the earlier years, children need the most safeguards and protectors from stressors and adverse experiences. These children depend on parents for just about everything, initially. Caregivers are the children's protectors, entertainers, teachers, and assessors of health and well-being.

Building the healthy cornerstones of child development includes attunement to what interferes with healthy growth. Below are steps caregivers may take to enhance children's experiences:

- Avoid frequent change in new caregivers or childcare providers.
- Reduce exposure to loud noises that startle young babies.
- Avoid frequent exposure to unfamiliar people.
- Isolate children from family conflict and violence.

A caregiver can increase an infant's sense of stability by countering threats to their well-being and creating a safe space in the home. Caregivers can help young babies self-regulate through reassuring, soothing voices, and caring actions. Gentle caresses or touches, using soft voice tones, hugging, and a gentle rocking motion may soothe the child and help children regulate their physical systems and reduce emotional stress.

ACTIVITY 10

Infants and Parental Incarceration		
Consider the importance of establishing routines for children. Consider also the importance of creating stability and a safe space for infants. Each of these practices help to minimize stress and aide children in healthy development. Now, reflect and answer the following questions: identify if the statement is True or False. Facilitators, use items 1 through 5 as a group discussion. What does the group think about how to address each scenario?		
1. A baby has not touched his morning bottle of formula. The baby is crying. Is the baby likely hungry?	☐ True	☐ False
2. The caregiver has changed childcare providers three times in the past year. This transition is likely to introduce anxiety for the child.	☐ True	☐ False
3. The caregiver's apartment is near a busy elevator. However, the caregiver moved the baby's crib to her bedroom, away from the loud noise. This step is considered a protective measure to reduce stress in the baby.	☐ True	☐ False
4. A baby's only form of communication is through talking.	☐ True	☐ False
5. A baby's primary goal is to survive	☐ True	☐ False

See Answer for Key Section 3.1, Activity 10, after Module 3 Reference list.

Section 3.2. Attuned and Attached

Section Focus | Case Example

The Lullaby

Jennifer is a new caregiver to a nine-month-old infant. The pair have been together for a couple of weeks since the baby's mom became incarcerated. Jennifer tucks the baby in bed and sings a lullaby each night.

Section Objectives

- ☐ Learn how to perceive an infant's needs through attunement
- ☐ Understand the importance of responding to children's feelings and behaviors
- ☐ Identify bonding practices for individuals new to caregiving
- ☐ Critically assess how new caregivers can use methods of soothing distressed babies

Overview

Some caregivers naturally are intuitive, exemplifying nurturing roles. The concept of *attunement* entails caregivers' awareness of and a matched response to a child's needs. Attunement means providing the appropriate reaction to a child's behavior. For instance, if a child is excited about an activity, then the caregiver's role is to reinforce the achievement, joy, and/or excitement. If the caregiver's response does not match the child's needs, then it is possible the infant feels they have done something wrong.

Foundational Learning

Attunement engages responsive parenting practices to ensure that a child's holistic well-being is considered. The good news is that many childhood risks can be managed through effective and attuned parenting. However, incarceration can introduce risks that are not always obvious.

Attunement is essential, especially if the caregiver is not the birth mother. Consider, when a child bonds with their mother, a chemical in the body is produced called oxytocin (Millason, 2016). This is a pleasure hormone that makes babies feel happy and content. This hormone is also produced through touch and physical contact and bonding with a significant attachment figure (such as their primary caregiver). The process of attunement also introduces these same types of comforts when a caregiver listens to the child, hugs, reassures the child.

Perceiving an infant's needs through attunement. Recalling that attunement means understanding a child's needs. While sometimes infant responses may seem utterly confusing, most of the time, if parents are listening, observing, and watching, they can figure out their child's needs. Keep in mind that attunement works both ways.

Babies become attuned to their caregiver's feelings and responses as does the caregiver toward the child. If the caregiver is happy, the child will sense that.

Responding to children's feelings and behaviors.

- Establishing calm and reducing stress in a child, might include co-regulation and soothing activities: hugging, rocking, reading, or singing to the child.
- Creating an environment with adequate lighting for daylight activities and nighttime sleep, coupled with noise reduction may offer babies and young children pleasant conditions and reduce stress.
- Caregivers for infants of incarcerated parents can combine attuned and positive parenting strategies to support child well-being. Over time, they may learn to warm up to their new caregivers.

Bonding practices for new caregivers. Caregivers who are new to raising children may wish, first, to observe the child and their behaviors. Infants tend to communicate verbally and nonverbally. This type of monitoring can help develop a baseline for children's typical behaviors. Attunement provides a way to identify how a child is feeling, what they need: if they are in distress, sad, or happy. As a caregiver, the goal is to help the child to feel understood and address their physical, emotional, and social needs. Addressing these needs can build a foundation of trust, where the child eventually learns that the caregiver has their best interests in mind.

Activity 11

Infants and Parental Incarceration

Read the case example 3.2 *The Lullaby*. Now, consider how Jennifer's ritual of singing a lullaby can benefit the child. Some benefits include:

- Shows the infant that they are the object of attention and affection.
- Soothing tones can help the baby to self-regulate and reduce stress.
- Singing and cuddling the child helps to build attachment (secure attachment of safety and bonding).
- Shows affection toward the child.

Critical Thinking Exercise

Consider the following changes in the case scenario. Under this new scenario, what steps could Jennifer take to soothe the baby? Address these questions as an individual exercise or group activity. Use the Notes section to respond. Please note that there is no answer key for this critical thinking exercise.

Case Scenario: Jennifer is a new caregiver to a nine-month-old infant. The pair have been together for a couple of weeks since the baby's mom became incarcerated. Jennifer tucks the baby in bed. *The baby's room is a shared space. The television volume is typically loud, and the baby is cranky and crying most of the time.*

QUESTIONS:

1. What can Jennifer do to establish calm?
2. What can Jennifer do to reduce the baby's stress?
3. What impact, if any, does the volume and/or lighting of the television have on the child?
4. What are the possible impacts of the mother's incarceration?

See Answer for Key Section 3.2, Activity 11, after Module 3 Reference list.

Notes:

Section 3.3. Parental Incarceration: Taking Inventory of the Impacts on Babies

Section Focus | Case Example

BABIES HAVE FEELINGS, TOO

Young children experience a wide range of emotions. They can feel happiness, sadness, grief, frustration, and fear, among other emotions. Parents can give these emotions a name and help children manage and develop the mastery of self-regulation.

Section Objectives

☐ Deepen knowledge about infant emotional development
☐ Understand the importance of using Responsive Parenting
☐ Learn how incarceration might affect infants and how caregivers might identify a baby's temperament and signs of grief

Overview

INFANT EMOTIONAL DEVELOPMENT

The first 12 months bring rapid developmental growth for the child's body and mind. This growth includes developing emotions. Socioemotional development involves mimicking caregivers' love and bonding skills (Zero to Three, 2021). The social skill of interaction is largely learned through reciprocal caregiver-child engagement. Babies experience emotions long before verbal skills develop. Talking to children with positive affirmations enriches their emotions, self-esteem, and confidence. Phrases like "You're smart," "So cute," and "You're loved" can foster strong bonds. Additionally, practicing responsive parenting can foster positive growth.

RESPONSIVE PARENTING

- **Allow children to grow, with safeguards.** Let them try, fail, and try again, like learning to walk. Caregivers can provide support while nurturing courage.
- **Learn About Your Baby.** Understand temperament, preferences, routines, and play activities.
- **Build Relationships.** Foster connections with your child, help others understand their preferences, especially if the child will be in others' care.
- **Support Holistic Development.** Encourage physical, emotional, and social growth. Provide play and emotional understanding opportunities.

Foundational Learning

As noted earlier, infants communicate through verbal and nonverbal cues. Crying, clenched fists, and facial expressions convey emotions. Attuned caregivers observe normal behaviors based on their baby's temperament. Happy and content babies may:

- Show happiness and joy through laughter and cooing .
- Sleep fitfully and soundly (barring their scheduled feeding times, etc.).
- Have healthy eating habits.
- May have a happy demeanor.
- Start to show a wide array of expressions (joy, contentment, surprise, anticipation).

Incarceration and signs of infant grieving. Caregivers also should pay careful attention to an infant who might be sad or grieving a parent's absence. The baby may show emotions through the following actions (Cerniglia et al., 2014):

- Search for Someone: Seek the parent.
- Crying and Discomfort: Express distress.
- Changed Eating Habits: Altered feeding patterns.
- Fearful Appearance: Display fear.
- Emotion Suppression: Show no emotions (flat affect).

Understanding infant emotions and behaviors supports children's development. Remember, love and caring are the foundations of building secure attachments.

ACTIVITY 12

Infants and Parental Incarceration

As children grow, caregivers can help children understand their feelings. Some parents may think that babies do not experience a wide array of emotions. However, research counters that notion by indicating that babies can feel emotions such as grief (Cerniglia et al., 2014). Parents can help their infants understand their emotions, even if a baby does not know or understand the language. For example, saying "happy baby" identifies happiness as an emotion. Or, saying "you are sad" identifies sadness as an emotion. Parents should not fear identifying and naming emotions.

DISCUSSION QUESTIONS

In this exercise, you are asked to relate and identify infant emotions. Consider how babies express their needs and feelings. Please finish the bulleted statements about babies.

- A baby is happy when….

- A baby expresses hunger by….

- The baby is sad when he/she….

- The baby shows anger when he/she….

- The difference between the baby crying for food and needing attention is….

- When babies are afraid, they react by….

Now, consider that a baby's mom or dad is imprisoned. What signs of distress might the caregiver look for, related to the child's behavior? List at least three signs of distress and note why these behaviors are likely or possible.

1.

2.

3.

Now, list at least three signs that a child is feeling content.

1.

2.

3.

Please note that there is no answer key for this critical thinking exercise.

References

Center on the Developing Child at Harvard University (2015). *Reducing the effects of significant adversity.* https://developingchild.harvard.edu/science/key-concepts/resilience/.

Cerniglia, L., Cimino, S., Ballarotto, G., & Monniello, G. (2014). Parental loss during childhood and outcomes on adolescents' psychological profile: A longitudinal study. *Current Psychology*, 33(4), 545–556. DOI: https://link.springer.com/article/10.1007/s12144-014-9228-3.

Iuele, L. (2018). A guide to parent-infant bonding in the neonatal ICU. Academic Festival, Event 139. https://digitalcommons.sacredheart.edu/cgi/viewcontent.cgi?article=1208&context=acadfest.

Millason, M. (2016). *What is attunement (and why it is important in parenting)?* Retrieved from http://www.simplynaturalmama.com/2016/12/what-is-attunement-and-why-it-is-important-in-parenting/.

Trout, M. (2018). They took my parent away: Little ones affected by incarceration speak. In Gordon, L. (Ed.), *Contemporary research and analysis on the children of prisoners*, 116–133. Newcastle upon Tyne: Cambridge Scholars.

Walker, L.J. (2013). Bonding with books: The parent-infant connection in the neonatal intensive care unit. *Neonatal Network*, 32(2), 104–109.

Weller, D., & Shaver, P.R. (2010, July). Attachment, parental incarceration and possibilities for intervention: An overview. *Attachment and Human Development*, 12(4), 311_331. Doi. 10.1080/14751790903416939.

ZeroToThree.com (2021). *Find resources and services.* Retrieved from https://www.zerotothree.org/.

Answer Key for Section 3.1, Activity 10.

1. [F]; 2. [T]; 3. [T]; 4. [F]; 5. [F]

Insights regarding Section 3.1, Activity 10., True/False Questions:

1. A baby has not touched his morning bottle of formula. The baby is crying. Is the baby likely hungry? Consider this: There can be many reasons that a baby will not drink from his bottle. The baby may not be feeling well. If the child has *not* touched the bottle, there could be something wrong with the formula. The caregiver will need to work through ruling out what could be wrong. The child may need to be held and comforted. Always check with a pediatrician when in doubt.

   2. The caregiver has changed childcare providers three times in the past year. This transition is likely to introduce anxiety for the child. Consider this: While changing childcare providers sometimes cannot be avoided, try to minimize frequent changes. A caregiver might also try to introduce themselves beforehand to become familiar with the new caregiver and environment.

   3. The caregiver's apartment is near a busy elevator. However, the caregiver has moved the baby's crib in her bedroom away from the loud noise. This step is considered a protective measure to reduce stress in the baby. Consider this: This caregiver realized that while she may not be able to change the layout of the apartment, she can minimize the impact of the noise.

   4. Baby's only form of communication is through talking. Consider this: No. An infant cries, coos, and kicks and uses several other ways to communicate.

   5. A baby's primary goal is to survive. Consider this: As noted in the Module overview, a baby's earliest forms of language are crying, cooing, and kicking. This communication helps a baby inform their caregiver that they need food, attention, proximity, and warmth. Routines and rituals introduce predictability, familiarity, and safety. Additionally, when the caregiver addresses a baby's needs, this increases trust.

Answer Key for Section 3.2, Activity 11

1. What can Jennifer do to establish calm? *Use bonding activities such as reading a book and talking with the baby. Also employ modes of reflection to better understand the relationship.*

2. What can Jennifer do to reduce the baby's stress? *Try to isolate sleeping quarters from the noise. Reduce the volume of the television to prevent startle responses. Also, determine the baby's needs and the reasons for the crying and stress response.*

3. What impact, if any, does the volume and/or lighting of the television have on the child? *Noises can cause distress in some babies. High volume and noise may cause startle responses.*

4. What are the possible impacts of the mother's incarceration? *It is possible that the baby misses their mother. Offer reassurance, safety, and nurturing to address the baby's needs and trust and bonding may develop over time.*

Toddlerhood: The Brain, Body, and Stress

MODULE FOCUS

- Section 4.0. Toddlers. Explore toddlerhood developmental milestones aligned with self-identity and verbal and nonverbal expressions.
- Section 4.1. Sympathetic | Parasympathetic: "The Doggie and Brain." Introduce the alignment of fear, stressors, separation anxiety, and the nervous system responses.
- Section 4.2. Managing Internalized and Externalized Behaviors. Consider options used to manage toddlers' behaviors during prison visits.
- Section 4.3. Fight or Flight: Jenny Is Nervous. Discuss the importance of predictability and consistency in daily schedules to reduce stress and extend the discussion on co-regulation.

Resources

Read Guidebook: Hart-Johnson and Johnson (2025) | Chapter 4, "Toddlers, Temperament, and Prison Visits"

Introduction

The brain is a marvelous organ. It is the foundation for children's physical, emotional, and social growth and development. Caregivers who are informed about how these processes work together are better positioned to understand pathways towards optimal parenting.

The module places a particular focus on Toddlers. This module covers children's self-image and explores how children communicate using their nonverbal expressions. The section also suggests ways to help children restore calm. Concepts of internalizing and externalizing emotions are introduced. The section closes with a focus on stress reduction for fight-or-flight responses by introducing activities to enhance emotional regulation.

Section 4.0. Toddlers

Section Focus | Case Example

Toddlers

A toddler's sense of self (self-image) begins to develop during infancy. As time goes on, the child recognizes they are an individual. Children learn about regulation and behaviors from their caregiver's feedback. This development contributes to building elements of character and healthy self-esteem.

Section Objectives

- ☐ Understand what shapes a toddler's sense of self/identity
- ☐ Learn and identify toddlers' communication methods (verbal/nonverbal) and self-identity development
- ☐ Explore and identify strength-based caregiver feedback
- ☐ Critically assess and interpret toddler nonverbal behaviors

Overview

Toddler Self-identity

A child's image of self gradually unfolds with each passing day. Toddlers learn and discover their identities, likes, dislikes, and sense of awareness through their daily activities and feedback from caregivers. This wonderful world of discovery is enhanced and conditioned, based on daily engagement and interactions with others in their environments. The interaction between caregiver and child helps the child to establish themselves as individuals.

Children at the toddler age learn how to communicate with others while also building their self-image and self-awareness. These skills lay the groundwork for future engagement in social settings such as preschool or kindergarten. Communication and social skills in the educational setting is essential and the foundation for future academic accomplishments. Additionally, enhancing communication helps children to further develop their sense of who they are, their personality, and temperament.

Foundational Learning

Self-identity is concerned with the development of personality, likes, dislikes, a sense of autonomy as well as self-appraisal. Caregivers learn about a child's developing sense of self through communication. Because of a toddler's limited language skills, they mostly communicate through gestures and nonverbal language.

The caregiver and the child can learn much from each other during the toddler years. Nonverbal communication accounts for about 90 percent of communication occurring between toddlers and their caregivers (Fast, 1970). Since toddlers are mostly nonverbal, learning their behavioral communication is essential.

Toddlers use physical communication as they develop the critical social skills that enable them to advance in social and interpersonal development. Mirroring parents and those in their immediate environment enables toddlers to develop and master the language of social interaction. These children also learn to develop their self-identities further based on observations of their environment.

Toddler Nonverbal Behaviors. Toddlers' nonverbal reactions include using their bodies to convey their attitudes and emotions. Children at the toddler stage might express the following nonverbal communication:

- Smiles, laughing, or frowns
- Warm or cold stares
- Positive or disapproving facial expressions
- Physical proximity (Snuggles, hugs, affection) or distancing
- Eye contact or avoiding eye contact
- Attentiveness (listening) or ignoring
- Relaxed posture versus ridged posture, closing off (folding arms across their chests)
- Body orientation: relaxed stance or erect posture versus defensive posture (feet turned inward, slumped shoulders)

Strength-based caregiver feedback and fostering close attachment bonds are important relationship building tools. Caregivers can offer valuable feedback to their children using nonverbal cues, eye contact, body language, positioning, and facial expressions that are warm and caring. These methods of feedback show children that caregivers are tuned in. A caregiver's nonverbal feedback might include:

- Turning towards the child and giving them full attention
- Squatting down to a child's level rather than standing in a dominant position
- Positioning near the child
- Touching, holding, hugging, or caressing
- Smiling, nodding, taking notice
- Clapping, showing signs of praise

Each of these interactions help children understand expected behaviors. For example, a parent who turns towards a child, giving full attention, teaches the child how to perform the same process in school.

ACTIVITY 13

The Brain, Body, and Stress

In this activity, consider how children's self-image develops. Next consider children's nonverbal communication. Focus on what toddlers might convey about their feelings using their posture. Review 4.0. Foundational Learning, paying particular attention to *Toddler Nonverbal Behaviors*. Now, examine Figure 4.0, "The Toddler." Try to interpret and identify the non-verbal expression displayed in Figure 4.0. Name at least five non-verbal expressions.

    1.

    2.

    3.

    4.

    5.

The Answer Key for Section 4.0, Activity 13, follows Module 4 Reference list.

Figure 4.0. The Toddler (graphic image by Rhythm Bowers).

Section 4.1. Sympathetic | Parasympathetic: "The Doggie and Brain"

Section Focus | Case Example

The Doggie and the Brain

The toddler approaches the doggie. The doggie barks loudly. The toddler screams and runs toward the caregiver, jumping into the caregiver's arms.

Section Objectives

- ☐ Describe the connection between toddler independence and separation anxiety
- ☐ Grain knowledge about stress and fight- or- flight responses
- ☐ Learn about and describe caregiver's support and emotional co-regulation strategies to restore calm
- ☐ Critically assess and describe ways caregivers can attend to toddlers' separation anxiety and support emotional regulation to restore calm

Overview

The development of independence is a natural part of a child's maturation process. Around age three, children begin to rely less on their caregiver's constant physical presence as a safety net. As toddlers grow, they start understanding concepts like "gone," "work," "shopping," and "bye-bye," indicating comprehension of temporary absence. Children learn through repetition, that when left at a childcare setting, the parents will eventually return for them. This process builds trust during these separations fosters independence. Children, however, do experience stress that requires caregiver co-regulation.

As toddlers explore their world, they encounter stressors when separated from their parents. While children can handle some distance, being separated from their parents for lengthy periods can produce anxiety. Caregivers can support improving children's self-regulation by understanding the link between emotions and body reactions then responding with matched responses.

Foundational Learning

Separation anxiety, triggered by events like an arrest, can affect children. Witnessing a parent's arrest can be distressing due to the uncertainty of the parent's whereabouts and return. Some signs that children are affected by separation anxiety include:

- Worry or unease
- Fear (scared appearance) or dread
- Crying and fussiness
- Tantrums and disruptive behaviors

Stress events and the body's [fight or flight] response. Additionally, for those unfortunate circumstances, a toddler witnessing parental arrest followed by sentencing can trigger fear and separation anxiety. Children are unique and may react differently resulting from separation from their parents. Stress from separation and loss can manifest emotional as well as in their bodies. A child's body responds to stress through the sympathetic and parasympathetic nervous systems. Sympathetic reactions include trembling, sweating, clenching, fleeing, clinging, and more (e.g., tantrums, wetting themselves, tummy aches, appearing scared, crying/panting while sucking in air). Parasympathetic responses aim to restore calm and are thought to be opposite of the stress responses.

> Consider, Doggie & Brain. The toddler approaches the doggie. The doggie barks loudly. The toddler screams and runs toward the caregiver, jumping into the caregiver's arms.

In this scenario, the toddler is adventurous and is learning about animals. He has no history of adverse reactions, so he approaches the doggie. However, the doggie, is likely as frightened as the toddler, barking as a reaction. The toddler runs to the caregiver, with his heart racing, fear of the doggie's reaction, and the toddler believes that his caregiver is his protector. The child likely returns to calm through the caregiver's co-regulation techniques of holding, soothing, and using quiet tones of comfort.

Caregiver interventions to restore calm. Monitoring and reassuring children during separation anxiety is crucial. Let children know they're safe and not in danger. If new to caregiving, assure the child you won't leave permanently. Gradually increase separations to build tolerance. Other interventions include introducing comfort objects (soft stuffed animals, blanket, etc.), fostering relationships with temporary caregivers, keeping promises, using clear statements, and teaching relaxation exercises. Finally, a toddlers' separation anxiety might be a phase they grow out of with caregivers' attentive support. Toddlers require some basics such as rest, routines, clear rules, praise, and security. Familiar routines offer safety, and reassurance during stressful times.

Activity 14

The Brain, Body, and Stress

Review the case vignette 4.1 *The Doggie and the Brain*. Read the simple scenario and consider the content presented in this section, *Foundational Learning*. Now, consider the toddler's stress response. Think of a stress event where a toddler needs their caregiver's support and emotional co-regulation to restore calm. Identify 3 ways that the caregiver can help restore calm in the child—list these strategies aligned with co-regulation below.

1.

2.

3.

Now, consider the seriousness of witnessing a parent's arrest as a toddler. What are the ways that caregivers might restore calm in the child? Document your ideas in a reflection below. Consider the following resource as a guide: *Safeguarding-Children-of-Arrested-Parents-Final_Web_v3.pdf (theiacp.org)*: https://www.theiacp.org/sites/default/files/pdf/Safeguarding-Children-of-Arrested-Parents-Final_Web_v3.pdf

See Answer Key for Activity 14, after Module 4 reference list.

Reflection

Section 4.2. Managing Internalized and Externalized Behaviors

Section Focus | Case Example

BLAKE

At nearly four years old, Blake began visiting his dad at the prison. His grandmother accompanied him. At the end of the visit, Blake was upset, as illustrated by kicking and screaming tantrums. Over time, Blake continued this behavior with tantrums and acting out at home. He then began sucking his thumb and developed challenges with potty training.

Section Objectives

- ☐ Understand how children internalize and externalize stress
- ☐ Use critical reflection and role-play to help children understand prison visiting rules

Overview

The case example focuses on a prison visit. During a first prison visit children may experience a wide array of emotions that are internalized and externalized. A visit with parents in prison can be a great bonding experience. Children naturally want to express their joy and happiness. They also may display their fears, concerns, and worry. The conditions of the prisons are generally not the culprit. Children tend to overlook conditions that parents might consider important (i.e., rules regulations, or how the prison looks). Instead, they want to be near their parent. Proper planning and preparedness may help to enhance the visit and to ensure that the child and the caregiver experience the best outcome possible.

Foundational Learning

Not all prison visits go smoothly. As mentioned, sometimes, children do not understand the rules and protocol. This calls for their caregivers to prepare them for the visits. Otherwise, children my exhibit internalized behaviors or externalize their feelings. Internalized behaviors might result from not understanding conditions. Externalized behaviors might include reactivity toward restrictions. Children might act out and become hyperactive. However, when children understand what to expect, they may try to impress their caregivers and parent by complying. Offering praise for positive behavior can go a long way and reinforce expectations.

Managing internalized and externalized stress behaviors. The caregiver can serve in a role of an emotional coach and help children self-regulate. Preparing for and debriefing after the visit is an opportunity for the caregiver to help children understand their emotions while also setting expectations.

Prison visits usually require a long journey. Children might be tired, hungry, scared, nervous, and exhibit other conditions related to the trip itself. When nervous, toddlers sometimes regress to behaviors they have overcome and regulated, such as having tantrums, bed-wetting, thumb-sucking. These are likely behaviors that will not persist. Responding to each of these conditions could offset adverse reactions during a time designated for bonding. For example, co-regulation might include offering reassurance and taking preventative steps such as extra restroom breaks. Additionally, talking with children before and after the visit can provide insights on having a better experience. Examples of prompts for a discussion include:

Preparation: Example of explaining prison rules that visitors must follow:

- Prisons have special rules to be followed. [share examples that the child already understands]
- The visiting rules require us to sit in chairs facing daddy. Let us practice. I will pretend to be Daddy. You did a good job following the rules. Good job! [positive reinforcement]
- Practice breathing out the anger when frustration ensues … one, two, three. [self-regulation techniques]
- When help is needed, I'm here. [establishing safety and trust]

Debrief (after the visit) examples:

- Sometimes, it is hard to say goodbye, but it is not okay to kick and scream at Grandma and Daddy. [showing empathy, yet remaining firm regarding behavior]
- "Blake, you seem angry (frustrated, sad, or whatever the emotion) when you leave Daddy." [acknowledging without passing judgment]
- Let us take a deep breath. Now, what do you wish you could have done during the visits? Try to explain your feelings. [assisting with emotional regulation]

ACTIVITY 15

The Brain, Body, and Stress

Review the case vignette 4.2 *Blake*, and the Overview. Now, consider the experience during the prison visit. Review the list of possible prompts for discussion with Blake (in **Managing internalized and externalized stress behaviors**). Role-play holding a discussion with Blake with the goal in mind to (1) help him understand prison visiting rules; (2) help Blake to use a method of emotional release rather than having a tantrum; and (3) explain why Daddy cannot get up and leave. Make sure your chosen language is age appropriate. List your responses and thoughts on role-play below. Remember to focus on the examples listed under *Managing Internalized and Externalized Behaviors*.

Using Age-Appropriate Language, Role-Play:

1. Help Blake understand prison visiting rules;
2. Help Blake to use a method of emotional release rather than having a tantrum; and
3. Explain why Daddy cannot get up and leave.

See Answer Key with suggested discussion points and explanation after Module 4 Reference list.

Section 4.3. Fight or Flight: Jenny Is Nervous

Section Focus | Case Example

TODDLERS AND CO-REGULATION

Jenny was four years old. Jenny was naturally a nervous child. However, when her dad became incarcerated, she began having nightmares, wanting Mom to leave the night light on. She also became fearful in some situations that seemed unreasonable. For example, she began hiding behind Mom's leg whenever someone visited.

Section Objectives

☐ Understand emotional co-regulation strategies
☐ Deepen the knowledge and understand the linkage between stress and fight-or-flight responses
☐ Learn about the do's and don'ts of emotional regulation
☐ Use critical reflection to identify co-regulation skills that can help both the caregiver and child reduce stress

Overview

Children's nervousness is a natural response to unknowns. Fortunately, caregivers can provide love and safety to protect children and ease their fears. Informed caregivers are attuned and strategize on how to reach a happy medium when responding to their children's fears.

Learning about emotional regulation tools can assist caregivers. Learning the science behind emotional regulation, followed by a few *Do's and Don'ts*, can be helpful for caregivers and their children.

Foundational Learning

Some caregivers can help children to develop emotional regulation skills. The first step in emotional regulation development in children is to understand how the body responds to stressful situations and learn how children can regulate their feelings.

Fight-or-flight. Child development experts often explain the body's stress reactions (fight-or-flight) and emotional regulation using a metaphor of a car's "gas pedal" and "brake." When a child becomes upset, their emotional "gas pedal" activates. Fear of unknown situations or people can activate the gas pedal. This acceleration can be compared to the body's sympathetic nervous system's fight-or-flight response. When a response activates the *emotional brain*, it then accelerates into high gear, placing children in stress mode. Generally, children's stress responses are not extreme unless the conditions are extreme.

Many caregivers may recall their toddler having a "melt-down." In such cases, during stress mode, out of self-preservation from fearful events, the child's heart rate increases. The child may become sweaty as the blood flows to the large muscle groups (gearing for fight-or-flight), their cheeks may feel flushed, the pupils dilate, and the breathing may become quickened (this may also be displayed by crying, sniffing and panting breaths).

Co-regulation strategies. Physical responses can be regulated or co-regulated through caregiver practices. The parts of the brain that slow the stress response and help the children calm down and regulate are analogous to the "brake pedal." The following are a few steps to enable the "brake pedal" and to help children regulate:

- **Provide comfort** (physical and verbal) to children who are experiencing intense emotions. A hug, physical embrace while rocking them, or using soothing tones of reassurance
- **Be responsive** and use direct caring toward children while not discounting their feelings
- **Validate children's feelings** by acknowledging them
- **Teach children** how to express their feelings

Table 4.3.0 contain a few Do's and Don'ts when parenting children.

Table 4.3.0. Caregiver Do's and Don'ts of Emotional Regulation	
Do	*Don't*
Use empathy	Ridicule (i.e., "boys don't cry")
Discuss feelings	Punish children for their reactions
Validate children's emotions	Invalidate children's emotions
Teach breathing techniques (for calming)	Ignore the child, letting them fend for themselves
Manage conflict in the home	Demonstrate aggressiveness

When children similar to Jenny have nightmares, try to reassure them as best possible, informing them that the monster is not coming for them. Remind them that you are their protector. Help them to develop their social skills (see also Section 5.0) to reduce stress when in new environments. Talk out their concerns using age-appropriate language. When they do have success, reward their accomplishments.

Activity 16

The Brain, Body, and Stress

Developing emotional coaching skillsets requires parents to model the behaviors they wish to see in their children. It also requires parents to understand their children's emotions and respond accordingly. Enhancing co-regulation skills can help both the caregiver and child reduce stress. Consider the list of Do's and Don'ts and think of how caregivers might add to this list. Search the Internet on parenting and co-regulation and list at least 5 "Do's" and 5 "Don'ts" to the list below. *Facilitators, use these activities for group discussion.*

DO'S

    1.

    2.

    3.

    4.

    5.

DON'T(S)

    1.

    2.

    3.

    4.

    5.

Review the scenario about four-year-old Jenny, described in, 4.3 *Toddler and Co-Regulation*. As an emotional coach, the caregiver can become more empathic by better understanding the child's feelings, thoughts, and behaviors. On a separate sheet of paper or in a notebook, draft an outline of talking points on how Jenny's mom can help her child overcome her anxiety of sleeping alone. What are the talking points? In what ways might the incarceration of the parent influence this talk? How, if at all, could the child be impacted by the separation between her and her father?

The Answer Key for Section 4.3, Activity 16 follows Module 4 Reference list.

References

Fast, J. (1970). *Body language: The essential secrets of non-verbal Communication*. New York: MJF.

The Answer Key for Section 4.0, Activity 13

1. Frowning
2. Avoiding eye contact
3. Closing off (folding arms across their chests)
4. Body orientation (feet turned inward)
5. Disapproving facial expressions

The Answer Key for Section 4.1, Activity 14

Event Example of a Stress Event: A Child Has a New Caregiver

1. Assure the child you will not leave permanently. Try to expose the child to the caregiver before leaving for an extensive time.
2. Introduce the caregiver first. Consider leaving security objects (stuffed animals, blanket).
3. Keep promises "I'll be back by dinner time."

The Answer Key for Section 4.2, Activity 15

Reflection:

- After a child witnesses arrest, help to restore calm through lots of reassurance that you will keep them safe and remain their caregiver.
- Explain that the parent has gone with the police to talk about important matters
- Create and maintain a predictable schedule
- Show attunement to the child's needs
- Love and care and support the child

The Answer Key for Section 4.3, Activity 16

DO'S

1. Use co-regulation techniques, like hugging and embracing the child.
2. Use calm voice tones
3. Acknowledge your similar feelings (like sadness or fear)
4. Paraphrase what your child has expressed feeling (showing understanding and empathy)
5. Give children's feelings a name.

DON'T(S)

1. Use spanking to address stressful behavior
2. Implement scare tactics ("If you don't stop, a monster is coming for you.")
3. Threated to take away toys (express wanted behavior)
4. Use high intensity shouting tones when reasoning
5. Use mean words—especially those that are lasting and imprinted in memory.

Cultivating Well-Being in Children

MODULE FOCUS

- Section 5.0. Preschoolers: Children's Stories. Examine preschooler developmental milestones and consider stories as tools for building emotional literacy.
- Section 5.1. Being Social and Confident. Explore modeling and teaching self-acceptance, self-confidence, and enhancing self-esteem.
- Section 5.2. Protecting the Critical Window of Development. Explore brain development, language, and emotions and understand how experiences shape the brain.
- Section 5.3. The Roadmap to Recovery and Resilience. Learn about the using protective factors in the context of witnessing parental arrest.

Resources

Read Guidebook: Hart-Johnson and Johnson (2025) | Chapter 5, "Throwing Crayons"

Introduction

The heart of this workbook centers on providing caregivers with tips and recommendations gathered from our primary research, empirical literature, and child development specialists for children. Through activities and interventions, caregivers can help shape children's lives in a manner that positively impacts their growth and future interactions with others.

Children learn and develop uniquely, yet there are common expectations that can be used as guidelines for anticipated cognitive (brain development) and physical growth. This section focuses on caregivers with children in the preschooler age range (three- to five-years old). As you read this section, consider the following principles (Brain Balance, n.d.):

- The brain and the body function as a team!
- Young children's brains and experiences are linked.
- Parents can influence their child's brain development.
- Each child is unique.
- The uniqueness of each child drives their needs.

- Children's emotions impact their comprehension and their development of social-emotional competencies.
- Stressful conditions affect a child's ability to learn about the self and the world.

This module returns to the importance of children's holistic care and well-being by reinforcing main ideas related to physical and mental health. The section reinforces that it is crucial to think of the child's mind, body, emotions, and environment as a part of the same team. A child needs exposure to an environment that contributes to healthy brain development, an environment that provides essential nutrition, safety, and physical health. Adults can model emotional regulation, secure attachments, and provide a pathway for children's intellectual development.

Section 5.0. Preschoolers: Children's Stories

Section Focus | Case Example

PRESCHOOLERS (3–5 YEARS)

Communication and emotional connections between caregiver and child are established through actions and verbal and nonverbal language. Early exposure to words can build a child's literacy skills, comprehension, intellect, and enhance social skills.

Section Objectives

- ☐ Discuss preschooler language development and emotional vocabulary
- ☐ Learn about social skills building blocks for intelligence and social engagement
- ☐ Critically reflect and apply the use of the Emotional Wheel

Overview

LANGUAGE DEVELOPMENT AND EMOTIONAL VOCABULARY

Preschoolers absorb sensory information from their parents and others in their environment. This process includes learning language skills through observation, mimicking, and practice. Language enables a preschooler to access a repository of words that allow them to describe who they are, what they are feeling, and what they wish to do or say. Language opens the door to a wonderful world of discovery.

Some child development specialists indicate that the first 1000 days of a child's life are critical in forming intellectual, emotional, and relational development. This development occurs in the body's central command center: the brain.

The brain's cognition advances during the preschooler age, when children begin to understand how to associate words as descriptors of objects. At the preschooler stage of development, children generally increase their vocabulary from about 500 to 2,000 words. They should be able to speak in simple sentences. Children can begin to better communicate with others around them. For example, they may describe their hair, face, shoes, colors, and other simple objects. Children at this age also enjoy books and stories. This time frame is optimal to expose preschool children to literature, as building blocks for intelligence and social engagement and expressing themselves. Books help children to:

- Build and enhance empathy.
- Develop an affinity for learning.
- Provide a platform for discussing sensitive topics.
- Enhance parent-child bonding.
- Promote imagination and creativity.
- Enhance listening skills.

Foundational Learning

Language acquisition allows most children to become more social as they advance in age. With these skills, preschool-aged children begin to interact with other children

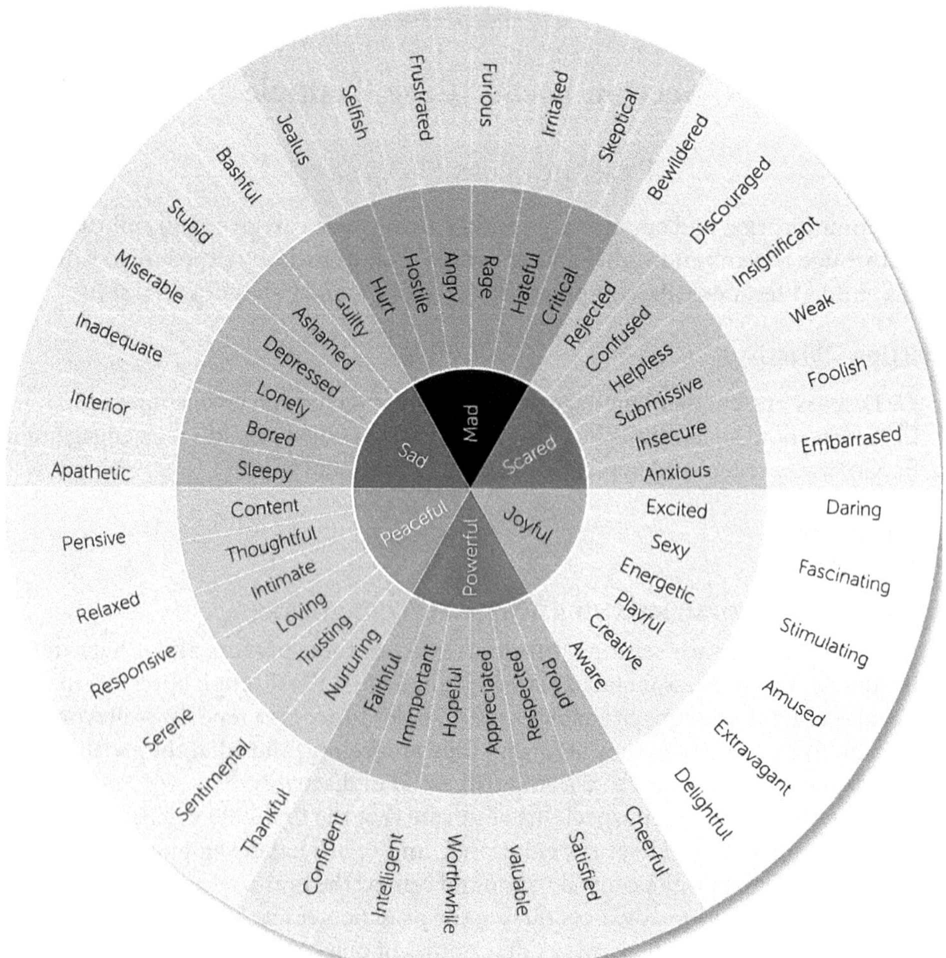

Figure 5.0. Icfyb.com (n.d.). Feelings [Emotional] Wheel (adopted from icfyb.com |These-usstar, Wikimedia Commons, CC BY-SA 4.0).

rather than play independently. At this stage, their emotions and interactions converge. For example, children may become temperamental, where they are happy one minute and angry the next. They may feel emotions such as joy, sadness and guilt, fear, and anxiety. However, not all children at the preschool age know how to describe these feelings. At this stage, parents can help children begin to understand these emotions by giving them a name and talking about the associated feelings.

One method of teaching feelings is by using an emotional wheel that helps to explore granular levels of primary emotions.

Emotional awareness can enhance, lead to self-expression and building interpersonal skills to bond with others. This process helps to build children's as well as their caregiver's emotional vocabulary. When children recognize such feelings as warmth, joy, empathy, confidence, and feeling cheerful, they can bring these emotions to social relationships. At the same time, children are building cognition, self-awareness, and emotional intelligence skills. Parents can enhance these skillsets by:

- Encouraging children to play with others, using emotional awareness of their feelings.
- Teaching sharing behaviors.
- Teaching kindness.
- Helping children to understand safe behavior during play.
- Explaining and modeling good proper social skills.
- Teaching children how to take turns (rules).
- Encouraging children to learn empathy (for example, when another child cries or gets hurt).
- Establishing group rules (teaches morals).

The emotional wheel can also be used to help children better understand feelings illustrated in storybooks. Use the word list for an open discussion about the storybook characters as they align or differ from children's feelings.

Activity 17

Cultivating Child Well-being

Associating words with persons, places, and things can be an engaging learning activity between caregivers and children. One example includes caregivers using the emotional wheel and asking their child to draw a picture of the associated emotional expressions. Caregivers can also draw a picture of an emotional expression and ask the child to guess what feelings are displayed. For example, the following icon illustrates a happy emotion.

Figure 5.0.1. Smiley Face.

Help your child create their own emotional wheel.

1. Have your child draw a large circle.
2. Divide the circle similar to a pie chart (*see* Figure 5.0 emotional wheel as an example).
3. Together, name as many emotions that they can think of.

Note: Caregivers can add to the list of identified emotions to help build emotional literacy. Please note that there is no answer key for this critical thinking exercise.

Engaging young children early and often may provide them a means of decoding their emotions and interpreting the emotions of others. Note the difference between the inner descriptors and the outer labels on the emotional wheel (Figure 5.0). The inner portion of the wheel demonstrates extremes or elevated emotions. The outer bands represent the initial feelings before escalation. If intervention is applied before the escalation, it is possible that one may not ever reach the full-blown emotional expression. For example, consider the first week of a diet and you are feeling "weak" and tempted to eat snacks. Before getting to the point of feeling helpless to temptation, you might try to remove the snacks and replace them with a healthy substitute. Or, yet another example: If a child feels envious (and potentially leading to *hurt* feelings) over a sibling's new birthday toys, you might explain how sharing in the excitement of a sibling's birthday might generate excitement about their own upcoming milestone. This may thwart the child becoming hurt and eventually angry. Using the emotional wheel can be helpful in many ways, but mainly to understand the variation and degrees of emotions.

Section 5.1. Being Social and Confident

Section Focus | Case Example

Socially Accepted

A child's self-love, self-respect and social acceptance is shaped in part by the feedback received from the world around them. However, their primary sense of self-acceptance comes from their parents. Caregivers can show children acceptance through their engagement, listening, responses, and empathy.

Section Objectives

- ☐ Understand modeling and teaching social acceptance: self-confidence, self-love, self-acceptance, and self-respect
- ☐ Deepen knowledge about children's social skills-building
- ☐ Role model and practice using play activities to build children's social skills

Overview

Children's self-love and self-respect are bolstered by supportive people who reinforce the idea that children are lovable, have positive qualities, and are admired by their close bonds (friendships) and social circles. These factors help foster children's self-acceptance.

Before children extend to the larger societal context, they learn from their family-related connections. Children's worlds and networks of connection may be limited to family members, neighborhood friends, and other closely connected people. Each of these networks offers feedback in a variety of ways. Therefore, the primary caregiver and other family members can positively influence children, as these connections play a central role.

Foundational Learning

Social acceptance is the integration and acceptance into groups, clubs, social networks, or assimilation in peer networks (Sam, 2022). Children learn how to smile, have conversations, and engage with others based on their influencers. This acceptance is particularly important for children who might be at risk for being stigmatized because of the status of parents. Developing strong interpersonal skills and confidence might thwart the risks of children becoming isolated without healthy interaction to form friendships and be accepted in peer groups. These are important skills that mitigate the risks associated with stigma often aligned with parental incarceration.

Children with positive social skills display: collaborative sharing, self-reliance, and a positive affect [positive display of emotions] (Aguiar & Aguiar, 2020, p. 4). Benefits include experiencing group connections, learning from peer engagement, and feeling a part of a social network of friends.

Caregivers can help children in building social acceptance. Simple phrases such as, "I am so proud of you," "Good job!" and other forms of praise can go a long way. Through this engagement, children enhance their self-worth. Teaching children about morals, acceptance, competence, and developing self-esteem can help them develop self-confidence and social engagement tools.

Recall that a child's view of themselves can affect their sense of worth and self-esteem. If a child feels appreciated and competent, they may gain a sense of agency and accomplishment. If a parent is too busy or lacks interactions and engagement, the message to their child is that "you are not as important as my task," "I am busy," or "I don't have time for you." On the other hand, caregivers can nurture the relationship with the child by actively listening to them, demonstrating empathy, and helping their children to master skills on multiple levels. Skills development activities can include constructive play, role modeling, problem-solving, and comprehension.

Build Self-Confidence

Building social skills can help children to feel a sense of belonging as well as enhance self-confidence. Social skills can help children learn to engage with others appropriately. Brain Balance (n.d.) provides ways to improve a child's social skills in a fun and beneficial manner.

- Understand your child's personality. Not every child is born to be an extrovert or social butterfly. Respect your child's preferences for engagement.
- Teach children how to become self-aware of their body language. Then role- play social engagement. For example, role-play interacting with guests.
- Teach children the basics of asking questions related to the individuals with whom they are engaged or interacting. By asking questions, uncomfortable silence is avoided.
- Teach your child empathy and compassion. These are skills that can enhance interpersonal bonds.
- A child's sense of self- worth and value is enhanced when they have a sense of agency or choice. When children have a say in decision-making, it can be empowering, knowing that their choices matter.

Explore the child's hobbies and affinities; identify their talents. Perhaps, they can learn to play an instrument or play sports. Each of these activities promotes group activity and collaboration.

Again, social relationships and interpersonal skills are first modeled by caregivers. Modeling may be one of the most effective methods of teaching children's social skills.

ACTIVITY 18

Cultivating Child Well-being

Social acceptance and self-esteem seem to be closely related. Many social skills are acquired by children through the teachings of their parents and family members. Teachers and others who engage with children influence these skillsets as well.

Consider activities and play exercises that build children's social skills and acceptance. Review the list of activities that caregivers can use to help children build self-confidence and acceptance.

Activities List

Role Model and Practice: Separately note on paper or in a journal/notebook, your ideas and create a 3-step plan on how to perform, engage, and interact with children when performing any of the following activities. For example, non-competitive play might include *"Simon Says." Facilitators*, groups of two or more can take turns discussing their views and ideas on role modeling activities. Please note that there is no answer key for this critical thinking exercise.

ROLE PLAY ACTIVITY:

- Physical: Encourage group non-competitive play and participation.
- Constructive Play: Play-Doh, building activities, and many games provide children with the opportunity to make choices, share ideas, take turns, and match objects.
- Problem-Solving: the use of puzzles and books to anticipate sequence work through complexities. Make sure that the information to solve the problem exists in the book.
- Comprehension: Reading to children; ask questions that encourage critical thinking. For example, when reading about a character in a book, ask, "What do you think will happen next?" "Why?"
- Practice Social Skills: Learn manners, teach kindness, teach cooperation and goal setting. Offer and teach appropriate feedback and listening skills. Use repetition and practice.

Role Model and Practice: (use separate paper/journal to record your ideas).

Section 5.2. Protecting the Critical Window of Development

Section Focus | Case Example

On the Same Team

The brain affects every area of a child's life. The brain and body are on the same team! A child's physical, emotional, and cognitive development are part of the same central system. The brain grows and develops based on children's environment.

Section Objectives

☐ Explore concepts of healthy brain development
☐ Learn about the caregiver influences that shape and co-construct children's healthy brain development
☐ Critically assess the impact of stress on children and how both positive and negative experiences shape the brain

Overview

While it may seem that the mind, body, and intellect seem magically to come together in harmony to contribute to a child's development, science explains this mystery. The first years of a child's life greatly influence the physical architecture of their brain. A caregiver can significantly influence a child's healthy brain development during this critical period.

The caregiver is considered the gatekeeper of child development. Science confirms that caregiver interactions contribute to building the physical architecture and wiring of a child's brain. The engagement, communication, and role modeling between caregiver and child help to shape the child's brain and lay the framework for future mental health and well-being. It is reasonable to say that caregivers can co-construct healthy brains.

Foundational Learning

Both positive and negative experiences shape the brain. Positive experiences such as warm and comforting interactions, structured and unstructured play, and communication stimulate the child's brain to grow positively. Negative experiences might include exposure to conflict, neglect, prolonged stress, and abuse.

A Critical Window

Children's brains develop in spurts called critical periods. The first occurs around age two, with the second major significant spurt occurs during adolescence. At the start of these periods, the number of connections (synapses) between the brain cells (neurons) doubles. Two-year-olds have twice as many synapses as adults. Because these connections between brain cells are where learning occurs, twice as many synapses enable them to learn faster than at any other time in life. Children's experiences during this phase have lasting effects on their development [Sriram, 2020, p.1].

One of the primary sources that shape children's experiences is stress. Surprisingly, some stress is good. For example, preparation for a new task or taking the first steps to perform a task, e.g., readying for the first day of daycare. This stress is considered good because it is motivational.

However, other stresses such as abrupt transitions can be more serious. Specifically, recurrent changes which upset children's routines may cause distress, equating to challenges to safety and security. For example, frequently changing caregivers will likely be stressful for children. This may cause a child to be consistently in a high-stress mode especially when they are constantly seeking a caregiver's safety, comfort, and protection. This point of concern reinforces the importance of routine and consistency in child development.

SEVERAL INFLUENCES SHAPE CHILDREN'S BRAIN DEVELOPMENT:
1. genetic makeup
2. interaction with the primary caregiver
3. life experiences and exposure
4. brain circuitry

The Center on the Developing Child at Harvard University (2015a) informs the following:

- Genes provide the foundation for brain development. However, earliest experiences will determine the blueprint for a child's future.
- Interaction with primary caregiver. The child's earliest experiences with a caregiver(s) will affect physical and mental health, behavior, and temperament.
- Life experiences and exposure. Life experiences and recurring exposure to learning opportunities can enrich the child's life. For example, consider the benefits of advancing problem-solving skills when introducing new words and language, and activities that enhance the memory of persons, places, and things.
- Brain circuitry. The architecture of the brain is comprised of circuitry made of neurons. Repetition reinforces and builds strong neuron connections. A child's environment dictates which circuits get the most use and become robust. Therefore, those primarily used circuits will become a part of a child's long-standing architecture. Others with less use get pruned away. These foundational neurons provide the pathway for motor skills, visual, emotional, behavioral regulation and control, and more!

ACTIVITY 19

Cultivating Child Well-being

The Centers for Disease Control and Prevention (CDC, 2021) indicated that caregivers can contribute to healthy brain development and overall health and child well-being by using the following strategies:

Read to children.

Develop age-appropriate tasks.

Use positive discipline with explicit language to help children learn rules and appropriate behavior.

Help children develop communication skills through modeling complete sentences and helping them to communicate their thoughts and ideas.

Allow children to make choices (e.g., picking out a shirt to wear, selecting a toy, game, or book).

Make sure children have proper nutrition.

Allow for plenty of rest.

Keep children's environments safe and free of hazards.

ACTIVITY 1:

Consider the statement: *both positive and negative experiences shape the brain.* With that thought in mind, answer the following questions with a true or false answer.

1. Caregivers have the ability to help children shape children's brain architecture in a manner that will serve children well into their adult years.	☐ True ☐ False
2. When caregivers help children to understand the challenges occurring in their lives, they can minimize or reduce stress in children.	☐ True ☐ False
3. The following factors influence and shape children's brain development: genes, caregiver-child engagement, life experiences and exposure and brain circuitry.	☐ True ☐ False
4. A child who has more negative experiences during early developmental years will likely be impacted by these circumstances unless a caregiver intervenes.	☐ True ☐ False

See Answer Key for Section 5.2, Activity 19 after Module 5 Reference list.

Section 5.3. The Roadmap to Recovery and Resilience

Section Focus | Case Example

WITNESSING PARENTAL ARREST

Becky was five years old when her father was arrested and sent to jail. The whole family and guests were in the middle of a picnic when police officers stormed the backyard and handcuffed Becky's dad. Becky witnessed the arrest and handcuffing. She is now afraid of police officers. She once hid behind her mother when she saw a security guard at the mall. Her mother had to calm her down.

Section Objectives

- ☐ Understand resilience and apply techniques to help children better understand the arrest of a parent and the role of law enforcement
- ☐ Deepen understanding related to how children develop resilience
- ☐ Critically reflect and devise strategies for role play discussion with children who witnessed parental arrest

Overview

Witnessing the arrest of a parent can be traumatic. It is unclear how many children in America have witnessed their parent's arrest. In the Hart-Johnson and Johnson (2022) study, among the 22 caregivers who took part in focus-group interviews regarding parental incarceration, at least three participants indicated their children had witnessed an arrest. The good news is that there are efforts underway in some jurisdictions (e.g., Buffalo, NY) to conduct child-sensitive arrest protocols. However, there is more work to be done.

Foundational Learning

Seven percent (7%) of America's youth will experience parental incarceration during childhood. Some of these children will witness their parent's arrest in the home. These adverse experiences could impact children's future social and adaptive developmental milestones (Poehlmann-Tynan et al., 2021).

Even though witnessing a parent's arrest can be devastating, children can recover. Children whose caregivers/parents intervene, may help children to recover and adjust from the adverse event.

Not every child will respond to an adverse event such as witnessing a parent's arrest in the same way. Some children can develop *resilience*.

Resilience refers to how well a child adapts to stressors or difficulties occurring in their lives. When adversity occurs in a child's life, the counterbalance is the application of positive actions taken, known as *protective factors*. Children who have been exposed to protective factors tend to overcome many life challenges. A child who has at least one positive, supportive relationship can help balance out the *risk factors* associated with negative experiences. Children build their resilience through healthy relationships, provided by loving, supportive caregivers. A few ways to enhance resilience in children include:

- **Supportive adult relationships** (Securely Attached): When children face adversity, a supportive adult can help them to find hope, self-regulate, and gain reassurance that they are going to get through the experience.
- **Teach children to manage stress**: Some stress is good. Over time, with exposure to low-level stress, children learn to adjust and manage their emotional responses. Successful adaptation assists in handling future stress response(s).
- **Early development of resilience**. While resilience can be developed at any age, the earlier a child learns to cope with life stressors, the better he or she will fare. According to the Center on the Developing Child, "The brain and other biological systems are most adaptable early in life, and the development that occurs in the earliest years lays the foundation for a wide range of resilient behaviors" (Center on the Developing Child, Harvard University, 2015a, p. 1).
- **Cultural rituals and traditions**. Use of rituals and traditions passed down and shared among the family can bolster hope, faith, and belief in a better tomorrow (e.g., faith-based examples and stories that offer hope can foster resilience).
- **Use scaffolding**. Help children build from prior learning by reinforcement, repetition, and continuity. In other words, when children experience adversity, teach them skills to recover from each event as a teachable moment. Over time, children develop their own coping skills leading to resilience.
- **Strengthen self-regulation and adaptive skills building**. Continue to help children regulate their emotions through role modeling and reassurance. Talk with children, ask about their feelings, and help them cope through engagement, optimism, and support.

Even if a child has not had positive relationships in the past with the caregiver, cultivating a loving relationship that helps to build resilience can start at any time. The Center on the Developing Child (2015b) offered that even children who are extremely sensitive to adversity have responded exceptionally well when introduced to resilience-building conditions.

ACTIVITY 20

Cultivating Child Well-Being

In this activity, read first the strategies below. Then reflect upon methods of calming children after they have witnessed arrest of a parent or family member. You are asked to role play individually or in a group. Please note that there is no answer key for this critical thinking exercise.

STRATEGIES FOR DISCUSSION

Strategies for Youth (Connecting Cops & Kids ®) offers the following guidance for children who have *witnessed the arrest* of their parents (Strategies for Youth, n.d.).

Acknowledge the parent-child relationship: *I know you love your Mommy and Daddy.*
Speak in age-appropriate, loving tones.
For children over 4 years old, convey that the parents are going with the police to talk, but do not make promises (like, "They will be home tomorrow").

Further, parents can help children better understand the arrest of a parent through understanding the role of law enforcement in society. Upon arrest, children might internalize feelings of shame and guilt. They may develop distrust, dislike, and fear of police officers. Therefore, the following tips are offered (Strategiesforyouth.org, n.d.):

1. Parents should comfort their children and explain the basic nature of the arrest.*
2. If children appear traumatized, seek formal intervention such as the support of a therapist. It is possible to locate a community organization that provides these services without imposing fees.
3. Speak to the child on their level (bend down or sit at eye level)
4. Explain why the police have come to the home. For example,
5. "Daddy/Mommy is going with the police to discuss important matters." "They are going to be okay." "This is not your fault."
6. When answers to questions are unknown, refrain from making things up. Instead, reply that the answer is not known at this time, but it will be discussed when made available.

Note: Parents do not have to explain the details of the alleged crime. It is more important to reassure the child about the parent's safety and explain that the parent's arrest is not their fault.

Other tips include the following.

Help young children to calm down by:

- Give them a favorite toy (stuffed animal) as a distraction and comfort
- Offer reassuring hugs and comfort
- Help the child take deep breaths to calm down

Look for signs of Trauma:

- Sleep disturbances
- Separation anxiety
- Hypervigilance
- Physical complaints (stomachache or headache)
- Irritability
- Emotional (upset, anxiety, fear)
- Flat affect (showing no emotion at all)
- Trouble concentrating

Reflections

Journal what stands out as substantive and note why. Role-play how you would:

1. Explain the arrest of the parent.
2. Use strategies to calm the child.

Facilitators: Pair the members of your group and ask them to role-play (one person in the role of the caregiver, the other in the role of the child).

References

Aguiar, A.L., & Aguiar, C. (2020). Classroom composition and quality in early childhood education: A systematic review. *Children and Youth Services Review*, 115, Article 105086. Doi: https://doi.org/10.1016/j.childyouth.2020.105086.

Brain Balance. (n.d.) *6 ways to improve your child's social skills*. Retrieved from https://www.brainbalancecenters.com/blog/ways-improve-childs-social-skills.

The Center on the Developing Child at Harvard University. (2015a). Resilience. Retrieved from https://developingchild.harvard.edu/science/key-concepts/resilience/.

The Center on the Developing Child at Harvard University. (2015b). The impact of early adversity on children's development. Retrieved from https://developingchild.harvard.edu/wp-content/uploads/2015/05/-inbrief-adversity-1.pdf.

The Centers for Disease Control and Prevention. (2021). Early brain development and health. Retrieved from https://www.cdc.gov/ncbddd/childdevelopment/early-brain-development.html.

Hart-Johnson, A., & Johnson, G. (2022). Caregivers' family relations assessment and communication strategies. *Science Publishing Group*, 11(5), 157–168. https://www.sciencepublishinggroup.com/article/10.11648/j.pbs.20221105.12.

Poehlmann-Tynan, J., Muentner, L., Pritzl, K., Cuthrell, H., Hindt, L.A., Davis, L., & Shlafer, R. (2021). The health and development of young children who witnessed their parent's arrest prior to parental jail incarceration. *International Journal of Environmental Research and Public Health*, 18(9):4 512. Doi: 10.3390/ijerph18094512.

Sam, N. (n.d.). Social acceptance. *The psychology dictionary*. Retrieved from https://psychologydictionary.org/social-acceptance.

Sriram, R. (2020). Why ages 2–7 matter so much for brain development. Retrieved from https://www.edutopia.org/article/why-ages-2-7-matter-so-much-brain-development.

Strategiesforyouth.org. (2022.) How to explain arrest to a child age 1 to 4. Retrieved from https://strategiesforyouth.org/sitefiles/wp-content/uploads/2014/10/Sills-What-to-Anticipate-Chart-for-Police.pdf.

Answer Key for Section 5.2, Activity 19:

1. Caregivers have the ability to help children shape children's brain architecture in a manner that will serve children well into their adult years.	☑ True ☐ False
2. When caregivers help children to understand the challenges occurring in their lives, they can minimize or reduce stress in children.	☑ True ☐ False
3. The following factors influence and shape children's brain development: genes, caregiver-child engagement, life experiences and exposure and brain circuitry.	☑ True ☐ False
4. A child who has more negative experiences during early developmental years will likely be impacted by these circumstances unless a caregiver intervenes.	☑ True ☐ False

Nurturing Self-Esteem in Children

MODULE FOCUS

- Section 6.0. Middle Childhood: Cape of Confidence. Review middle childhood development aligned with personality development, self-worth, and self-esteem.
- Section 6.1. Self Worth and Resilience. Explore concepts of enhancing self-esteem and developing social connections and building resilience.
- Section 6.2. Assimilating and Belonging. Discuss the importance of children developing social-emotional skills.
- Section 6.3. Self-Appraisal, Shame, and Guilt. Review the connections between self-appraisal, loss, grief, and social-emotional identity.

Resources

Read Guidebook: Hart-Johnson and Johnson (2025) | Chapter 6, "Everyone Else Had a Mom and Dad"

Additional Resources

Plummer, D. (2007). *Helping Children to Build Self-Esteem: A Photocopiable Activities Book*, second edition. Jessica Kingsley.

Introduction

This module focuses on how children in the middle childhood age group can benefit from caregivers helping them to develop a positive self-image and a sense of self-worth. Selected activities enhance caregivers' awareness of children's developing personalities and self-esteem while illuminating their individualism and uniqueness. Self-esteem entails how a person views and judges their self-image. Caregivers will explore how children, learning through engagement and interaction with parents, will develop positive or negative feelings about their own abilities, appearance, physical skills, emotional, and cognitive intelligence. The module reinforces notions that caregivers provide contributions to a child's feedback loop. Finally, emphasis is placed on processes of building self-confidence and helping children to have a sense of belonging while exploring strength-based parenting methods, focusing on children's strengths rather than deficits.

Section 6.0. Middle Childhood: The Cape of Confidence

Section Focus | Case Example

The Cape of Confidence: Self-esteem

Self-esteem is an evaluation of oneself. A positive self-image contributes to building self-esteem. Self-confidence involves trusting one's ability to make the correct decisions, use judgment, and believe in oneself. Building self-confidence comes with practice, setting goals, and achieving them.

Section Objectives

☐ Differentiate between self-image and self-esteem
☐ Identify and difference between high and low self-esteem
☐ Summarize caregiver interventions for enhancing children's self-esteem
☐ Demonstrate how S.M.A.R.T. goals can be applied to life skills planning for caregivers and children

Overview

During middle childhood, children's self-identities and maturation feature prominently. This age group is between six and ten years old. During middle childhood maturation, development aligned with personality, self-worth, and self-esteem evolve.

Children in this age group continue to shape their individual personalities. Along with this development, their ideas on perceived value or self-worth advance.

While *self-image* and self-esteem are closely related, the former is a *description*, and the latter is an *evaluation* or judgment. A person's self-image is how they view or see themselves as individuals. However, self-esteem is the attachment of label, value, and perceived self-worth as an individual. A person with high self-esteem has the following characteristics:

- Self-like
- Unconditional self-love
- Assertiveness
- Self-confidence
- Makes choices (trusting instincts and judgments)
- Does not feel inept if someone disagrees with them
- Takes pride in who they are as individuals
- Strong principles (morals)
- Realistic
- Not ashamed to ask for help
- They do not need to prove themselves to others (to obtain validation)

- Accepts compliments and warm regard
- Treats themselves with dignity and respect

These are just a few of the attributes aligned with high self-esteem. Caregivers can nurture these elements in their children.

Children with *low self-esteem* may not have confidence and require a bit of support. For various reasons, they may not feel accepted and respected for who they are. Their interactions with others may be limited and they may prefer isolation. Children who could benefit from building positive self-image might display the following behaviors:

- Lack self-acceptance
- Low appreciation for personal accomplishments
- Lack unconditional self-love
- Lack confidence or has low confidence in abilities
- May not accept compliments
- Pessimistic
- Low aspirations or goals
- Feel unlovable
- May not take risks or try out new challenges
- May avoid leading team activities
- May lack confidence and the ability to trust their own decisions
- Self-destructive
- Self-sabotage

Foundational Learning

Enhancing children's self-esteem. The middle childhood years are marked by children's needs to belong and fit into social groups (Bailey, 2000). A child's sense of self is first influenced by their caregivers and environment. Caregivers' positive interaction with children helps them to develop a sense of personal value. For example, a caregiver can use strength-based parenting skills and an affirmative voice, declaring, "You are loved and regarded as a valuable member of this family." Positive affirmations related to children's strengths can serve as an intervention to enhance children's self-esteem.

The National Library of Medicine indicated the following premise regarding influencing children's self-esteem and self-image:

- The internal thoughts of self-image shape behaviors.
- Self-image can be shaped and molded using new and reframed thoughts.

Both the conscious and unconscious mind and opinions about self-image can be reshaped and reconditioned. Caregivers can help to shape the self- image held in a child's mind (consciousness) and bolster a child's self-esteem through strength-based parenting. This process is especially important for children who demonstrate the warning signs of low self-esteem. Some examples of strength-based parenting intervention (to build self-esteem) include:

Boost Self-Esteem.

- Helping children to develop a personal list of achievements.
- Helping children to identify their talents, strengths, and abilities.

- Teaching children to understand levels of expectations and the advancement through practiced routines.
- Helping the child set small incremental goals and celebrate them.
- Offering praise for accomplishments; even if the task is not completed, the effort can be acknowledged.
- Providing opportunities to develop skills and confidence.
- Helping children to make eye contact and accept compliments.
- Giving positive feedback (e.g., "I notice that you are really learning a lot about goal setting. I am so proud of you.")

These practices can help children during their early years when they are seeking acceptance and a sense of belonging. Early childhood educators generally practice these processes, as well. The processes of affirming feedback can help children grow into confident adults. Children's self-esteem generally strengthens as they accomplish goals and receive positive appraisals for their deeds.

Activity 21

Nurturing Self-Esteem in Children

Structured activities can help children bolster self-esteem. For example, children can be introduced to the concepts of goal setting. By teaching children S.M.A.R.T (specific, measurable, attainable, realistic, and time-based) goals, they can begin to appreciate managing expectations.

To demonstrate how S.M.A.R.T. goals work, consider yourself a caregiver with the desire to practice some of the interventions and life skills listed in the "Boost Self-Esteem" list. Create two S.M.A.R.T goals that you could use to help children improve their self-esteem. Please note that there is no answer key for this critical thinking exercise.

Example:

"I will meet with my child on Saturday mornings after breakfast (time-based) and help them to develop a weekly list of small incremental goals and acknowledge their achievements (specific), identifying at least one personal achievement each week (measurable, attainable, and realistic)." Keep the content succinct by making it fit in the cloud.

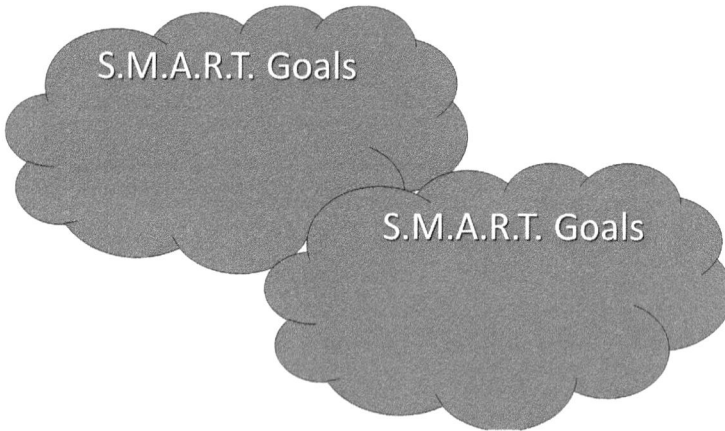

Fig. 6.0

Section 6.1. Self-Worth and Resilience

Section Focus | Case Example

SELF-WORTH AND RESILIENCE

Caregivers who impart kind words can help children to feel loved and appreciated. Kind words can be the foundation for building self-worth and self-esteem. Caregivers can help children to overcome failed attempts to accomplish tasks by teaching children to master related skills. Additionally, caregivers can help children to understand that failed tasks are a part of learning. They do not equate to low personal value or worth. Overcoming failure and setbacks foster resilience.

Section Objectives

- ☐ Understand how children build social connections and potentially associate ideas of self-worth with parental incarceration
- ☐ Review and gain knowledge about expected development during middle childhood years
- ☐ Learn about caregivers' tips for supporting children of incarcerated parents and offering reassurance for children who have experienced life stressors

Overview

During the middle childhood years (ages six to ten), a child's world expands beyond the family to include social connections and engagement, as well as acceptance by others. With this expansion comes the desire to integrate into groups, form friendships, and be accepted by peers. Under normal circumstances, children evaluate and compare themselves to other individuals. The notion of self-worth emerges. Fitting in and belonging is vital to children, especially during this stage of development. At this stage, children may equate their sense of belonging to their personal worth. Developing critical thinking skills, reasoning, and tools to build self-confidence are critical to offset negative appraisals of themselves.

Foundational Learning

During the middle childhood stage of growth, logic and reasoning skills are developing. Children who have experienced parental incarceration need honesty and trusted relationships. They can benefit from understanding their individualism versus life circumstances. Children impacted by incarceration need to clearly understand that their parent's actions are not their own. Further, these circumstances do not define who they are, what they will become, or their personal self-worth.

Children tend to feel stigmatized after parental incarceration has been disclosed to others or is public knowledge. Caregivers can help children to better understand the concepts of stigma and shaming, as well as family privacy. By creating a safe space for children to talk about how they feel and discuss related emotions can be helpful. Children can learn through developing compassion and empathy for others. Through this process they learn that stigma is concerned with a lack of empathy, knowledge about a topic, and most importantly, it does not define them as a person.

Middle childhood. Children at this age may begin to develop trusting friendships and want to share information about what is happening in their lives (e.g., such as information about their incarcerated parents), without understanding the ramifications of disclosure. This is where concepts of privacy become critical. Teach children that family members have private affairs that are not for public discussion. See Module 7.3 for more information regarding privacy issues.

Unfortunately, some children have been shamed, bullied, and embarrassed because their parents are incarcerated. It may be wise for caregivers to inform their children of the possible social reactions to incarceration while also helping children to realize that the issue does not define them as individuals. The previous exercise (Section 6.0 The Cape of Confidence) helps to practice strategies for building children's self-esteem. These exercises might help children develop a stronger sense of self-confidence and positive self-image (which derails stigma).

Caregivers' tips for supporting children. As reinforced throughout this workbook, children need to know that their caregiver is in their corner and appreciates them as individuals. Caregivers can offer reassurance to children during this stage of growth, especially if they are dealing with issues such as parental incarceration and the accompanying stigma. Support might be offered in several ways as they go through this defining stage of development:

- Be unwavering in providing love and support.
- Be affirming, listening to children's concerns.
- Be supportive and offer encouragement.
- Help children manage anger and model appropriate responses.
- Ask children about their feelings.
- Ask children for their input and ideas.
- Share kind words of appreciation and help children to develop grit when they fail (give hope and be optimistic).

ACTIVITY 22

Nurturing Self-Esteem in Children

As an activity, recall the discussion regarding how children in the middle childhood years are developing. This activity builds upon the previous activity in Section 6.0 *Boost Self-esteem*, and provides opportunities for giving children positive feedback using affirming words. For this exercise, make a list of the child's strengths and associated accomplishments. Try to think of at least 5 strengths. Review the example and add your own below. Please note that there is no answer key for this critical thinking exercise.

Strengths	Accomplishments	Kinds Words or Phrases
Example. The child is: "Dedicated"	Completes homework on time	"You have done such a good job completing homework each day. I am proud of you!"
1.		
2.		
3.		
4.		
5.		

Section 6.2. Assimilating and Belonging

Section Focus | Case Example

ASSIMILATING AND BELONGING

Children learn their first social skills from the people in their lives. A parent or guardian can help children develop skills that foster connection with others. This engagement starts by being accepted as a valuable member of the family. Affirm children's value and worth. Teach children interpersonal skills to engage with others and express their individuality.

Section Objectives

- ☐ Deepen knowledge about middle childhood socio-emotional development (age 6 to 10 years)
- ☐ Learn about parenting tips to influence children's social competence and social acceptance
- ☐ Demonstrate how caregivers' parenting tips and strategies can be applied to helping build children's social competence

Overview

MIDDLE CHILDHOOD SOCIO-EMOTIONAL DEVELOPMENT

As noted, during the middle childhood years children seek social acceptance. Children in this age range are gaining a stronger sense of self and want to be accepted and liked. Social acceptance includes assimilating in teams, to be considered valued members of a group, and to form close friendships.

Children in the middle childhood age group who are closer to 10 years old are forming a greater self-identity, differentiating themselves from their siblings and parents. They have their own likes and dislikes, such as favorite foods, and color preferences. Social-emotional development includes understanding and managing self-temperament and building attachment relationships. Temperament is concerned with how children interact with people in their environment. Their emotions, sensory reactions, personality, and even their attention levels factor in. Their attachments involve how they relate and bond with others. These are key factors that relate to assimilating and belonging.

Foundational Learning

Children's interpersonal and social skills continue to develop during middle childhood. Children at this age care about what others think of them. Their image and belief systems about themselves (and others) are forming and maturing. They care about their clothing, how their hair looks, what their friends think of them, and these thoughts shape opinions on self-image.

Affirming parents can help children to develop a strong sense of self, based on emotional/cognitive grounding. Helping children to see their strengths and qualities provides a foundation for other interpersonal relationships. Parents who model morals, honor rules and fairness, and show proper social etiquette can provide children with a template to follow.

Parenting tips to influence children's social competence. The Centers for Disease Control and Prevention (CDC) (2020) offers the following *parenting tips* to build social-emotional skills and social competence:

- **Hold discussions about the social value** of friendship, family, school, and other social interactions. Discuss how children are doing in each of these areas.
- **Help children develop personal responsibility and accountability.** Help children to have greater responsibilities by assigning age-appropriate chores. Accountability might include a task completion list where the child receives praise for accomplishments.
- **Teach patience.** Help children develop patience through sharing and taking turns. Play games that reinforce waiting for others to complete a task before their turn.
- **Affirm and praise positive behavior.** When a child accomplishes goals, tasks, or other assignments, offer praise for what was completed or accomplished.
- **Engage in family activities.** Doing things together fosters a sense of belonging. This sense of connectedness helps children who might otherwise struggle with assimilation with others. This process teaches social engagement, even in the family system.
- **Read to each other.** Reading should be a pleasurable and insightful activity between caregivers and children. Teach children through example that reading opens a whole world of access and adventure and information.
- **Support a child's goal setting.** For example, some children have "dance-off" or "walking challenges" to fundraise for their school. Support children and cheer them on. Praise their academic goal setting and help them to set reasonable and attainable goals.
- **Encourage extra-curricular activities.** Encourage a child to get involved in clubs and in community and social groups. Social activities help children develop their own identities and voices while building social engagement.
- **Teach respect, morals, and sound judgment.** Children are not around their parents every minute of the day. Children need to develop social skills, respect for others, and moral values to make good decisions. Talk to children and help them to understand by personal example. Teach them how to make good decisions by allowing them to make choices and by offering support when they do not quite get it right. Remember, life lessons can be gleaned through failed attempts as well. Model respect by teaching children's manners and valuing family, friends, and others. Using sound judgment also enhances a child's belief in themselves, bolstering self-confidence.

ACTIVITY 23

Nurturing Self-Esteem in Children

In this activity, consider the list of Parenting Tips to Influence Children's social competence in 6.2. Foundational Learning. For each Activity Domain below, list at least one action to help the child develop the associated skill. Draw examples from the provided tips. An example follows. The activity continues on the following page.

ACTIVITY DOMAIN [EXAMPLE]	ACTIONS
SOCIAL VALUES	Demonstrate how to engage in conversation during family dinners.
	Apologize when mistakes are made and take responsibility for actions.
	Model demonstrating grit by persevering through challenges and explaining the importance of not quitting before starting.

Activity continued on next page.

Now, create a list of personal examples, below. Provide at least one action aligned with the activity domain. The goal is to add at least one example that caregivers can use to help children build social competence and social acceptance. Please note that there is no answer key for this critical thinking exercise.

ACTIVITY DOMAIN	ACTIONS
Social Values	
Personal Responsibility and Accountability	
Teach Patience	
Affirm/Praise Positive Behaviors	
Engage in Family Activities	
Read to Each Other	
Supporting Goal Setting	
Encourage Extracurricular Activities	
Teach Respect, Morals, and Empathy	

Section 6.3. Self-Appraisal, Shame, and Guilt

Section Focus | Case Example

Loss, Grief, and Parental Incarceration

Not all children will be affected by a parent's incarceration in the same way. Some will not fully understand, or question why a parent is away in jail or prison. Others may feel grief and envy toward those who have intact families or free access to their parents. Caregivers can help children adjust to the child's individual circumstances, alleviating children's fears of loneliness with love, assuring them that parental incarceration is not any fault of their own.

Section Objectives

- ☐ Learn how children's feelings associated with parental incarceration and loss can influence self-appraisal and self-blame
- ☐ Apply knowledge and tips related to offsetting the adverse impacts of stigma on children
- ☐ Differentiate between guilt and shame
- ☐ Critically reflect and list actionable steps caregivers can take as preventable strategies that offset the stigma associated with mental health, childhood trauma, bullying, feeling flawed, and coping with failure

Overview

The loss of a parent can manifest in several ways in the lives of young children. Children need guidance to redirect negative thinking and offer them clarity when they are confused. Children with incarcerated parents tend to feel guilty for their parent's confinement. With this idea, they tend to blame themselves. Neuman (1998) indicated that young children tend to believe that they are to blame for all sorts of life events: divorce, incarceration, and even death The natural progression from self-blame is self-evaluation or self-appraisal. Children with low levels of self-esteem may be harsher on themselves than a child with a high level of confidence. Caregivers can help children understand that they are not to blame for the incarceration by first explaining that the situation is not their fault.

Foundational Learning

Offsetting stigma. Remember, children in the middle childhood years seek to belong. Incarceration of a parent might cause them to feel like they are "different" from peers who have intact families. When they feel different, they may feel like an outcast. Children who feel different from others may sometimes rebel, seek acceptance in other groups, or internalize the shame and stigma.

Caregivers can monitor their children's behaviors and attitudes. Additionally, caregivers should consider keeping an eye on their young children's social engagements to ensure that they are not experiencing the aftermath of stigma. When children feel the shame associated with their parent's condition, it may cause them to shy away from relationships or even invent a life fantasy built on untrue realities. While fantasy is certainly a part of children's imagination, it is important for them to deal with the present and truth of situations. Talk with children and help them realize that, sometimes, bad things happen to good people. Teach them coping skills as reinforced throughout this workbook.

Guilt and shame. Sometimes, children will feel guilty about a parent's incarceration. This is a normal reaction. Some adults feel the same way. Because guilt and shame are often used interchangeably, the terms are clarified here. Guilt is a feeling aligned with values and falling short of responsibility. It suggests that a person feels they did something wrong or did not live up to expectations. Shame is a value judgment of oneself or circumstances.

Shame is feeling *less than* and appraising oneself as less than others. This feeling may come with specific ideas and negative self-talk concerning oneself (self-appraisal):

- self-worth
- rejection
- lack of appreciation
- not being good enough
- not liked
- not fitting in

Shame also refers to feelings of dishonor and embarrassment. Each of these feelings could align with parental incarceration. Talk to children and help them understand the differences between guilt and shame. While reinforcing that they are not to blame for their parent's choices.

By using age-appropriate language, caregivers can explain that, sometimes, people do things that violate rules, laws, policies, and values. A caregiver acting as a child's emotional coach, can prepare a child for the world they will live in independently as adults. Teach children the value of character and honoring good behavior.

ACTIVITY 24

Nurturing Self-Esteem in Children

In this activity, consider the list of parenting tips in 6.3 *Foundational Learning*. For each Activity Domain, below, list at least one action to help children develop the associated skill in the listed domain. Examples are:

- Mental health issues: Teach children that mental health is akin to physical health and that checkups and doctor visits are a normal means of addressing health issues.
- Childhood trauma: Seek professional assistance and/or counseling.
- Bullying: Nurture self-esteem and teach children to assimilate in peer groups. Reinforce self-esteem and building confidence.
- Feeling flawed: Draw upon children's strengths and share those attributes with them.
- Not coping with mistakes or failure: Teach tolerance and instruct children how to set reasonable and attainable small goals.

ACTIVITIES:

List actionable steps as preventable strategies caregivers can take for each Domain. Enter your ideas in the "Examples of Preventative Actions" column. *Please note that there is no answer key for this critical thinking exercise.*

Activity Domain *How do you help a child address* *feelings related to:*	*Examples of Preventative Actions*
Mental Health	
Childhood Trauma	
Bullying	
Feeling Flawed	
Coping with Failure	

References

Bailey, B.A. (2000). *I love you rituals*. HarperCollins.

The Centers for Disease Control and Prevention. (2020). Middle childhood (6–8 years of age). Retrieved from https://www.cdc.gov/ncbddd/childdevelopment/positiveparenting/middle.html.

Hart-Johnson, A., & Johnson, G. (2022). Caregivers' family relations assessment and communication strategies. *Science Publishing Group*, 11(5), 157–168. https://www.sciencepublishinggroup.com/article/10.11648/j.pbs.20221105.12.

Neuman, G. (1998). *Helping your kids cope with divorce the sandcastles way*. Random House.

Plummer, D. (2007). *Helping children to build self-esteem: A photocopiable activities book second edition*. Jessica Kingsley.

Communication: "Lost for Words"

MODULE FOCUS

- Section 7.0. Life Happens. Explore the challenges and methods associated with holding difficult discussions.
- Section 7.1. Intra-Family Communication. Discuss the importance of communication related to balancing priorities and family life.
- Section 7.2. Communication Redo's: Help I Told My Child a Lie! Examine the consequences of compassionate deception and explore ways to mitigate harm.
- Section 7.3. Boundaries and Family Privacy. Introduce concepts of personal information versus public disclosure of private information.

Resources

Read Guidebook: Hart-Johnson and Johnson (2025) | Chapter 7, "Caregiver-Child Communication"

Additional Resources

Appendix C: Communication Strategies

Introduction

Communication is the foundation of learning, encompassing more than mere words—it involves body language and emotions. Attuned listening is key, ensuring all parties are heard and understood, as emphasized by the United Nations Convention on the Rights of the Child [CRC] (1989) (UNICEF, 2011). Children have individual rights, including age-appropriate communication.

Research study overview. In 2018, we conducted a research study on caregiver-child communication linked to parental incarceration (Hart-Johnson & Johnson, 2022). A principal finding highlighted that caregivers prioritize a child's overall well-being before discussing complex topics like parental incarceration. Caregivers in the study recognized the importance of addressing children's emotional, social, and physical states before tackling sensitive subjects. Our research unveiled four **primary communication strategies** employed by caregivers in discussing parental incarceration:

> **Direct Communication:** This involves straightforward, age-appropriate discussions, respecting boundaries, and considering timing of discussions.
> **Indirect Communication:** Sometimes, discussions are indirect or avoidant,

relying on passive communication. Caregivers may withhold certain information to protect children.

Abstention/Abstaining: Some caregivers choose not to share any details with the child, fearing the child is too young or not ready to comprehend matters currently. This approach can lead to further misinformation or imagined scenarios created by children's imaginations.

Reflection: Caregivers may reflect on past communication, seeking ways to better support children. Apologies, forgiveness, and honesty play a role in this strategy.

NAVIGATING DIFFICULT DISCUSSIONS

Difficult conversations are challenging, but essential for understanding, reasoning, and finding meaning in tough circumstances. Although uncomfortable, mastering communication during sensitive topic-related discussions can be achieved through practice, role-play, or self-preparation.

MODULE FOCUS

This module covers communication strategies, emphasizing healthy boundaries. It touches on the C-FRACS (Caregivers' Family Relations Assessment and Communications Strategies) theory, shedding light on how caregivers prepare for discussions about parental incarceration.

Section 7.0. Life Happens: The Big Talk

Section Focus | Case Example

LIFE HAPPENS: THE BIG TALK

The way incarceration unfolds in the lives of affected families is not generally neat and orderly. Parents sometimes make mistakes, exercise poor judgment, and commit unlawful acts. Similarly, others get arrested, accused, and incarcerated for crimes they did not commit. Either way, it can be a tricky situation for caregivers and their children to manage. Communication can be the key to helping children understand life events.

Section Objectives

- ☐ Understand how family members and children might react to holding discussions about parental incarceration
- ☐ Deepen and understanding about how children's behaviors may be telling of their feelings related to parental incarceration
- ☐ Learn why caregivers may withhold information about parental incarceration from children
- ☐ Advance knowledge and critically reflect on the challenges related to holding difficult discussions

Overview

Part of the lived experience of being children is to grow through good times as well as life's challenges. Parents and family members can help young children learn they will survive situations such as embarrassing mishaps, not reaching an athletic goal, or a recital gone bad. There are also life skills that can be learned even when parents are incarcerated.

REACTIONS TO DISCUSSIONS ON INCARCERATION

When discussing their parent's incarceration, even with the best of intentions and well scripted discussion points, children may not respond as anticipated. Family members and children may react in nuanced ways, including the following:

Denial: In their innocence, children may assume that their parents will be "coming home soon." They may refuse to believe that their parents are going to be away for a while (indefinitely), even if the parent is serving a life sentence. This can be a defense strategy to prevent deeper pain from ensuing. A caregiver's response might include saying, "There are many children whose parents are incarcerated, and they think they will come home the next day. It is normal to have those types of wishes." Responses such as, "I am sorry that this is something that is not likely to happen soon." "Let's try to stay in touch and write a letter and tell Mom/Dad that you miss them."

Anger: Children get angry when they are sad, hurt, frustrated, lonely, and a host of other reasons. Tell your child that the frustration is a normal response to a disappointing situation. Caregivers can then work to help children modulate and channel their emotions in positive ways. Remember, anger is a communication of underlying feelings.

Regression: Feeling overwhelmed and stressed may cause children to regress to former behaviors such as bed wetting, thumb-sucking, and self-soothing activities. If children's regression advances to prolonged and repeated adverse behaviors, check with a helping professional such as a counselor or the child's general doctor.

Acceptance: The family may anticipate the discussion and react in a manner that accepts circumstances at face value. Over time, they may recognize that there is a great degree of uncertainty with having a loved one who is incarcerated. The family may plan future events and strategies accordingly. When dealing with the circumstances head on, it may be less stressful than having high expectations for something that may not occur.

Children's behaviors can be telling. While children's behaviors may be telling of their feelings and emotions, caregivers may still need to speak with them about their emotions and responses to the incarceration. Recognize that some discussions will be challenging because children may feel displaced and unknowingly direct anger or frustration toward other family members/persons to vent or act out.

Also, keep in mind (as mentioned throughout this workbook) that even though children may not admit it, they may feel to blame for the parent's incarceration. It is easier to look at themselves and blame themselves rather than to blame the incarcerated parent or the caregiver who is providing support.

Foundational Learning

Talking about incarceration is not easy. Explaining difficult topics to children is typically hard, especially when young people do not have a prior frame of reference or life experience that assures them that they will survive the event. Caregivers can reassure children that they can adjust and manage their feelings.

The way information is shared is essential. For example, deception is rarely a good tactic. Over time, this approach may result in a child developing trust issues. The element of mistrust may extend beyond the family, where a child considers most adults as deceitful, or at the least, hard to accept or trust.

Lastly, there are times when caregivers may withhold information from children for the following possible reasons:

Communication can be emotionally taxing for all involved: One way to address emotionally taxing discussions is to prepare for the discussion and practice through role-playing and rehearsal. Practicing might entail going over the talking points in one's minds or by preparing while looking in the mirror. Difficult discussions are generally challenging because people struggle to find the right words to say. Practice choosing words that fit the content and try to anticipate questions that may follow.

Insufficient information: When preparing for a discussion with an adult or child, recognize that not having all of the information should not be a reason to avoid the discussion. Recognize this by admitting that "I do not have the information, but here is what I know." "Once additional information becomes available, we can return to this discussion." Also, refrain from "making up information" to sound informed. This alternative might cause children to distrust future content and information.

Not wanting to burden the information receiver: Generally, people do not want to discuss bad news or any information about a child's parent that entails separation. However, a caregiver should consider their role as the child's emotional coach and teacher. In that case, this is an opportunity to model information sharing in a manner that does not tax or burden the child.

Holding the discussion on parental incarceration. Remember to frame the information in an age-appropriate way and do not feel compelled to share alleged details about the crime. Instead, focus on words of encouragement by using talking points similar to what caregivers in our research study recommended:

Toddlers and Younger:
- "Mom/Dad will be gone for a while. I am here to take good care of you."
- "When the time comes, you can talk to Mom/Dad on the phone/video/during a visit (modify as appropriate)."

Older Children
- "Daddy or Mommy is in a place called jail or prison."
- "Mom/Dad made inappropriate/bad decisions and broke adult rules or laws."
- "Remember we discussed the importance of following rules and obeying the law.... Mom/Dad did not follow some of these rules."

Difficult Discussions

Check-in. Before concluding the discussion, be sure to ask children how they are feeling and use their answers as an opportunity to help them learn about emotions. For example, "I noticed that you are sad after we talked. Let's talk through what you are feeling...."

Negotiating the communication message and strategy. Perhaps negotiating the importance of being truthful is a communication strategy between all caregivers and the incarcerated parents. Sometimes, the incarcerated parents do not want the children to know where they are. However, if a caregiver withholds this information, it is best not to lie. Sharing that the parent "...is away and will not be home for a couple of birthdays" might be better than saying nothing at all.

The discussion is uncomfortable. The discomfort associated with communication is generally due to feeling ill-prepared with words, content, and conveying messaging in age-appropriate language. Practice, practice, practice. Then, plan and practice using age-appropriate language for children.

What's information is important? Generally, children do not need to know details about the parent's crime. They need to know their parent is safe. This clarity might be an alternative to saying something untrue. Think in "abstracts" rather than "detail." Abstracts are broad ideas and are generalized. For example: "Your mom/dad is in prison, and they will be there for a long time. I know it hurts; I will be here for you."

Compassionate deception. Finally, the struggle to tell children that their parent is in a place called "prison" is a hard thing to do for most parents and caregivers. Just saying the word "incarceration" out loud is a challenge. To some caregivers in our research study, making up a plausible story seemed better than telling the child the facts. During focus groups (Hart-Johnson & Johnson, 2022), the authors heard from some caregivers who believed that compassionate deception or telling "white lies" to children was far better than explaining a painful truth. So, instead, some caregivers made up untrue narratives about the parents or told the children mistruths. A few caregivers told their children that the incarcerated parent was in college. One parent offered that the incarcerated parent was in the military. These alternative truths are known as *compassionate deception*. While compassionate deception might buy time and perhaps delay telling the hard truth, be mindful of how a child might feel when they learn otherwise.

ACTIVITY 25

Communication

Choosing a communication style that matches the discussion is essential for age-appropriate talks with children.

Discussing parental incarceration can be challenging, yet it can be less stressful when incorporating planning, practice, and a bit of role- play. First, consider how children might feel following separation from parents. Further, consider how the child might miss the daily routines with parents and other family members. Ponder the importance of maintaining bonds or maintaining long distance relationships with the incarcerated parent. With these ideas in mind, complete the following activity.

Step 1: Review the four (4) types of communication styles identified in our research, outlined in Module 7.0 (primary communication strategies). Reflect on variations of approaches.

Step 2: Now, write a reflection on how you most identify when holding sensitive discussions. What steps do you consider effective? Now, role play in the form of a written script, telling a 7-year-old child their parent is incarcerated. *Facilitators:* For group activities, ask members to discuss their preferred communication styles during sensitive discussions and share why it is their preference. Ask volunteers to role play holding a discussion with a 7-year-old child regarding their parent's incarceration.

Please note that there is no answer key for this critical thinking exercise.

Reflection:

Section 7.1. Intra-Family Communication

Section Focus | Case Example

Breathe Again

The phrase, "sucking the oxygen out of the room," generally refers to someone grandstanding, leaving little room for others to communicate or contribute. The opposite of this metaphorical phrase is to replenish resources and energy through communication strategies that support healthy interpersonal relationships.

Section Objectives

☐ Examine concepts related to intra-family communication
☐ Deepen an understanding related to the role of intentional self-care maintenance and well-being processes for caregivers
☐ Examine ways to enhance family bonds, improve communication, and identify family support systems

Overview

Intra-family communication using a holistic focus involves understanding family support needs, resources, and the health and well-being requirements of all involved. When families have a crisis involving another family member, given their compassion and concern, the focus may consume and overwhelm them, with very little attention paid to other components of the family needs (including their well-being and mental health). In some cases, extended family and friends may provide support and help during a family emergency. However, people tend to return to their personal responsibilities because their own lives require attention and management of priorities. With this awareness, family communication among and between members is of importance.

Foundational Learning

The role of intentional self-care maintenance. This book is about the effects of incarceration. Most people will agree, it takes a great deal of intentionality to focus and balance life events during such occurrences. When a crisis remains the dominant focus, some caregivers indicated, it "sucks the oxygen out of the room" (Hart-Johnson & Johnson 2022). However, with proper attention, balance can be achieved. With purposeful planning and effective communication, a caregiver might be able to balance the priorities of the family, while supporting loved ones who are incarcerated.

One method is to intentionally focus on family health-maintenance, self-care, financial management, intra-family communication, and spiritual and emotional needs.

Here are a few ideas designed to enhance the family's wherewithal:

S TRATEGIES

- **Communicate:** When possible, include children in the decision-making during family member communications (noting that there is a two-way process during discussions). Plan talking points using language that is empowering, while avoiding words that cause defensiveness. Use phrases such as "May I suggest" or "Perhaps we might" rather than "I need you to" or "You had better." Keep the conversation on track by establishing boundaries for discussion. Avoid phrases such as "you," "always," "never," "every time" "everybody" and "no one." These phrases are defense-producing as well.
- **Assess:** Examine the needs and requirements of the most vulnerable first; then work towards stabilizing the more robust and mature family members. A young child may need the most significant support during a crisis. Work to stabilize them and help them feel safe.
- **Schedule:** Establish self-care routines for all involved, including family time, outings, and social engagement.
- **Engage:** Be fully present when engaging with children and family members. Children can tell when caregivers are preoccupied. The unstated messaging is that you are not listening because more critical matters are at hand.
- **Budget:** Make a budget and stick to it. Budgets include meal plans, dwellings, phone time, and even budgeting prison travel and visits. Incarcerated family members can contribute to budget preparation as well. This may reduce the feelings associated with cutting or limiting expenses such as phone calls, if decisions are made as a collective family unit.

By examining the family's communication, assessing needs, prioritizing a schedule and budget, engaging the family might become a productive meeting. Each of these areas might be stressors that contribute to ineffective focus on the topic at hand.

A note on communication: People tend to communicate with underlying emotions. These emotions may not be conscious thoughts, but they are there. In general, when individuals are well rested, have a balanced life, and healthy perspectives, they tend to think and speak logically. Remembering to remain self-aware of emotions can help with managing them. On the other hand, when a person lacks sleep, has high stress, and is emotionally dysregulated, they will likely have problems thinking clearly and communicating effectively.

ACTIVITY 26

Communication

Review Sections 7.1. *Foundational Learning,* strategies. In this activity, consider the importance of intra-family communication. Consider the importance of establishing boundaries for discussion and choosing words and phrases that invite dialogue rather than defense producing reactions. This activity involves examining ways to enhance family bonds, improve communication, and identify family support systems. Please address the following discussion questions:

    1. Identify five ways to communicate and implement boundaries for intra-family discussions (making note of the impact of schedules, budgets, assessing needs, or communication).

    2. Consider ways to ensure healthy outlets for the family to avoid over-consumption with a single focus on crisis.

    3. Consider what formal and informal resources can help the family stabilize (i.e., community support groups, nonprofits, faith-based institutions, and other supports).

    4. Develop a list of self-care strategies for the family. List at least three ideas caregivers can implement.

      a.

      b.

      c.

Note: There are no right or wrong answers for this activity. This exercise is intended as a personal reflection. Consider this reflective work, as critical thinking exercises. Please note that there is no answer key for this critical thinking exercise.

Section 7.2. Communication Redo's: "Help, I Told My Child a Lie!"

Section Focus | Case Example

WHITE LIE

A "white lie" is considered harmless to some people. In the case of discussing incarceration, a stated mistruth might be used to avoid hurting others in disclosing the truth.

Section Objectives

- ☐ Learn about risks related to telling mistruths to children
- ☐ Gain insights about why caregivers may use mistruths
- ☐ Learn and practice strategies for addressing mistruths (white lies)
- ☐ Consider methods of corrections when children are told mistruths (addressing a lie)
- ☐ Critically reflect and apply caregiver options that consider acknowledging, apologizing, and asking children for forgiveness

Overview

Most people want to avoid hurting or insulting others. Many of us are guilty of telling what are thought to be: harmless "white lies." Often, these mistruths are designed to prevent embarrassment, hurt feelings, or even deeper emotions. It is, therefore, understandable that caregivers might use the same approach when discussing sensitive information around parental incarceration.

Emotions can run deep for the child and caregiver when these discussions take place. However, on a positive note, these serious discussions can introduce problem-solving methods for young children (Morin & Lockhart, 2021). Given that children model their behaviors from behaviors of their caregivers, it may be best to illustrate telling the truth under difficult circumstances. Also, truth telling can entail setting boundaries while maintaining integrity, and credibility.

Foundational Learning

THE RISKS OF TELLING MISTRUTHS TO CHILDREN

Effective parenting entails helping children to develop morals and trust. Parents generally want their children to be truthful with them. A foundation of truthfulness might include establishing patterns and teaching children techniques to be honest using effective communication (even when discussions are difficult). This approach can help children build character.

While everyone likely makes excuses at some point in time, consider the impacts of consistent behavior aligned with mistruths. It is possible that practicing mistruths will teach children how to master deception rather than truth-telling.

Reasons for using mistruths. People tell mistruths for many different reasons. Morin and Lockhart (2021) suggested that the following are a few reasons why alternatives to truth are shared:

Fantasy

Sometimes, it is easier to create a fantasy based on hope; it is easier to look at the world through "rose-colored-glasses." Sometimes, incarceration is so overwhelming that caregivers and their children may create fantasy. They might tell others, "Mom/Dad are coming home by Christmas." This might be wishful thinking and perhaps not intended as a white lie, yet it still may be untrue. This form of pretense might be harmful if the child begins to believe that, indeed, mom or dad will be coming home. It is probably wiser to manage expectations.

Avoiding Responsibility

It is difficult to tell the truth sometimes if it hurts emotionally. Caregivers might lie to their children to avoid the responsibility of telling hard truths. Alternatively, a caregiver might believe that the responsibility belongs to the incarcerated parents. However, telling lies, using omission, wishing the situation would go away, or telling partial truth are all forms of compassionate deception or perhaps, shirking responsibility.

Addressing a lie. It may seem insurmountable to correct the potential damage that a lie can cause. The following tips may help.

Correct and apologies: The first step to address a mistruth or lie is to apologize and own the action. Declare from that point forward to be honest and truthful with the child. Telling the truth and sharing the fears and concerns that influenced the deceptive behavior might also be helpful.

Acknowledge challenges: A caregiver might share why it was so difficult to share this sensitive information in the first place. For instance, the caregiver may admit they did not have the words to say or that they were overwhelmed. This admission models honesty.

Ask for forgiveness: Asking for forgiveness may help the child to know that their feelings matter, and that the caregiver truly cares. By asking for forgiveness, the child also learns how to grow beyond disappointments and move on.

ACTIVITY 27

Communication

Reflect upon the section content 7.2. Consider the consequences of telling a mistruth. Mindfully rehearse and note below how a caregiver could acknowledge, apologize, and ask for forgiveness related to mistruths told to a child regarding their parent's incarceration. Use the Notes section to write your rehearsed script. Facilitators: For group activities, ask the learners to share their answers using a flip chart or whiteboard. Please note that there is no answer key for this critical thinking exercise.

Notes

Section 7.3. Boundaries and Family Privacy

Section Focus | Case Example

FAMILY BUSINESS

Families of the incarcerated have private lives, too. Teaching children privacy rights and guidelines is an opportunity to cultivate personal values and foster household privacy protocol and boundaries in the family system.

Section Objectives

- ☐ Deepen the understanding and assess when its "on or off limits" when sharing personal information related to family privacy
- ☐ Review and understand tips on teaching children about their privacy rights versus family secrets

Overview

Humans are highly social. They share information among friends, colleagues, and others. However, within that social context, families generally need marked boundaries that establish what personal information is in or outside of scope for public sharing. As noted, some personal issues within a family system are not suitable for public disclosure. Examples include family finances, medical history, mental health status, and personal identifiable information (PII) that could be potentially damaging, embarrassing, or sensitive information. ThePrivacyParent.com (TPP) advised that caregivers of children teach privacy protocol early in life. In the current social media age, private matters can be disseminated using the Internet or an app, to a worldwide audience in seconds (TPP, 2022). Once personal information is shared, it is hard to retrieve and delete. It is often better to retain security than try to get it back once it has been lost or exposed.

Foundational Learning

One of the first steps in teaching children about privacy is helping them to differentiate between privacy and secrets. Privacy and personal rights are concerned with protecting private and confidential information, but it also extends to understanding personal boundaries. Hernandez and Ebersole (2021) indicated that families bond through shared experiences of privacy and therefore have privileged information linked to their experiences of crisis and recovery. This information is not necessarily to be shared with others. The authors further suggested that issues of privacy and confidentiality, if not managed, could cause division, mistrust, and feelings of betrayal among family members if not handled properly. Therefore, it is wise to establish boundaries or conditions of disclosure before such situations arise. Considerations of personal and private information might include (Hernandez & Ebersole, 2022):

- **Personal whereabouts** (i.e., disclosing a person's location).
- **A person's right** to express emotions in private. For instance, a person has a right to cry behind closed doors.
- **A family member's health** status.
- **Personal Identity:** Social security, driver's license; birth certificates.
- **Family member incarceration** status.
- **Children's grades**, education records; health records.
- **Financial records** and budgets.

This list contains only a few considerations. The list could easily be extended to include such domains as digital privacy and password protections. Family concerns and other considerations of the family's well-being might also be off-limits. For example, finding out that a household member has an illness is something family members may not wish to make public until they have sorted out how to manage the situation. Another example causing embarrassment might be a family member's arrest.

Privacy and secrets. Privacy is different from secrets. A secret involves intentional acts to hide, deceive, protect, and/or prevent knowledge about a situation (generally thought to be shameful or harmful if revealed). Secrets held within the family domain can sometimes also be harmful to children who are asked to carry the burden of secrecy.

Establishing guidelines and having open communication in the family about ways to manage privacy and confidentiality are one way to clear up confusion and prevent thick walls surrounding the idea of disclosure from happening.

Petronio et al. (2013) indicated that families have established a perimeter or a boundary representing what is inside or outside disclosure. Figure 7.3.0. Family privacy, secrets, and disclosure. Family privacy, secrets, and disclosure are represented in the center of the micro context. This linkage represents how family privacy may extend to close peers, extended family, friends, and in other social contexts such as school, work, etc. However, perhaps only some information is shared with those links. The decision to share could be situational in these contexts. Perhaps, the family decides that they will keep some "healthy secrets" that are off limits to extended family; and for others, they will employ a "family privacy rule" as applied to sharing information in the workplace, school settings, and community. Consider the following scenarios related to secrets and privacy:

EXAMPLES OF SECRECY VS. PRIVACY

Secrets: The family intentionally holds a secret about a surprise birthday from Sally's *peers*. They invite Sally and her peers under the ruse that they are meeting for other reasons.

Privacy: The family decided that it is best not to share that they will need to move to a new home, for financial reasons. This information is not to be disclosed until there is certainty where they are moving.

Secrets: Everyone believed that Darnell was going to earn a scholarship to a top ten school. However, he found that was not the case. The family decided to intentionally not let the *extended family, friends, and peers* know about the situation until Darnell is ready. He prefers to keep this information hidden. Note: This could also be considered a privacy matter as well.

Privacy: The family just learned that they would need to downsize because of financial reasons. They are uncertain if they will find a smaller home or rent an apartment. The caregiver informs the children that until they are ready, this information is to be kept private.

PLANNING FOR PRIVACY

The following ideas might help develop a framework to institute as family guidelines. Consider the following:

- Everyone in the family should have a right to privacy. Generally, minor children's privacy should be protected by their parents/caregivers.
- Privacy is not a secret. Privacy considers rules and rights. In contrast, secrets are choosing not to reveal information.
- Consider what information is off-limits to the public.
- Consider methods to teach and help children understand how to frame responses when people ask questions outside of the family privacy boundaries.
- Secrets are not all "bad"—some secrets can establish solidarity among family members (Caughlin et al., 2013).

When discussing privacy rules and protocol, be sure to ask children if they understand the rules; allow them to discuss their ideas and provide input.

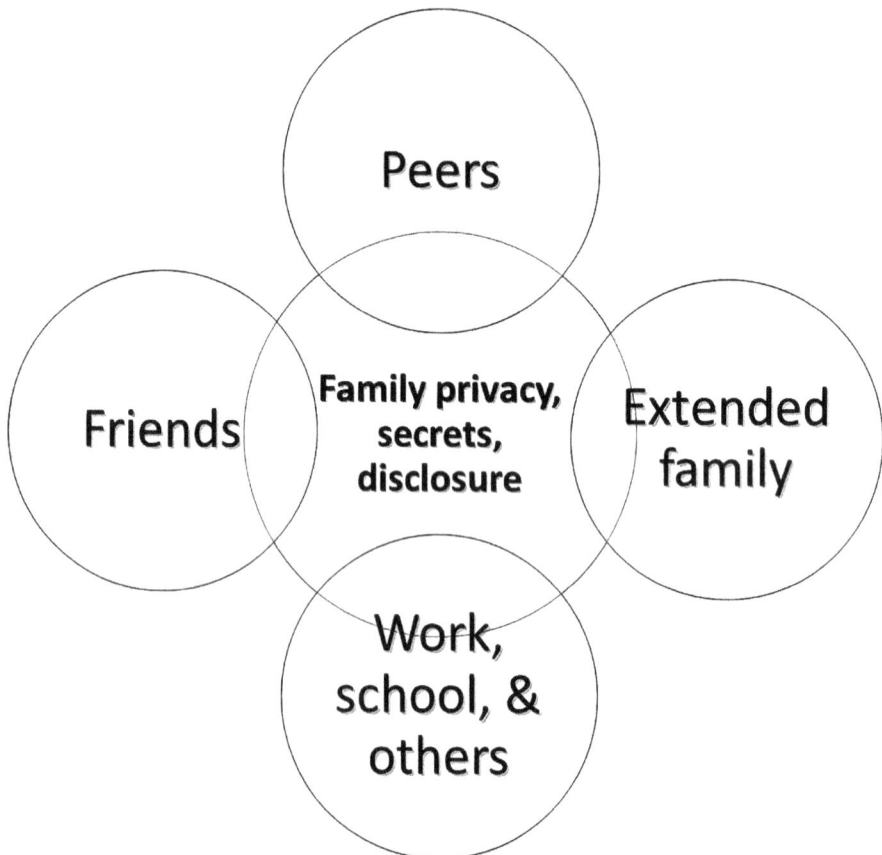

Figure 7.3.0. Family Privacy, Secrets, and Disclosure.

ACTIVITY 28

Communication
In this activity, you will consider some principles of privacy for families. This activity involves identifying boundaries for information sharing by reviewing the personal information type, information privacy, and family information for public discussion. Mark the column with the designation "on/or off limits" for public disclosure using a Y/N designator. This exercise could be used as a guide for family privacy discussions as well (remembering that the answer is unique to families).

Personal Information	*On/Off Limits? Y/N*	*Information Privacy*	*On/Off Limits? Y/N*	*Family information for public discussion*	*On/Off Limits? Y/N*
Medical data		Social security		Divorce and separation	
Mental health data		Security codes and passwords		Family member incarceration status	
Personal, photos		Financial records		Academic challenges	
Education records		Address		Threats to the family	
Digital narrative (containing family member information) in memes, posts, blogs		Phone numbers		Major family decisions (decided or pending)	
Vacation plans		Birth certificates		Marriage proposals	
Diaries/journals of family members		Driver's licenses		Family disagreements	
Text messages		Phone contacts lists		Overheard conversation	

The Answer key for Section 7.3, Activity 28, follows Module 7 Reference list.

References

Caughlin, J.P. (2013). Family communication standards: What counts as excellent family communication and how are such standards associated with family satisfaction? *Human Communication Research*, 29(1), 5–40.

Hart-Johnson, A., & Johnson, G. (2022). Caregivers' family relations assessment and communication strategies. *Science Publishing Group*, 11(5), 157–168. https://www.sciencepublishinggroup.com/article/10.11648/j.pbs.20221105.12.

Hernandez, R., & Ebersole, D. (2022). Parents' and children's privacy management about sensitive topics: A dyadic study. *Journal of Family Issues*, 43(1), 73–95.

Morin, A., & Lockhart, A.T. (2021). *10 steps to stop a child from lying*. Retrieved from https://www.verywellfamily.com/steps-help-child-stop-lying-tell-the-truth-1094945.

Petronio, S. (2013). Brief status report on Communication Privacy Management theory. *Journal of Family Communication*, 13(1), 6–14. https://doi.org/10.1080/15267431.2013.743426.

Petronio, S., Caughlin, J.P., Braithwaite, D., & Baxter, L. (2006). Communication privacy management theory: Understanding families. Braithwaite, D.O., & Baxter, L.A. (Eds.), *Engaging theories in family communication: Multiple perspectives* (pp. 35–49). Sage.

ThePrivacyParent.com. (2022). *Your kid deserves data privacy*. Retrieved from https://www.privacyparent.com

UNICEF. (1989). The United Nations convention on the rights of the child. Retrieved from https://www.unicef.org/child-rights-convention.

UNICEF. (2011). Communicating with children: Principles and practices to nurture, inspire, excite, educate and heal. https://resourcecentre.savethechildren.net/document/communicating-children-principles-and-practices-nurture-inspire-excite-educate-and-heal/

Off Limits = generally this information is shared on a need to know basis. Generally people do not share personal identifiable information because they risk personal breach of records and risk misuse.

Depends on the family's choices/decisions = families decide whether this information should be available for the public, close friends, or others.

Personal Information	On/Off Limits? Y/N	Information Privacy	On/Off Limits? Y/N	Family information for public discussion	On/Off Limits? Y/N
Medical data	Off Limits	Social security	Off Limits	Divorce and separation	Depends on the family's choices/decisions
Mental health data	Off Limits	Security codes and passwords	Off Limits	Family member incarceration status	Depends on the family's choices/decisions
Personal photos	Depends on the family's choices/decisions	Financial records	Off Limits (generally, yet conditional)	Academic challenges	Depends on the family's choices/decisions
Education records	Off Limits	Address	Depends on the family's choices/decisions	Threats to the family	Depends on the family's choices/decisions made with law enforcement and others.
Digital narrative (containing family member information) in memes, posts, blogs	Depends on the family's choices/decisions	Phone numbers	Depends on the family's choices/decisions	Major family decisions (decided or pending)	Depends on the family's choices/decisions
Vacation plans	Depends on the family's choices/decisions	Birth Certificates	Off Limits	Marriage proposals	Depends on the family's choices/decisions
Diaries/journals of family members	Depends on the family's choices/decisions	Driver's Licenses	Depends on the family's choices/decisions	Family disagreements	Depends on the family's choices/decisions
Text messages		Phone contacts lists		Overheard conversation	

Ambiguous Roles

Module Focus

- Section 8.0. Parents and Helpers. Explore the significance of roles within family systems, parentification, and role boundary disturbances.
- Section 8.1. Family Member Roles. Extend the focus on functional responsibilities in the family system.
- Section 8.2. Mirror-Mirror Reflections. Discuss the intersection between caregiver role modeling, parenting styles, and parenting children.
- Section 8.3. Family Support Inventory. Consider criterion for choosing family support systems.

Resources
Read Guidebook: Hart-Johnson and Johnson (2025) | Chapter 8 "Ambiguous Roles and Child Parenting"

Introduction

There are many ways to describe the concept of "family." Some households consider family members to be all the individuals who dwell in the home. Others consider the extended family members who live inside and outside of the home. Incarcerated family members are still a part of the family.

Gibson considers the uniqueness of each family as a gift (Gibson, 2013). She posited that family narratives are a collection of events, memories (fond, and even hurtful) that make up the family's identity. This shared identity generally defines who is in and out of the family system. Within this context, shared rituals, holidays, celebrations, and memorials all contribute to the family unit's unique identity and ties to one another. However, incarceration tends to challenge this notion of togetherness and identity and leave a void.

To balance the effects of incarceration, the family can examine roles and determine how to manage the shift in household configuration. Gibson (2013) advised, after the shift in family dynamics, remaining family members can seek clarity on how they contribute to sustaining relationships and bonds through role identification. Role identification is important for all who are emotionally connected. For instance, if the father of the family always read to the children before they went to sleep, then, someone can fill that role; otherwise, the child may feel the void. Or, consider a mom who always attended activities at the children's school and is now currently absent; perhaps, grandmother will need to fill that role.

Section 8.0. Parents and Helpers

Section Focus | Case Example

THE CHILD-PARENT

A five-year-old changed diapers for her nine-month-old sibling, incrementally, throughout the day and well into the evening. She poured formula when the bottle became empty, occasionally spilling the liquid on the floor. She warmed the baby bottle in the microwave. When her three-year-old sibling misbehaved that evening, she put him on timeout in the apartment hallway.

Section Objectives

- ☐ Learn about the concept: "parentification"
- ☐ Learn about boundary disturbances (how children's roles in the family structure can morph into responsibilities beyond their capacities)
- ☐ Critically reflect and apply knowledge related to the concepts: parentification, boundary and role disturbance

Overview

Crisis tends to effect a family's equilibrium. When the family seeks to stabilize and regain its balance, it may call for an all-hands-on-deck approach, meaning that everyone in the home may need to contribute to helping out, children included. However, when the roles in the household become blurred and children's responsibilities exceed their capacity, it is referred to as *parentification.*

Parentification also describes caregiver-child role reversal of emotional and functional responsibility (Winton, 2003). Emotional responsibility might include a young child listening and empathizing with a lamenting parent who seeks sympathy and emotional support. Functional roles might entail taking on chores that require critical thinking skills beyond the child's standard capabilities and capacity. In this section, we explore ways to balance the roles to prevent this outcome.

Foundational Learning

During times of challenge, it is normal for families to request the support of everyone in the home. Perhaps, children and teens may become more involved in caring for the younger siblings to save on finances. The adult(s) in the home may need to work or take on additional forms of employment.

To be clear, families have had exchanges in roles and household responsibilities as a general practice worldwide. For instance, in some Asian families, children provide financial support and care of parents. Hispanic children in the United States may serve as translators for their parents. African American children generally take on chores at an early age and they fare well in developing related skillsets. When the responsibilities become out of balance and potentially harmful, however, there are **boundary disturbances**. This means that children have been tasked with functional and emotional responsibilities beyond their cognitive, physical, and emotional development. Examples include:

- Parents who are emotionally unavailable to care for children and who place that burden on one of their children instead.
- Requiring children to parent their siblings.
- Parents expecting emotional support from developmentally immature children.
- Parents who require children to fill roles they are not mentally equipped to do.

Winton (2003) considers examples like these as degrees to which parentification may encroach on family member roles and distort those boundaries. Each of these examples assumes that children can perform the role; yet it exceeds their abilities to do so. These responsibilities may also deny children the opportunity to have well-paced childhood experiences where growth and development coupled with responsibilities are gradually introduced and perfected over time.

ACTIVITY 29

Ambiguous Roles

This activity explores the vignette 8.0 Child-Parent and reflects upon the dynamics of a child in a parentified role. The risks of parentification include boundary disturbances associated with family member roles.

Step 1: Review the scenario, Part I, Table 8.0 Child Parent Analysis below.
Step 2: Consider the analysis of parentification, boundary and role disturbance, and the *critical thinking and reflection* analysis.
Step 3: With this content in mind, answer the following questions and note under the section titled "Reflection."

Reflective Questions:

- What stands out to you the most about the 5-year old's responsibility and why?
- What is the most concerning about the 5-year-old's responsibility and why?
- Place yourself in the role of the caregiver. What would you do to maintain boundaries in the home?

Part I Child Parent Analysis

Table 8.0 Child-Parent Analysis

Scenario	Is This Parentification?	Is This a Boundary and Role Disturbance?	Critical Thinking and Reflection
A 5-year-old changed diapers throughout the day, well into the evening for the 9-month-old sibling.	Maybe. The tasks could morph into parentification. The child provided care for her sibling, an adult responsibility.	This is boundary disturbance because the child is thrust into the role of the caregiver to determine timing and care related to the diaper change.	Changing a diaper requires an understanding of schedule expectations. Assessment during the change might include understanding if the baby requires ointment to address any rash or chafing. Fine motor skills might be needed to fasten the diaper.

She warmed the baby bottle in the microwave.	Maybe. This could morph into parentification. The child provided care for her sibling, an adult responsibility.	This is boundary disturbance, and a safety issue.	This task potentially requires height to reach the microwave. Safety risks of standing on a chair or other furniture increase the falling concerns.
			    This task requires an analysis of the timing to heat the formula. Preschoolers have not mastered concepts related to time.
			    This task requires determining what is too hot for the infant to consume—the analytical skills and baseline for determining lukewarm, hot, too hot conditions.

Scenario	Is This Parentification?	Is This a Boundary and Role Disturbance?	Critical Thinking and Reflection
The 5-year-old refilled formula when the bottle became empty, occasionally spilling the liquid on the floor.	Yes, this might be considered parentification.	This is boundary disturbance and also a safety issue.	The spillage is a safety hazard. The toddler may also feel guilty for spilling the liquid on the floor. While this task is clearly beyond the expectations of a five-year-old, they may still believe that they should be able to perform the task.
When her 3-year-old sibling misbehaved that evening, she put him on timeout in the apartment hallway.	Maybe. This could morph into parentification. The child provided care for her sibling, an adult responsibility.	This is boundary disturbance and also a safety issue.	A 5-year-old likely modeled the caregiver's discipline practices but misinterpreted differences between timeout in rooms in the apartment versus outside the apartment unit. The child could be inadvertently harmed, traumatized, or abducted. However, these concepts are likely beyond the reasoning skills of the preschooler.
It is unclear where the caregiver was on this day.	Yes. This is parentification which includes the child assuming responsibility for managing the home without the parent's guidance.	This is boundary disturbance and also a safety issue.	A 5-year-old should not care for a 9-month-old and a 3-year-old. Generally, a child should be pre-teen before they are considered competent as caregivers for young children. This scenario poses many risks, with the top concern as safety.

Please note that there is no answer key for this critical thinking exercise.

Reflection:

Section 8.1. Family Member Roles

Section Focus | Case Example

WHO FILLS THE FAMILY GAP?

When a parent is absent from the family, the caregiver may look to their children, family members, and others for support. Augmenting the family's resources is reasonable and expected. However, a careful balance is required.

Section Objectives

☐ Learn about the risk for parentification during family crisis
☐ Develop ideas about balancing functional roles in the family system
☐ List the pros and cons related to the assignment of children's functional responsibilities

Overview

FUNCTIONAL ROLES: THE RISK OF PARENTIFICATION DURING FAMILY CRISIS

Some children appear to be wise beyond their years. They possess remarkable skills and seem to excel in providing practical support to the family. Their eagerness to become the caregiver's helper is ever apparent. Learning and fulfilling functional roles might include performing age-appropriate tasks such as toddlers dressing themselves, putting away toys or asking a child in the middle childhood age group to tidy the home or to set the table. Caregivers generally are the best positioned to understand a child's skills and capabilities. *Parentification* is when functional and emotional roles overstep the boundaries of children's capacities to perform the task. Children need cognitive skills to perform specific functional roles or tasks in the home. They may need critical thinking skills, understanding of concepts of time, and more. Children need to mature into these roles. Assignment of some tasks is a great opportunity to learn new skills, while others may leave the child feeling inept or unprepared.

Foundational Learning

Balancing functional roles. During family crisis, children may sometimes be requested to perform tasks outside their general responsibilities and functions. These task requests may occur at times when a parent is overwhelmed and needs support; no one else may be available. An example might include a ten-year-old making a simple dinner of sandwiches and chips for siblings.

If the task requires a child to make a dinner which requires critical thinking, judgment, and past experience, this same task could be dangerous when children lack supervision of the task. Consider the scenario of the ten-year-old making a sandwich. Now, introduce the complexity of using a knife to add chopped ingredients. In this scenario, there is a need to slice ham, tomatoes, and lettuce, using a sharp knife. Judgment and advanced precision along with the use of fine motor skills are needed. Building on this example, if the ham must be cooked first, the step involves critical thinking in terms of choosing utensils, using protective gear (cooking mitts), selecting temperature control, and determining, based on history of cooking this meal before, what is considered to meet the family's preference (well- done versus medium, etc.). Therefore, it is fair to say that decisions about functional task assignments are situational and that some chores are beyond children's abilities and might infringe on their capacities.

Not all challenging task assignments are inappropriate. Some assignments help children to develop skills. There are pros and cons associated with assigning functional responsibilities to children as listed below in 8.1.0 Pros and Cons of Functional Responsibilities.

Table 8.1.0 Pros and Cons of Functional Responsibilities	
Pros	*Cons*
Opportunity to learn advanced skills at a young age	Failing at the task can introduce feeling incompetent
May develop self-confidence and critical thinking for some children	The child may not have the physical, cognitive, and emotional skills to perform the tasks
May promote self-regulation skills and stress-management for some children	The requirement could place excessive stress related to the demands related to the task's time, energy, and resources
May result in caregiver praise and positive feedback	Lack of reciprocity from caregivers
May provide decision-making opportunities	It may be overwhelming for the child to make critical decisions

The important takeaway for caregivers is always assess the child's ability, consider the safety risks, and determine if the skill will hurt or help the child.

Activity 30

Ambiguous Roles

Review and scan section Module 8 through 8.1. Now, consider the pros and cons of children performing functional roles in the family identified in Table, *Pros and Cons of Functional Responsibility.*

Step 1: Read each scenario for 1 through 3 in the assignment.
Step 2: Decide if the scenario is a Pro (e.g., opportunity to advance skills) or Con (Potentially harmful and might lead to role confusion)
Step 3: Explain your rationale under "Explanation."

Pros and Cons
of Functional Responsibility

Scenario	Pro or Con?
1. A mother of a six-year-old asks the child to make his bed.	
Explanation:	
1. A nine-year-old is tasked with child-care responsibilities once a month while the mother participates in a two-hour-long virtual meeting.	
Explanation:	
1. The father of a seven-year-old requests that she assist her five-year-old brother with finding his shoes, clothing, and preparing a backpack lunch for school every morning.	
Explanation:	

See Answer Key for Section 8.1, Activity 30 after Module 8 References

Section 8.2. Mirror-Mirror Reflections

Section Focus | Case Example

Mom's Parenting Style

Mom applies makeup every day. She sits on a stool in front of a vanity with a mirror when getting dressed. She applies her makeup there, with bright red lipstick as the last part of the application. Bobbie, the active toddler, is always nearby, playing with toys. On this bright and sunny Monday morning, Mom walked toward her vanity to find Bobbie sitting there with red lipstick all over the vanity. The red lipstick, now broken from its base, lay on the vanity. Mom shouted, "Bobbie, you ruin everything you touch!"

Section Objectives

☐ Understand caregiver role modeling
☐ Learn about the concept: scaffolding
☐ Obtain knowledge about positive parenting
☐ Critically reflect on parenting styles: authoritative, permissive, or authoritarian

Overview

Caregiver Role Modeling

The caregiver's behaviors provide cognitive (intelligence) and emotional learning models for children. Caregivers are often the first role models for young children. Children absorb their surroundings like sponges. They observe parents and imitate their behaviors. As children grow, they explore their worlds with curiosity, as illustrated in the scenario, *Mom's Parenting Style*. Bobbie's curious behavior is similar to most toddlers, who are observing, discovering, and experimenting. Children of Bobbie's age range tend to mimic their parent's behavior while not yet knowing the cause and effect of their actions. A caregiver's careful guidance can direct children toward desired behavior.

Using age-appropriate guidance can support young children's understanding of boundaries and rules. Such commands as "Bobbie, do not play with Mom's perfumes and makeup," or "You can play with your toys, but makeup can make you sick or cause your skin to itch." In other words, explain to the children the possible adverse consequence of the behavior using age-appropriate guidance.

Foundational Learning

Children learn through *scaffolding*. This term refers to building a foundation of knowledge and integrating additional information as a learning process. This approach refers to how children learn from caregivers' support and through demonstration and modeling behaviors of parents, teachers, and other people in their environments.

Positive parenting (strength-based parenting) requires caregivers to find the good and focus on a child's strengths rather than deficits (Bailey, 2000). The parenting techniques associated with this mode include (Betterup.com, 2020).

- When rendering positive discipline*, use tactics that make sense to the child.
- Validate children, use empathy and sympathy.
- Use language that makes sense to the child.
- Help children learn from their mistakes.
- Treat children as individuals.
- Provide gentle, yet stern warnings (rather than threating ultimatums).
- Establish clear boundaries and expectations.
- Help children to learn what to do and why rather than what not to do.
- Be positive and affirming.
- Be consistent and maintain integrity.
- Be loving and firm.
- Use humor when appropriate.
- Consider both developmental and age appropriateness.
- Manage your feelings.

Problem-solving and comprehension are the cornerstones of child development. Communication and interpersonal engagement shared through caregiver-child interactions provide the foundation for social skills. Using age-appropriate and developmentally aligned language helps children understand boundaries and core life skills.

Finally, caregivers may wish to consider the importance of carefully selecting age-appropriate guidance and language. Children remember how words make them feel long after the incident or situation. They sometimes carry these words in their memory well into adulthood, reminding them of how parents value them. All parents make mistakes. Be forgiving of these errors—give yourself a pass to begin again and strive for efficiency.

Parents should consider: (1) choosing words carefully; (2) being mindful of personal emotions and temperaments; (3) factoring a child's immaturity; and (4) choosing empowering words rather than disempowering terms.

*Positive discipline refers parents using clear communication with children, stating desired behaviors, pointing out inappropriate behavior, and rewarding/acknowledging children for good behavior.

ACTIVITY 31

Ambiguous Roles

Return *Module 1, Section 1.2, "Parenting Styles: Sally Learns to Cook."* Pay particular attention to the different parenting styles.

In the case vignette, *Section 8.2 Mirror-Mirror Reflection*, re-read the vignette, noting *"Mom's Parenting Style."* Make note of your assessment of the mother's parenting style.

Is it authoritative, permissive, or authoritarian? Recall that Mom has morning routines while her toddler, Bobbie, is generally nearby, playing with toys. Recall that after Bobbie observes Mom's makeup routine and then applies mom's lipstick to surfaces nearby, it becomes apparent that Bobbie is not precisely modeling Mom's behavior.

Activity:

Step 1: Put yourself in Bobbie's position and consider what it is like to be a toddler. How might Bobbie interpret Mom's words: "...Bobby, you ruin everything you touch!"?

Step 2: What can Bobbie's mom do to correct any misappropriated words she may have stated?

Facilitated Group Discussion: With parenting styles in mind, what steps can the mom use as an alternative reaction to Bobbie's behavior? How could the mom use a different approach to inform Bobbie of her displeasure regarding the smeared lipstick?

Please note that there is no answer key for this critical thinking exercise.

Section 8.3. Support Inventory

Section Focus | Case Example

SEEKING SUPPORT AND TRUST

If given the opportunity, people will use their strengths, intellect, and talents to solve problems. However, when a crisis emerges, such as incarceration, individuals may feel confused and out of sorts.

—Avon Hart-Johnson

Section Objectives

☐ Learn about the characteristics of support groups
☐ Identify evaluation criteria for support group selection using a support inventory list
☐ Brainstorm, assess, and list criteria for selecting family support groups

Overview

As indicated in earlier sections, seeking help is not a sign of weakness, but rather a means to remain strong and grounded. Support groups provide additional benefits that are different from interpersonal relationships. These groups are designed to be unbiased and neutral. Organizations with case management usually have trained staff who take into account privacy and confidentiality. They also tend to consider the "whole" person or whole family (using a person-centered, strength-based approach). They review the whole situation and its resultant impact on the family's life. The primary goal of most advocacy support groups who work in the domain of parental incarceration and supporting impacted families is to enhance or restore their quality of life. These groups are also in place to prevent current life situations from escalating into something worse. For example, family well-being includes the mental health of all of its members; meeting people where they are. Untreated conditions could manifest into more dire situations.

Foundational Learning

Characteristics of support groups. While many support groups have emerged over the past four decades for families of the incarcerated, there are general criteria that families and their children may wish to consider when seeking formal or informal support groups. Scanning a group's website and understanding their philosophies and belief systems might be helpful. The following is a list of considerations when browsing websites for a peer support group. Review the support group inventory used to determine a good fit:

PEER SUPPORT INVENTORY LIST

- Uses guidelines for engagement (i.e., privacy, creating a safe space, requests that group members not share legally damaging information)
- Uses language to describe people rather than the problem (i.e., families of the incarcerated rather than families of prisoners)
- Practices empathy rather than sympathy
- Uses a strength-based modality
- Refrains from labeling people—label behavior, instead
- Creates a sense of privacy and safety
- Reduces power differentials so that all members feel valued
- Practices non-judgmental support
- Promotes agency and self-determination
- Refrains from sensationalizing stories of lived experiences
- Refrains from making a poster child from group members to elevate its mission
- Has a confidentiality protocol for social media shares, photos, content publication, and other information that could trace back to the individual contributor

ACTIVITY 32

Ambiguous Roles

Review the Section 8.3 *Foundational Learning,* peer support inventory list. These are basic recommendations when choosing a support group. Consider developing a personalized list of requirements when seeking out a support group. Considerations might include culturally informed groups such as those who are bilingual. In your opinion, what other requirements should caregivers consider when joining a support group? Brainstorm and list at least five requirements:

1.

2.

3.

4.

5.

Please note that there is no answer key for this critical thinking exercise.

References

Bailey, B.A. (2000). *I love you rituals.* HarperCollins.

Betterup.com. (2020). *Want to be a better parent?* Retrieved from https://get.betterup.com/for-individuals.

Gibson, D. (2013). Ambiguous roles in a stepfamily: Using maps of narrative practices to develop a new family story with adolescents and parents. *Contemporary Family Therapy: An International Journal,* 35(4), 793–805. https://doi.org/10.1007/s10591-013-9258-2.

Hart-Johnson, A., & Johnson, G. (2022). Caregivers' family relations assessment and communication strategies. *Science Publishing Group,* 11(5), 157–168. https://www.sciencepublishinggroup.com/article/10.11648/j.pbs.20221105.12.

Winton, C.A. (2003). *Children as caregivers: Parental & parentified children.* Bacon.

Answer Key for Section 8.1 Activity 30, Pros and Cons

1. It depends. This scenario could be a pro or a con. It could be beneficial for a child to learn the core of making a bed. It might be a con if the child does not possess the physical ability to do so.

2. It depends. The nine-year-old who watches the younger sibling for two hours is likely a con. However, it is again situational. The caregiver is the better judge to determine if the child is capable of keeping an "eye" on the younger sibling. As long as the mother is nearby.

3. Most likely a Con. The seven-year-old has the responsibility of attending to his brother, finding his shoes, clothing, and preparing a backpack lunch for school every morning. This is a big responsibility for a child who must also learn to prepare for school each day. Occasional assignments of helping little brother are likely okay. However, consider the burden and stress of meal preparation and wardrobe planning. It might be a bit much for a seven-year-old to do every day.

MODULE 9

The Importance of Play

MODULE FOCUS

- Section 9.0. A Play Funeral. Reflect upon the connection between children's emotions and symbolic play.
- Section 9.1. The Power of Make Believe. Understand modes of play (tactile, visual, auditory).
- Section 9.2. Play Interventions. Learn about the power of play therapy.
- Section 9.3. Reflection: What We Know About Play and Resilience. Learn how play activities serve as coping mechanisms and building resilience.

Resources

Read Guidebook: Hart-Johnson and Johnson (2025) | Chapter 9, "Why Are They Still Playing?"

Introduction

This module is all about play. It helps caregivers to understand the application of play as it relates to building cognition, physical growth and development. Emotional and social well-being are also discussed. The section covers the importance of imaginative play as well as key factors of how play contributes to children learning to process their world and understanding the people around them.

Play may be one of the most underestimated and undervalued developmental tools for children. There is much to understand about this critical and necessary element for building children's physical, cognitive, emotional, and social well-being.

Play is essential in helping children to communicate their emotional states. Consider an adult with unaddressed emotional issues, buried deep, festering. When adults talk through the issue, they may experience somewhat of a cathartic (emotional) release. The same holds true with children and play. When children use play activities, they sometimes use actions and integrated thoughts to process what they have experienced. As an emotional release, children might draw pictures of something that scared them. They may talk to their figurines and dolls to make sense of the event. They may act out aggression and expressions using play objects.

Playing is natural for children of all ages. A child may play when happy or sad. Children's play is most creative when they are happy. When they are sad, they may appear subdued or anxious. This situation occurs because when playing, children may be seeking answers to allay their fears and confusion. Sometimes, this process is demonstrated when children talk with their toys. They are, in essence, communicating how they feel or role-playing what they may have seen or heard in their environment.

As children develop, they use different forms of play to communicate (physical, imaginative, creative, and social play). Young children eventually add sound and language while playing. Physical play engages gross (large muscle movement such as walking, running, lifting) and fine motor (smaller muscles such as holding, grasping, writing) skills and associated muscle groups. Imaginative and creative play uses abstract and symbolic thought processes; innovative problem-solving (and may include goal setting). Older children engage in social play and may use social skills and core life skills during group play and competitive sports. Each of these skills contributes to children becoming fully actualized individuals.

Section 9.0. A Play Funeral: "The Military Man"

Section Focus | Case Example

THE MILITARY MAN

My father passed away, and we didn't think it affected the middle child. I mean, it affected him, of course, because his grandpa passed. But about two weeks after the funeral, he was in his room, and he had gotten a little box and one of his military figures and he put it in the box and covered it. It was like he was burying it. That was him acting out the funeral, basically. He never said anything. He didn't appear to be depressed about anything, but he did act it out. So, like the other [caregiver in the focus group] said, whether they know what they are seeing or not, those young ages are still traumatic.

—Focus Group Caregiver

Section Objectives

- ☐ Understand how play is used for developmental learning & enhancement
- ☐ Gain an understanding about the linkage between play and processing grief
- ☐ Learn how play enhances cognitive development
- ☐ Learn how caregivers can encourage play

Overview

For years, understanding the link between children's play and their thoughts, memories, symbolizing and feelings has been the focus of researchers, scholars, and practitioners. Forensic specialists use toys and drawings to help children tell their stories about abuse. Play is also an essential component in academic and community-based settings.

PLAY AND DEVELOPMENTAL LEARNING

Play therapy has emerged as a viable intervention for traumatized children (Malchiodi, 2015). Children use functions of play to process their understanding of people, places, and things. Play allows children to tap into their sensory functions, using toys, dolls, and drawing and games and other objects as a means of self-expression. For instance, when a child reenacts a scenario aligned with trauma exposure, they are processing and releasing potentially pent-up emotions. Play has also been used to help children process grief.

Play can be an effective developmental learning process. Even infants engage in developmental and recreational play. Infants use rattles, and other stimulating toys and objects to engage sensory skills in undirected play. They develop motor skills, sharpen their senses, and begin to understand their sense of control over objects. Hence, a caregiver might hear a baby uttering or mimicking adults as they play with toys through various scenarios. Even babbling contributes to building developmental milestones. For example, babbling while playing or otherwise, exercises a baby's vocal cords and prepares them for speaking and language execution (Lillard, et al., 2011).

Play and processing grief. Play activities have several benefits for young children. Through this mental and physical activity, children develop cognitive abilities: logic, critical thinking, talking, and making sounds, and they refine physical skills. Play is a means of reprieve from grief as well as making sense of death and non-death related loss. According to Izumi-Taylor et al. (2021), play can have healing benefits.

When children experience a stressful, traumatic, or emotionally draining event, it is important that they have the right toy objects, activities, or materials to help them work out their feelings. For example, in The *Military Man*, the grandchild used the military figures to emulate and participate in his grandfather's memorial, a form of symbolic play. In his own private way, the child used his toys to metaphorically bury his grandfather.

Foundational Learning

The Care Course School [TCCS] (2016) guides early childhood educators in understanding six important components of play-based intervention that are fundamental to developmental learning: motivation, routine, physical environment, interaction, activities, and families. This practical advice can be helpful for caregivers/parents who seek to better understand the power of play as a system of healthy growth and maturity.

The first component, motivation, has to do with action-reward interaction. For example, children become motivated to play a game based on receiving or winning a prize (TCCS, 2016). Routine is important because children need structure. Letting children know (even during sad or difficult times) that it is okay for playtime can enable them to play without the pressure of stressing (or feeling compelled to openly grieve like others). Children should have opportunities for individual (self-directed, self-initiated) play routines. At times, structured play is beneficial [versus child-centered play] where children solve simple problems such as using puzzles.

Physical environments to practice play include the home, at school, at playgrounds, and designated safe outdoor areas. Interaction entails how children socially engage with others, including their caregivers.

Finally, children at play should be encouraged to use social skills such as sharing, courtesy, respect, and fairness. Some examples of activities involve age-appropriate games, goal-oriented sports, or using constructive toys, which should be tailored to fit the maturity of the child.

Play enhances cognitive (brain) development. There are many cognitive benefits to encouraging and supporting play activities in a child's life. Research indicates that children's engagement in play can boost their intellectual abilities. Additionally, directed play as an intervention can help children to self-regulate and overcome behavioral difficulties (Kestly, 2016). Directed play might include engaging in directed sports activities where a coach teaches rules of the game. Perhaps, the best component of the play process is that, while engaged, the child places the outside world on hold, temporarily allowing them to go to that creative space in their minds where they are safe and self-directed and without pressure (Drewes & Schaefer, 2010).

What can caregivers do to encourage play? Integrative tools such as children's storybooks are beneficial as they can engage the caregiver and the children in focused activities. Children can learn pattern and color matches using colorful books and other interactive objects to enhance their cognition.

Safe physical play allows children to engage their muscles and enjoy the health benefits of these activities. The following are tips for caregivers regarding play activity considerations:

> **Encourage the use of building blocks for play.** Encourage building blocks for young children to build structures.
> **Children should have the power to choose** which toys they engage with and have time for undirected and unstructured play. Additionally, parents do not need to rely solely on store-bought, commercial toys to encourage cognitive development and learning. Do not underestimate the possibilities of miscellaneous objects for play (string, stones, sticks, and other safely vetted objects).
> **Allow children to fantasize and imagine during play.** Caregivers can encourage creativity that stimulates abstract ideas and sequencing. Play stimulates children's creativity and intuitiveness, aligned with the brain's right hemisphere. When reading a story or using figurines and toys, encourage the child to share what the object is doing/expressing/feeling. Ask where the characters are going and inquire about what is happening next. These steps focus on emotions, sequencing, and concepts regarding anticipation/expectations. As a follow-up, ask children if they relate to the content.
> **Refrain from using play restrictions or discipline.** The role of discipline is to provide a foundation for decision-making and competence development. Discipline should provide an understanding of morals, right from wrong, and information that helps children model appropriate behavior and caregiver guidance (Effective Discipline for Children [EDC], 2004). "The purpose of effective discipline is to help children organize themselves, internalize rules and acquire appropriate behavior patterns" (EDC, 2004, p. 2).

Self-directed, self-selected play, with voluntary participation is the most rewarding and valuable play. Competition sometimes brings on stress and takes the fun out of playing. There are times for games and team play; however, allow time for individual play.

Do not force playtime with children. Allow play to unfold organically with children. Children will insert themselves in self-selected, self-directed roles when they make the rules and enjoy play more freely.

ACTIVITY 33

<table>
<tr><td colspan="2" align="center">The Importance of Play</td></tr>
<tr><td colspan="2">To prepare for this activity, reflect on 9.0 Foundational Learning. Pay particular attention to section What can caregivers do to encourage play? Now, review the list of play activities, and in this self-check, identify if the statement is True or False.</td></tr>
<tr><td>1. Competitive games are the best form of play for young children.</td><td>☐ True   ☐ False</td></tr>
<tr><td>2. Playing allows children a sense of agency and choice. In this mode, they can control what happens next and how it happens, creating the rules.</td><td>☐ True   ☐ False</td></tr>
<tr><td>3. When a child misbehaves, it is best to call timeout by taking away playtime for a week.</td><td>☐ True   ☐ False</td></tr>
<tr><td>4. Trusting caregivers who do not infringe and direct activities provide a platform for children to play and presents an opportunity for children to express their emotions through actions.</td><td>☐ True   ☐ False</td></tr>
<tr><td>5. Play stimulates children's ideas, creativity, and intuitiveness, aligned with the brain's right hemisphere.</td><td>☐ True   ☐ False</td></tr>
<tr><td>6. Parents should always establish the rules of play and direct the child in all areas of the activity.</td><td>☐ True   ☐ False</td></tr>
<tr><td>7. Only store-bought, commercial toys encourage cognitive development and learning.</td><td>☐ True   ☐ False</td></tr>
<tr><td>8. Significant learning and development occur during children's formative years. While life can present everyday stressors, playing provides an outlet and possible relief in a child's life.</td><td>☐ True   ☐ False</td></tr>
<tr><td>9. When a child reenacts a scenario aligned with trauma exposure, they are processing and releasing the potentially pent-up emotions.</td><td>☐ True   ☐ False</td></tr>
<tr><td>10. At times, structured play is beneficial [versus child-centered play] where children solve simple problems. For example, a ten-year-old playing the board game, Monopoly, with older siblings may foster an understanding of financial concepts, enhance their math skills, and invite social engagement.</td><td>☐ True   ☐ False</td></tr>
</table>

The Answer Key for Section 9.0, Activity 33 follows Module 9 Reference list.

Section 9.1. The Power of Make Believe

Section Focus | Case Example

JUST PLAY

Play is our brain's favorite way of learning.
—Diane Ackerman

Section Objectives

- ☐ Learn concepts of play: tactile, visual, and auditory
- ☐ Increase knowledge about prison visits policy and program related to prison play spaces
- ☐ Learn about play activities that appeal to children's senses (sensory elements) using low-cost resources
- ☐ Reflect on how prison policy could be changed to make vising more child-friendly for children
- ☐ List creative ways to integrate low cost and creatives ways children can play focusing on tactile, visual, and auditory concepts

Overview

Play can be self-soothing and promote emotional regulation in children. Creative arts such as finger painting and drawing may offer comfort. Children may respond to different objects and textures that promote self-soothing to achieve calm, such as:

- Stuffed animal or cuddly blanket
- Working with colors and fabrics (creating collages using colors, sparkles, paints, and construction paper) for artistic creations
- Listening to soothing music
- Dancing

Foundational Learning

Concepts of play. There is power in play where the emphasis is placed on the play process. These areas include tactile, visual, and auditory play engagement.

Tactile play. Tactile play explores ways of using touch and texture to create spaces and opportunities for recreational engagement. Other modes include:

- Using the senses to explore touch, pressure. While touching to feel texture are the most prominent forms, children also may use their tongues and the inside of their mouths to feel sensations and textures (e.g., baby teething rings, pacifiers).
- Sprinkler systems are a joy in the summer!
- Ball pits are exciting tactile play!

Visual play experiences. Visual play involves using sight to explore pleasurable experiences. Visual play integrates the physical environment, creating a stress-reduction atmosphere.

- Colorful toys are inviting. Environments that are bright-colored and have play equipment and furniture sized for young children are welcoming rather than intimidating. Colorful graphics, textures, and child-friendly visuals invite children to engage, informing them that the space encourages them to play.
- Game mats, puzzle floor cover mats, and comfortable bean bags are fun for children.

Auditory play engagement. Auditory play involves using sounds, instruments, voice, hands, and/or muscle groups to generate sound.

- Digital music applications
- Patty-Cake (sounds of hand and body clapping)
- Hands Clapping (sounds of hands clapping)
- Music to sing to
- Musical Chairs
- Musical toys and instruments (age-appropriate)
- Tapping or stamping feet

Books. Why would a book about parental incarceration be used to discussed in the context of various modes of play? The answer to this question entails the following:

- Promoting healthy families and well-being
- Influencing prison policy to benefit children
- Helping children to adapt to prison rules and visits regulation
- Using role-modeling and visual play to explain difficult topics

Helping children adapt to prison rules and visits regulation. Parents visiting prisons with children can use play activities to help children maintain calm in carceral (detention) settings. Tactile play encourages children to use their senses: touch, taste, smell, and possibly, hearing, to engage in the process. Toddlers need stimulating activities to engage their senses—even during prison visits. Using attention-holding activities, caregivers can help the prison visit go a bit more smoothly. Tiffany Green, RISE Program Coordinator, mother and advocate, recommends using creativity to pique a child's interest and help engage the child during the visit. She illustrated that using products from the prison vending machine can serve as a source of discovery and play adventure. For instance, animal crackers, Cheez-Its, or Skittles can double as a fun activity. These snacks can be used to discuss geometric shapes, create fun patterns, inspire "pretend play," and engage in sorting shapes or colors. Crackers and snacks also serve as a tasty snack and a carbohydrate boost for tired and weary children.

Using role modeling and visual play to explain difficult topics. Parents can use visual play and role modeling to help explain and illustrate difficult topics. For example, parents can use various objects to help children understand the nature of prison visits and the protocol requirements.

- **Use toys such as miniature dolls' tables and chairs** to explain the seating requirements at the prison. Then role-play with the child/children, acting out the seating arrangements and restrictions. The game could include what happens when the rules are violated. Using this process creatively, parents can discuss how to behave during visits.

- **Use toys and other objects to explain that jail and prison are institutions.** Children can learn through toy configurations that a prison is a place where people live, exercise, eat, and sleep. Using objects, such as building blocks, Legos, doll houses, and other props, parents can explain the concepts of rules and how boundaries, including how the prison perimeter restricts both entry, movement, and exit.
- **Provide visuals to navigate feelings, post-prison visit:** Children may need to express their feelings after leaving the prison. There may be sadness and confusion. Drawings are a great way for children to express feelings. Read topic-specific books (see Modules 16 through 19 for examples) designed to generate discussion about prison and jail.

Making prison visiting more child-friendly: Influencing prison policy to benefit children. Prison reform policies can help contribute to child well-being. Prisons can be threatening and intimidating to young children who have not committed any crime or offense. Policy and program administration in prisons might consider the importance of providing children with environments (play spaces) that are not intimidating and offer stress prevention rather than trauma-producing experiences. Some children have witnessed their parent's arrest. Uniformed officers might be intimidating if their role is not explained in a plausible light. Other children may be living with new caregivers and have not seen their parents for a long time. Hence, children might already be stressed before visits. Children should be spared from triggers of past trauma as well as the risk for introducing new trauma during a visit. Children need environments that will evoke self-regulation and self-soothing behaviors.

ACTIVITY 34

The Importance of Play

This activity requires caregivers to consider using basic, no-cost or low-cost objects to engage their children in creative ways to de-stress and play. Imagine observing children with their parents in a park. In this scenario, the parents have not brought along toys. Close observation of the children might reveal that they will eventually find something to play with. They may use sticks and dirt, fiddle with something on the park bench, and twiddle with something on their mother's keychain. They will find creative ways to play. These actions signify three essential processes in the child: imagination, curiosity, and creativity. These imaginative processes involve tactile, visual, and auditory skills development. Consider the following objects (item) and match them to the sensory elements (tactile, visual, or auditory play) by writing in the correct domain match below. There may be one or more answers for the domain match.

ITEM	*DOMAIN MATCH* *[Tactile, Visual, or Auditory?]*
A cardboard tube saved from the paper towel center	
Play-Doh	
Walking in the sand on the beach	
A pre-recorded song from an incarcerated parent	
A jar of pebbles	
A fabric book	
Slime	
A plastic bucket of sand or dirt	
Rubbing two sticks together	
Shaking a plastic jar of beans	
Listening to birds	
Food	
Colored blocks	
Building blocks	
A song	
Animal crackers	
Stuffed animal	

See Answer Key for Section 9.1, Activity 34, after Module 9 Reference list.

Section 9.2. Play Interventions

Section Focus | Case Example

CREATIVE INTERVENTIONS

Childhood is, and always has been a vulnerable time.
—Bruce D. Perry, MD, Ph.D.
(Malchodi, 2015, p. x)

Section Objectives

☐ Learn about the role of play therapy
☐ Become familiar with the use of music and art therapy
☐ Learn how children's conditions may cause regression to prior behaviors

Overview

A child who experienced stress in the past can usually recover. Children can learn to cope and overcome adversity that trauma tends to leave in its wake. Traumatizing events could include death, violence exposure, natural disaster, medical illness, abuse, relocation, parental incarceration, and war.

Helping professionals (mental health, clinical social workers, play therapists, and other practitioners) can provide interventions to address the physiological distress aligned with trauma while also helping to stabilize a child's emotions and self-regulation. Interventions may include play therapy, which includes ways to communicate with nonverbal and verbal methods. Therapeutic modalities can help children express themselves in non-threatening and safe ways. This therapeutic work with children teaches practical coping skills and builds resilience, as well.

Foundational Learning

While there are many creative interventions available for children, we present two types in this section to inform caregivers of the related processes and expectations should they consider seeking out licensed practitioners. The role of play therapy provided here include:

1. Music therapy
2. Art therapy

MUSIC THERAPY

Music can be a source of healing, according to Dr. Russell E. Hilliard. Through this medium, people can feel connectedness, express their feelings, reflect on fond memories, and even make meaning of previous experiences gone wrong. Sometimes, emotions are so complex that even adults become lost for words where expressions such as, "I am feeling some kind of way" may make no sense to others. However, the expression means that a person lacks the words to express themselves.

This lack of articulation is similar to what young children go through when they do not have the words or vocabulary to share the complexities of their feelings. Grief, anxiety, and depression are complex conditions that may be multidimensional. Therapists are trained to help clients address these issues. Music therapy can help promote healing by the therapist-child team working through the grief process and other intense emotions.

Music therapy: What to expect
A music therapist's role is to assess a child's *holistic well-being* (emotional, physical, social, and communication skills). Treatment entails more than listening to music. The therapy may involve listening sessions (talk-sessions), imagery, songwriting, learning through music, and interdisciplinary therapy modalities.

Who performs the therapy
A licensed practitioner • RMT (Registered Music Therapist), CMT (Certified Music Therapist), ACMT (Advanced Certified Music Therapist) • Certification Board for Music Therapists: https://www.cbmt.org/

Where to find a music therapist
findMT@musictherapy.org

Where they work
• Hospitals • Corrections Facilities (prisons, jails, halfway houses, rehabilitation centers) • Schools • Community Centers

ART THERAPY

When children are traumatized, they may regress to behaviors aligned with their former years. For example, a 10-year-old might have incidents of bedwetting. Young children may become increasingly needy, while older children may become isolated. Concentration might suffer, and children may seem to need extra support performing basic tasks. Loumeau-May (2020) indicated that this type of regression is because of the many changes in the bodies and emotions of growing children, especially for 10- to 18-year-olds. The trauma may complicate or exacerbate their physical and emotional sensations.

Art therapy: What to expect
Working with an art therapist may involve a hands-on discussion with a licensed therapist. The first step is establishing comfort, trust, and rapport. The therapist will likely use a different medium for artwork, such as paint, pencils, crayons, markers, or clay. The work entails de-stressing techniques, building emotional coping skills, interpersonal connections, and a focus on client presenting concerns. Art therapy is a facilitator-led activity that combines human services and mental health modalities to form a nexus of creative art processes, using psychological theories and interventions.

Who performs the therapy
A licensed practitioner • Professional Art Therapist • Licensed Professional Counselor with Specialty Designation in Art Therapy • Registered Art Therapist with a License to Practice Psychotherapy • Art Therapy included in the Creative Arts Therapist License • American Art Therapy Association: https://arttherapy.org/about-art-therapy/
Where to find an Art therapist
United States 　American Art Therapy Association 　4875 Eisenhower Avenue, Suite 240 　Alexandria, VA 22304 | United States 　Phone: 888-290-0878 | 703-548-5860 　FAX: 703-783-8468 United Kingdom: 　British Association of Art Therapists—BAAT 　https://www.baat.org/About-BAAT/Find-an-Art-Therapist
Where they work
• Special Education • Charities • Community Centers • Private Practice • Social Services • Primary and Secondary Education

ACTIVITY 35

The Importance of Play

In this activity, review the Module content and complete the Fill-in-the-blank questions:

1. _____can be a source of healing, according to Dr. Russell E. Hilliard.
2. A child who experienced _____ in the past can usually recover.
3. The role of play therapy provided here include:

   1. _____
   2. _____

3. When children are _____, they may regress to behaviors aligned with their former years.

The answer key for Activity 35 follows Section 9 Reference list.

Section 9.3. Reflection, What We Know: Play & Resilience

Section Focus | Case Example

ADAPTIVE COPING MODELED BY CAREGIVERS

Children develop the skills they need to navigate the world through trial-and-error problem-solving, observing their caregiver's behavioral models, and learning by doing.

Section Objectives

- ☐ Gain an understanding about the links between resilience, play, and coping.
- ☐ Identify the building blocks of resilience
- ☐ Critically reflect and discuss the integration of play, children's emotions, and how children express themselves

Overview

RESILIENCE, PLAY, AND COPING

The main goal of coping mechanisms is to make the pain go away. Whether physical or mental pain, children want relief. Play allows children to experience or explore feelings safely. Children may not understand the associated emotions; however, emotional release in a safe space might provide the initial step towards healing. When a child engages in play with a supporting caregiver, this trusted environment allows for a child's emotions and feelings to emerge. Sometimes, children simply need to be heard to be acknowledged. When children express themselves and find relief in doing so, they come to realize they can and will get through other challenging situations in life. This process of self-discovery helps to build resilience and enhance coping.

Foundational Learning

According to Ginsberg and Jablow (2011), the fundamental *building blocks of resilience* and the ability to cope begin with:

- The love and unwavering support of parents/caregivers: A child who feels secure may take chances in the world, learning by doing, knowing the caregiver will be there to support them should they fall or falter.
- Encouraging appropriate goal setting and applauding successes. If caregivers applaud children for their successes, they may continue to excel. Stand by children and encourage appropriate goal setting and applaud their successes. As a result, the children will likely aim high and make the caregiver proud.
- Creating a positive environment. Children are like sponges. The environment children are exposed to will shape their development. Create an environment that protects children from abuse, risks, violence, bullying, and other threats.
- Model the adult you wish children to become. As a repeated theme, be the person you wish your children to become as adults.

ACTIVITY 36

The Importance of Play

In this activity, reflect upon the Section 9.3 Overview and Foundational Learning. Note three insights that stand out and the reasons why. There is no single right answer, as these reflections are situational. *Facilitators, for group discussion, ask each group to report what resonates as important key factors and why.* Please note that there is no answer key for this critical thinking exercise.

Reflections

Insights and Reasons:

<u>Overview</u>

   1.

   2.

   3.

<u>Foundational Learning</u>

   1.

   2.

   3.

References

The Care Course School, Inc. (2016). *The magic of play.* Distance learning for early childhood professionals. Author.

Drewes, A.A., & Schaefer, C.E. (Eds.). (2010). *School-based play therapy.* John Wiley & Sons.

Ginsburg, K.R. & Jablow, M.M. (2011). *Building resilience in children and teens: Giving kids roots and wings.* American Academy of Pediatrics.

Hart-Johnson, A. & Johnson, G. (2022). Caregivers' family relations assessment and communication strategies. *Science Publishing Group,* 11(5), 157–168. https://www.sciencepublishinggroup.com/article/10.11648/j.pbs.20221105.12.

Izumi-Taylor, S., Turner, S.B., & YeonSun, R. (2021). The healing power of play for children in crisis events. *Exchange* (19460406), 260, 14–16.

Kestly, T.A. (2016). Presence and play: Why mindfulness matters. *International Journal of Play Therapy,* 25(1), 14.

Lillard, A., Pinkham, A.M., & Smith, E. (2011). Pretend play and cognitive development. In U. Goswami (Ed.), *The Wiley-Blackwell Handbook of Cognitive Development, Second Edition*. Wiley-Blackwell.

Loumeau-May, L.V. (2020). Art therapy with traumatically bereaved youth. In S. Ringel & J.R. Brandell (Eds.), *Trauma: Contemporary Directions in Trauma Theory, Research, and Practice* (pp. 206–255). Columbia University Press. https://doi.org/10.7312/ring18886-009.

Malchiodi, C.A. (2015). *Creative interventions with traumatized children*. Gilford Press.

Nieman, P., & Shea, S. (2004). Effective discipline for children. *Pediatrics & Child health*, 9(1), 37–50. https://doi.org/10.1093/pch/9.1.37.

Answer Key for Section 9.0, Activity 33.

1. Playing allows children a sense of agency and choice. In this mode, they can control what happens next and how it happens, creating the rules.	☑ True	☐ False
2. When a child misbehaves, it is best to call timeout by taking away playtime for a week.	☐ True	☑ False
3. Trusting caregivers who do not infringe and direct activities provide a platform for children to play and presents an opportunity for children to express their emotions through actions.	☑ True	☐ False
4. Play stimulates children's ideas, creativity, and intuitiveness, aligned with the brain's right hemisphere.	☑ True	☐ False
5. Parents should always establish the rules of play and direct the child in all areas of the activity.	☐ True	☑ False
6. Only store-bought, commercial toys encourage cognitive development and learning.	☐ True	☑ False
7. Significant learning and development occur during children's formative years. While life can present everyday stressors, playing provides an outlet and possible relief in a child's life.	☑ True	☐ False
8. When a child reenacts a scenario aligned with trauma exposure, they are processing and releasing the potentially pent-up emotions.	☑ True	☐ False
9. At times, structured play is beneficial [versus child-centered play] where children solve simple problems. For example, a ten-year-old playing the board game, *Monopoly*, with older siblings may foster an understanding of financial concepts, enhance their math skills, and invite social engagement.	☑ True	☐ False

Answer Key for Section 9.1, Activity 34

ITEM	DOMAIN MATCH *[Tactile, Visual, or Auditory?]*
A cardboard tube saved from the paper towel center	Tactile & Visual Play object
Play-Doh	Tactile
Walking in the sand on the beach	Tactile & visual
A pre-recorded song from an incarcerated parent	Auditory
A jar of pebbles	Tactile
A fabric book	Tactile & visual
Slime	Tactile
A plastic bucket of sand or dirt	Tactile
Rubbing two sticks together	Tactile, possibly auditory
Shaking a plastic jar of beans	Visual and auditory
Listening to birds	Auditory
Food	Tactile, visual, possibly auditory
Colored blocks	Tactile, visual, possibly auditory
Building blocks	Tactile, visual, possibly auditory
A song	Auditory
Animal crackers	Tactile, visual

Answer Key for Section 9.2, Activity 35

Answer to fill-in-the-blank questions:

1. Music can be a source of healing, according to Dr. Russell E. Hilliard.
2. A child who experienced stress in the past can usually recover.
3. The role of play therapy provided here include:
    1. Music therapy
    2. Art therapy
4. When children are traumatized, they may regress to behaviors aligned with their former years.

PART II

Tackling the Big Topics

Offsetting Risks and Overcoming the Odds

MODULE FOCUS

- Section 10.0. Risks and Protective Factors. Understand factors that contribute to children's well-being.
- Section 10.1. Reframing and Rewriting the Story. Learn about strength-based perspectives to reframe life stories.
- Section 10.2. Co-Parenting. Explore and identify intentional parenting concepts, co-parenting from prison, and extended family relationships.
- Section 10.3. Let's Network: It Takes a Village!

Resources

Read Guidebook: Hart-Johnson and Johnson (2025) | Chapter 10, "Risks, Protective Factors, and Child Well-being"

Introduction

This workbook is designed to focus on protecting and promoting the child's well-being, while being mindful of caregivers' self-care. Informed caregivers who are equipped to recognize risk factors might favorably enhance children's developmental trajectories. Caregivers can benefit when they understand child protections that safeguard children and enable their chances for successful growth and development (benefits include reducing personal stress, as well).

Risk factors are threats to well-being. *Protective factors* are steps or actions taken to prevent adverse conditions from occurring. Protective factors contribute to building resilience. As indicated earlier, resilience is concerned with helping children to develop coping skills.

RESILIENCE

Building resilience is concerned with teaching and influencing children to recover after challenging setbacks or adverse events. Parents can help children develop resilience through their outlook and reactions to life. Some young children look to the parent to gauge how concerned, stressed, and upset they themselves should be. Of course, children will have their own reactions to adverse circumstances, but the parent/caregiver can quiet fears and provide guidance. Perhaps this ray of hope may help children to get through challenges.

It is not just the caregiver who contributes to children building resilience. Others in the family and outside the home contribute to helping children react to setbacks in life. They might include:

- Teachers
- Clergy or church members
- Mentors
- Extended family
- Community group peers and leaders

Resilience and Stress Responses

Stress comes in various forms and at different times throughout a child's life. Children's reactions to life events may vary based on their uniqueness and a host of other variables. They may use effective and ineffective coping to get through situations. Effective coping entails learning coping skills and developing belief systems that through contextualizing and framing difficulties in perspective, they can develop resilience. Conversely, if children are not taught effective coping, they may use alternative sources to cope such as over- or under-eating, sleeping, and withdrawal. Alternatively, they may learn turn to effective coping such as exercise, talking through their feelings, using mindfulness, incorporating deep breathing exercises, and other practices. These activities are also considered protective factors.

This section revisits previous concepts regarding resilience, self-care practices, the notion of co-parenting, family support, and an ecosystem of support. This module also covers the importance of understanding risks to child well-being. These risks are not always obvious and therefore, we point out some of the well-known risks through activities. The sections also introduce the idea of "reframing" through an activity. The activities ask readers to examine their ideas about life circumstances and perhaps, look at their lives through a meaning making activity to find a silver lining. The Module covers co-parenting and reinforces the importance of networking with others who are experiencing similar challenges and learning methods to overcome them.

Section 10.0. Risks and Protective Factors

Section Focus | Case Example

Risks and Protective Factors

Not all children will experience risks—threats to well-being—nor will they all respond in the same way. Children have different temperaments, parenting exposure, stress tolerance, and personalities. Protective factors are a means to counteract the potential harm that children may encounter.

<u>Section Objectives</u>

- ☐ Identify risks associated with parental incarceration
- ☐ Identify protective factors
- ☐ Gain an understanding of stakeholders who provide family support
- ☐ Reflect critically and list upon risk management techniques

Overview

RISK FACTORS OF FAMILY MEMBER INCARCERATION

Risk factors threaten well-being. The risks of parental incarceration are well-known. Researchers cite the following risks for affected children (e.g., Arditti & Johnson, 2022; Turney et al., 2018; Wildeman et al., 2018):

- Challenges with academic matriculation
- Mental health
- Physical health
- Financial challenges and, potentially, poverty
- Teachers lowering their expectations of children's academic achievement goals

RISKS ASSOCIATED WITH THE CAREGIVING RELATIONSHIP:

- Insecure attachments with children
- Disengaged parenting
- High internal conflict in the family system
- Caregivers' unfamiliarity with the risk factors
- Negative communication skills
- Negative parenting styles
- Poor social skills and interpersonal styles

Besemer et al. (2018) indicated that risk exposures can have long-term consequences to children's health and well-being. The authors further suggested that these risks do not stop with the children and that their caregivers also encounter stress while caring for young people. This strain exacerbates their own exposure to adversity.

Of all the risks experienced by children, the psycho-emotional and biological impacts can be the most concerning. Children's risk exposure during the formative years may infringe upon their ability to meet cognitive development milestones. It can be difficult to navigate these conditions if the whole family is experiencing distress that affects their mental health. Therefore, identifying risk factors early on and addressing them before they emerge in an escalated form is imperative.

Protective factors for children. Protective factors can offer stabilization and prevention. Additionally, the following actions may be helpful for children:

- Encourage strong supportive families.
- Preserve relationships and communication between children and their parents.
- Hold police departments and public entities such as social services accountable to protect and safeguard children's experiences.
- State and federal prisons and jails should be trained and aligned with family-friendly and family-preservation policies, programming, and laws.

Protective factors for caregivers. Protective factors are steps taken to reduce risks and prevent adversity. Some examples include the following:

- Maintain a cordial co-parenting relationship (between the incarcerated parent and caregiver) in the best interest of the child.
- Provide truthful and honest interpersonal relationships with affected children.
- Advocate for children at all levels of society.
- Provide the foundation for children to build resilience and coping skills.
- Seek resources that support the child.
- Observe and monitor signs of bullying.
- Ensure that early education centers and other community groups provide peer support and mentoring—where affected children realize they are not alone.

Foundational Learning

A repeated theme aligned with protective factors for children of incarcerated parents is "support." Children need caregivers and adults to assist them along the journey of life. They need the support of adults even more when they are facing risks that threaten their emotional, physical, and mental stability: their mental health, and intellectual growth. Support systems offer the kind of help that benefit families in a positive manner.

Stakeholders who provide family support. Stakeholders are considered people who have a vested interest in achieving a common goal. Stakeholders who support affected families must ensure that dignity and respect are integrated from the first point of contact and encounters, especially with children. Stakeholders who may provide tailored support for families and children include but are not limited to:

- Community advocates
- Law enforcement
- Corrections personnel
- Legislators
- Policymakers
- Educators
- Prison officials
- Media
- Courts
- Helping Professionals

Summers (2015) reminds helping professionals, as well as advises families seeking services, that they have rights. This is an especially important reminder since individuals who seek support are by definition in need of help and therefore, may be vulnerable. Intrinsic rights include privacy and informed consent, participation in the planning and needs assessments, and rights to self-determination. Each of these rights factor into understanding risk management processes and protective factors. See Appendix G, *Getting Support: What to Expect*, for helpful tips on what to expect from support personnel.

ACTIVITY 37

Offsetting Risks and Overcoming the Odds

In this activity, readers reflect critically upon risk management techniques and ideas. Risk management entails identifying the threats to well-being and applying ways to reduce the risk. In the home, caregivers can use common sense approaches to risk reduction. For example, if the risk entails children's exposure to conflict, they may choose to minimize the exposure. They may set aside time when children are not present to work through interpersonal conflict. If the risk is community violence, they may choose to accompany their children or assign someone to safeguard children when they are in public spaces (as well as teach children strategies for protection such as never walking alone, using confident postures, and avoiding being outside during late night hours).

For this assignment, review the table 10.0 Risk Exposure, below. Consider what steps a caregiver might implement to minimize the harm by applying protective buffers for children aligned with each identified risk scenario. Be creative and use intuition and common sense (remember, there is no wrong answer, as this activity is situational). However, for this activity, we do offer tips in the answer key.

Table 10.0 Risk Exposure

Risk Exposure	Protective Action │ Risk Mitigation Strategy
Classmates bully a child	
Since a new resident moved in the caregiver's home, there has been internal conflict.	
Since the incarceration of their mother, there have been challenges with each if the children's academic matriculation/progress.	
The grandmother noticed that her biological daughter uses harsh and negative parenting styles with the grandchildren when under stress.	
Upon reflection, the mother recognizes that she has felt disengaged and not able to completely concentrate. She fears not being fully present for the children.	

See Answer Key for Section 10.0, Activity 37.1, after Module 10 Reference list.

Activity | 37.1

Review, Section 10.0 and Appendix G. In this activity, learners will match the term with the brief definition. Please complete the following 10 questions.

	Term		*Definition*
A	Confidential	1	A legal right.
B	Insecure Attachments	2	Individuals have the right to contribute to insights and options towards their well-being.
C	Needs Assessment	3	Threat to well-being
D	Self-determination	4	People who have a vested interest in achieving a common goal.
E	Community Advocates	5	Steps taken to reduce the risk, prevent adversity, or negate the risks.
F	Risk Factor	6	A risk factor for children of incarcerated parents
G	Caregiver Support	7	Every individual has the right to free choice without coercion or interference.
H	Protective Factors	8	An example of a stakeholder.
I	Participation in Planning	9	The process of understanding client /constituent history, their unique situations, and requirements for restoration of personal well-being
J	Stakeholders	10	A repeated theme identified as a protective factor.

The Answer Key for Section 10.0, Activity 38, follows the Module 10 Reference list.

Section 10.1. Reframing and Rewriting the Story

Section Focus | Case Example

I Am Strong. I Am Capable. I Am Loved.

Our self-narratives tell us how to feel, respond, and act. Why not tell ourselves an empowering story that lifts us up from the depths of despair?

Section Objectives

- ☐ Learn about the benefits of strength-based reflection
- ☐ Gain Knowledge about rituals mindfulness practices
- ☐ Practice creative writing through journaling

Overview

The role of a caregiver can seem monumental at times and a breeze during others. Reflecting upon one's strengths rather than weaknesses or deficits can be empowering. Using a positive mindset is considered a *strength-based reflection* and perspective. Through a journey of self-awareness and reflection, one can revise thoughts and behaviors and develop habits that contribute to the holistic well-being of both caregiver and child. When mistakes or mishaps do occur, using a bit of self-compassion goes a long way.

Foundational Learning

Rituals. This section reflects and builds upon prior discussion on achieving self-care, self-awareness, and self-compassion. Setting goals and creating rituals may benefit caregivers and their families. Additionally, helping professionals who provide assistance and care can also benefit from rituals and self-care routines.

Rituals are considered practices or habits that, when repeated over time, can have "staying power." However, most importantly, these routines may contribute to recognizing ways to enhance personal health, fitness, mindfulness, and interpersonal relationships.

The following philosophies may help both caregivers and helping professionals to become more self-aware, engage in mindful practices toward self-compassion, and to practice self-care:

- Recognize that you are fully human with strengths as well as opportunities for growth;
- Emotional pain is not to be avoided but embraced and managed as a normal part of life;
- Recognize that life has cycles of happiness, sadness, joy, and grief;

- Embrace the love of family, friends, colleagues, and others who are in your inner circle and those who are not—respect their individualism;
- Be kind to yourself and treat yourself the way you would treat others, using empathy and caring;
- Do not seek to dismiss the suffering but rather understand and work through the suffering;
- Understand and set realistic expectations for yourself and others;
- Be truthful with oneself;
- Recognize the power of stress combined with burnout. For caregivers of children and for helping professionals with clients, this condition can be a high-risk factor associated with inadvertently hurting others (potentially through lack of sensitivity or being overworked and stressed).

Seeking help is not a form of defeat. When individuals have a great deal of responsibility and face stress beyond normal levels, they may feel exhausted. Consequently, many tasks can go unmet because the person is not functioning at optimal levels. Do not self-blame, but rather remember self-compassion.

Journaling can be a way of getting in touch with feelings and setting realistic goals. Small steps can become a lasting routine. For example, simply stretching each morning after getting out of bed may promote physical well-being and establish self-care discipline. Listening to soothing music can enhance mood and may help with de-stressing.

ACTIVITY 38

Offsetting Risks and Overcoming the Odds

There are two activities in this section. The first activity, Table 10.1. Goal Setting: Self-Reflection and Self-Awareness, entails reflection and self-awareness. Read the prompts listed in the table below and fill in the section with the answer (following the ellipses "..."), recognizing that there is no right or wrong answer. This exercise is individualized and pertains to you as an individual. In this reflective exercise, try to be honest and genuine. We each have strengths, likes, and positive attributes.

Table 10.1 Goal Setting: Self-Reflection and Self Awareness	
The following are my top 3 strengths....	When I feel strong I....
What I like about myself....	When I feel most loved I....
When I think of one life goal that I must accomplish in this lifetime, it involves....	What it feels like to achieve a baby step (completing an incremental step successfully)....
What I want to accomplish in a month....	What it feels like to commit....
The most positive thing about myself....	When I am in the "flow," this is the part of me that shines!....
My de-stressing rituals are (music, writing, doodling, stretching, walking, etc.)....	This activity always calms me and brings me back to my "center"....

Activity | 38.1

In this reflective and creative process, learners write a children's story. This is a two-part process designed to stimulate creativity and ideas. Part A entails writing a story. Part B requires the reader to draw a picture that represents the essence of the story.

Preparation and Materials:

Select blank paper, or flipchart, or device to record content.

Optional: Crayons, markers, or colored pens for the drawing portion of the assignment

Time: Allow at least a day to complete this exercise. This activity can be used also as a group exercise (shorter duration—complete in one setting), following the prompts below identified in Part A.

PART A (GROUP OR INDIVIDUAL EXERCISE)

Create a children's short story, focusing on helping build "self-compassion, self-awareness, and self-love." Consider the content covered in Section 10.1. With this overview and foundational learning, in mind, follow the prompts below.

- ° **Create a story for the age group, 7 to 10 years old (if you do not have children, write a personal memoir/essay/story).** Recall that children between the ages of 7 and 10 tend to be quite creative. This age group can understand events and sequenced ideas involving choices and consequences.
- ° **Integrate sensory elements** to make the story come alive (the smell of food, touching objects, colorful objects, etc.). You may also revisit Section 9.1 focusing on the various ways children engage with tactile, visual, and auditory play, to gain ideas.
- ° **Follow the prompts as guidance:**
  - Where does the story take place?
  - What time of year does the story take place?
  - Who is in the story?
  - Where does the story begin?
  - What is happening in the story?
  - Why is the story important?
  - What happens in the middle of the story that challenges the main character of the story (the point of no return)?
  - How are acts of self-awareness, self-compassion, and self-love illustrated?
  - How does the main character overcome the odds?
  - What is the silver lining?
  - How does the story end?
  - What is the final thought the reader must learn before reading "the end"? (This is the moral of the story or the reason the story is needed)

PART B
- ° Draw a picture that represents the essence of the story.

Please note that there is no answer key for this critical thinking exercise.

Section 10.2. Co-Parenting

Section Focus | Case Example

Intentional Parenting

Caregiving involves making sacrifices for children. Intentional parenting takes responsibility for both the challenges and the triumphs. My child said: I need you to comfort me, I'm sad. I don't know what to do. And then the other little one said, like, I need someone in my life. I want to do something, go places, and feel loved. In all of these situations, you have to interact with them.

—Focus Group Caregiver

Section Objectives

☐ Learn about tips for building healthy family systems and co-parenting strategies
☐ Gain knowledge about interpersonal relationships and communication
☐ Identify options related to co-parenting from prison

Overview

Parenting and co-parenting generally requires the adults to place their differences aside and focus on the child's best interests, and overall well-being. This collaboration may call for healthy interpersonal relationships underpinned with compassion, and respect, fostered by sound communication. A respectful exchange of ideas and information enables all members to have a voice and helps to build a foundation for a close-knit family system. With this healthy mindset, families can thrive and weather crises when strong foundations are in place.

In the case of parental incarceration, while it may seem difficult, even incarcerated individuals can contribute to family support, child upbringing, and household decision-making through co-parenting. As the case example calls out, children may call out for love and comfort. Parenting and co-parenting can provide the answer.

Foundational Learning

Co-parenting takes a village. In a unique framework, Hart-Johnson et al. (2018) introduced the concept of co-parenting from prison. In this schema, the authors indicated that co-parenting goes beyond the construct of mother and father, extending to stakeholder support. Their research findings suggested that community advocates, interventionists, policymakers, and parents/caregivers all bear responsibility in raising the child (Hart-Johnson et al., 2018). In this context, Hart-Johnson and colleagues indicated that stakeholders share a co-parenting responsibility of treating children with incarcerated parents with trauma-informed practices. However, it is not enough to be trauma-informed or trauma-sensitive; stakeholders must collectively enforce rules and protocol to ensure that children are the highest priority. An example includes school settings where children spend a great deal of time with teachers and coaches. Children are the most vulnerable in the adult-child equation, where co-parents can uplift children as they navigate different conditions in life.

Co-parenting from prison. The authors (Hart-Johnson et al., 2018) also offer the following insights and recommendations from practical fieldwork and advocacy:

- Consider the child's best interests
- Be reflective, and when necessary, use apologies, offer forgiveness, and negotiate.
- Use strength-based parenting practices (focus on strengths rather than deficits)
- Integrate safeguards to prevent children from feeling guilty
- Never "bad-mouth" or speak negatively about the other/estranged parent
- Demonstrate emotional regulation when communicating sensitive topics, especially in the presence of children (via phone, video, in-person, or even through written communication)
- Do not force co-parenting relationships on children
- Be supportive and be respectful of everyone's needs and goals
- Set realistic expectations

Additional options related to co-parenting from prison. The National Healthy Marriage Resource Center (n.d.) offers tips for enhancing interpersonal relationships that might support the co-parenting model. The following communication and engagement strategies can also support co-parenting strategies.

RELATIONSHIPS

- Treat family members as unique humans with unique needs
- Consider cultivating and modeling healthy relationships inside and outside of the family system (e.g., social network, friendships, extended family, and work relationships)
- Set realistic goals and expectations regarding raising children
- Establish foundations of trust
- Where possible, model warm behaviors and show examples of unconditional support

COMMUNICATION STRATEGIES

- Try to use respectful, clear, and forthright communication
- When discussing parental incarceration consider abstract versus detailed information sharing (details are not always necessary, but honesty and clarity matter)
- Consider the timing for communication
- Use person- and age-appropriateness
- Listen to others

Receiving Communication

- Consider the most efficient mode of delivery (face-to-face, phone, text message, video conference)
- Listen, and reflect
- Find common ground

The following insights are also offered from caregivers who participated in Hart-Johnson and Johnson's (2022) research study as findings related to effective family communication and engagement:

- Use direct communication and be truthful
- Find a place with little or no distractions when holding family conversations
- Actively listen, and paraphrase what the other person says
- Co-develop a plan or action to move forward
- Use supplemental resources to help explain complex content to family members and especially to young children
- Rehearse and role-play talking points

ACTIVITY 39

Offsetting Risks and Overcoming the Odds	
Reflect on Sections 10.2. Answer the following True or False statements. Circle the correct answer below. The answer key follows the Module 10 reference list.	
1. When holding difficult conversations, any place will do, as long as there is seating.	☐True ☐ False
2. A characteristic of building strong family bonds entails creating healthy relationships inside and outside of the family system.	☐True ☐ False
3. Parents should demonstrate emotional regulation when talking to children about complex topics.	☐True ☐ False
4. Three communication strategies are: Be respectful, clear, and forthright.	☐True False
5. Loving exchanges of support and affection in the family system demonstrate family bonding.	☐True ☐ False
6. When co-parents plan to discuss important topics with children, it is best to prepare and even role-play or rehearse.	☐True ☐ False
7. Reflection is an integral part of taking responsibility and accountability for actions.	☐True ☐ False
8. Children should have access to their parents, even if they are in prison or living outside of the home. However, never force children into compliance.	☐True ☐ False
9. Safeguard children from feeling guilty over adult relationship issues.	☐True ☐ False
10. Only parents with professional backgrounds can use trauma-sensitive, strength-based parenting skills.	☐True ☐ False

Section 10.3. Let's Network:
It Takes a Village!

Section Focus | Case Example

It Takes a Village

"Asiye funzwa na mamae hufunzwa na ulimwengu"
Translation: Whomsoever is not taught by the mother will be taught by
the world.

—Swahili proverb

Section Objectives

☐ Gain an understanding about "ecosystems" related to family support resources
☐ Learn about the importance and need for caregivers and their families having multiple levels of support
☐ Identify and create a personalized list of family support systems

Overview

The Swahili proverb above expresses the sentiment of many cultures that believe in the power of collective action. The inference made in the adage conveys that if learning does not occur in the home, indeed, the world will offer corrections through morals, laws, ethics, and social responses.

Bannink et al. (2014) indicated that a limited way to look at child-rearing is to consider that parents do this work alone. Bannink et al. indicated that children are raised in a larger social context that extends to the community, academic settings, extended family members, maternal and paternal relatives, and other natural extensions of the parent-child relationships. Each of these domains potentially influences how a child matures and grows in the world.

Foundational Learning

Ecosystem of support. Multiple levels of support can positively benefit family systems. Applying the concept of "it takes a village," the notion of neighbors looking out for each other's children was/is commonplace. Extended support systems might include institutions such as church (faith-based) affiliations, affinity clubs such as Boys and Girl Scouts, and other institutions (e.g., 4-H, community programs) beyond the family unit. In this context, support became a part of the extended family.

There are multiple levels of support. Other systems of support might include educational systems.

Educational systems also provide family support. At this level, teachers/educators and other personnel in school systems advocate for children. Trauma-sensitive and person-centered, strength-based approaches are essential to ensure that support is provided through a lens of dignity and respect.

School support and caregiver attunement include awareness of children's emotional and physical needs. Effective support includes:

- Encouraging children and uplifting them to their full potential
- Being nonjudgmental
- Incorporating ways to self-check biases and attitudes
- Establishing boundaries
- Creating a safe space to learn

Therapeutic support: Professional mental and physical support requires cultural awareness and ethical practice. Children whose parents have faced trauma and crisis require compassion and nonjudgmental support. Boilerplate options are not effective in addressing the individualized needs of children. Treatment planning and needs assessment should ensure appropriateness and contextual application. In other words, different cultures respond to crisis and family stressors in different ways.

Wrap-around support during challenges: With collective support and intervention of wraparound services, a crisis might strengthen families experiencing challenges. This support model entails addressing the family crisis and challenges from a holistic perspective (financially, socially, physically, emotionally, and even environmentally). Group support systems can enhance and even heighten the strengths within the family unit.

In a parent training class called the BRIDGES program, Weeks (2013) highlighted the importance of wraparound support systems and extended the focus to continuity of care that includes effective parenting practices. The following are a framework that supports holistic care of family systems:

- Develop a shared understanding of what families need as external support
- Develop goals that are client or family-driven
- Ensure that the intervention is understood and fits within the family goals strategy
- Establish a plan for follow-up and check-ins
- Make sure that there is a co-therapy intervention model where there are intermittent check-ins
- Develop an exit strategy for the termination of services

While interventions vary depending on the modality and therapist or helping professionals, common expectations include using strength-based modalities and integrating self-determination and client-centered strategies. Of critical importance is the continuity of services and a clear plan for an exit strategy. This process ensures that intervention can be continued as maintenance planning once the professional services have concluded.

ACTIVITY 40

Offsetting Risks and Overcoming the Odds

In this activity, we reinforce the importance of family support systems. Each family must decide if and when support resources are beneficial. This creative exercise helps to identify potential caregiver/family support systems.

Procedures:

1. This activity is called "A Family Support Tree."

    a. The Family Support Tree concept illustrates the metaphor that a family's network extends to friends, community members, and others. This idea aligns with the concept of "It takes a village." This adage means that we can work to support each other as a collective network.

2. Take a moment to review the tree's structure (Figure 10.3.0).

3. Every leaf should represent, by name, people and organizations who represent your current support system. Examples include:

    b. Family members (siblings, grandparents, aunts, uncles, godparents)
    c. Organizations (faith-based, community, educational, advocacy, nonprofit)
    d. Social Systems (social workers, caseworkers, attorneys, educators)
    e. Friends and relations (co-workers, close friends, and colleagues)

4. As you reflect, consider how each leaf could include names or groups (e.g., "My family" or "Jenny's school.)"

PARENT-CHILD ACTIVITY: Caregivers can perform this activity with children. Work individually or collectively with children to identify supporters. Label branches and leaves as support resources. See example below. Caregiver and children's support might be similar. Discussion can help the caregiver and child realize they have love and support and are not alone. Examples of children's responses might include:

- "My family"
- "My best friend"
- "Our dog"
- "My mentor"

A Family Support Tree

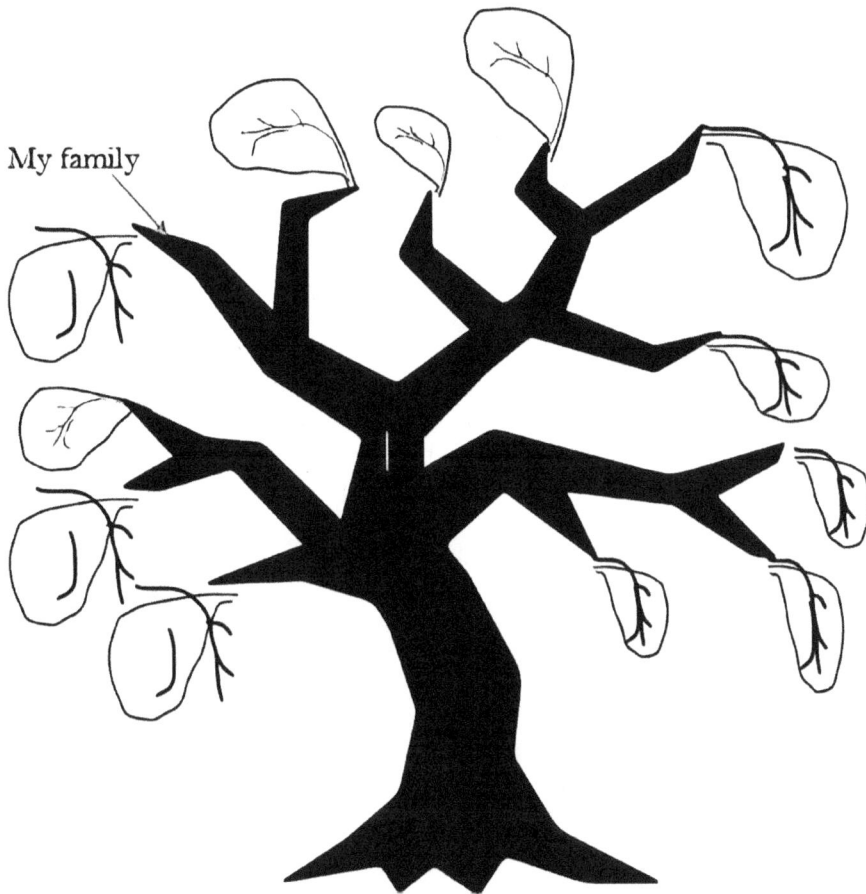

My family

Figure 10.3.0. Family Support Tree.

References

Arditti, J.A., & Johnson, E.I. (2022). A family resilience agenda for understanding and responding to parental incarceration. *American Psychologist*, 77(1), 56.

Bannink, R., Broeren, S., van de Looij-Jansen, P.M., de Waart, F.G., & Raat, H.(2014). Cyber and traditional bullying victimization as a risk factor for mental health problems and suicidal ideation in adolescents. *PloS One* 9(4), 394026.

Besemer, K.L., Van de Weijer, S.G., & Dennison, S.M. (2018). Risk marker or risk mechanism? The effect of family, household, and parental imprisonment on children and adults' social support and mental health. *Criminal Justice and Behavior*, 45(8), 1154–1173.

Hart-Johnson, A., & Johnson, G. (2022). Caregivers' family relations assessment and communication strategies. *Science Publishing Group*, 11(5), 157–168. https://www.sciencepublishinggroup.com/article/10.11648/j.pbs.20221105.12.

Hart-Johnson, A., Johnson, G. & Tate, M. (2018). *Prison staff who shape child and family visits: United Kingdom multiple case study*. In L. Gordon (Ed.), *Contemporary research and analysis on the children of prisoners: Invisible children* (pp. 241–265). Cambridge Scholars.

The National Healthy Marriage Resource Center. (n.d.). Home—Healthy marriage and responsible fatherhood http://www.healthymarriageinfo.org.

Summers, N. (2015). *Fundamentals of case management practice: Skills for the human services.* Cengage Learning.

Turney, K., & Goodsell, R. (2018). Parental incarceration and children's wellbeing. *The Future of Children,* 28(1), 147–164.

Weeks, S. (2013). Collaboration as wrap-around supports: Parents training. *Consultant Manual,* 24.

Wildeman, C., Goldman, A.W., & Turney, K. (2018). Parental incarceration and child health in the United States. *Epidemiologic reviews,* 40(1), 146–156.

Answer Key for Module 10, Section 10.0., Activity 37 (Hints).

   1. Bullying: Help children develop self-confidence and self-esteem. Impart strategies so that children are not singled out and targeted. Read books on bullying prevention.

   2. Conflict: Seek family counseling or conflict resolution. Establish ground rules for managing family disagreements.

   3. Support Academic achievements. Get involved in children's school and other educational pursuits.

   4. Negative parenting styles. Reflection is powerful and revealing. While many parents will follow their parents' methods, times have changed. Taking inventory of caregiver strengths and honoring a commitment to the child/children is the first step. Bibliotherapy and self-help parenting books can help with a strategy to improve parenting styles. Engage with children and find a balance between authoritarian styles and permissive parenting. Children need adult guidance rather than figuring out all life lessons independently.

   5. Disengaged: Listen; make eye contact; check in and ask questions. Schedule family outings, dinners, play games, and have a movie night.

The Answer Key for Module 10, Section 10.0, Activity 37.1

   A 1; B 6; C 9; D 7; E8; F 3, G 10; H 5; I 2; J 4.

The Answer Key for Module 10, Section 10.2, Activity 39

1. When holding difficult conversations, any place will do, as long as you have seating. False, choose a quiet space to enhance focus and concentration and allow authentic feelings to emerge.	☐ True	☑ False
2. A characteristic of building strong family bonds entails creating healthy relationships inside and outside of the family system. *True, having external sources of support may help, especially during a crisis.*	☑ True	☐ False
3. Parents should demonstrate emotional regulation when talking to children about difficult topics. *True. Parents should model how to discuss emotional or difficult topics by putting their own feelings in check while being authentic. It is possible that some conversations will involve the parent crying or showing sadness. These are authentic and expected behaviors. However, in contrast, acting out in disrespectful ways, using inappropriate language, and unchecked emotions are not effective strategies to model for children.*	☑ True	☐ False

4. Three communication strategies are: Be respectful, clear, and forthright. True. Being respectful, using clear and age-appropriate language as well as being forthright with children is important.	☑ True ☐ False
5. Family bonds are demonstrated through loving exchanges of support and affection in the family system. *True. Family members are better connected when they can freely show love and demonstrate affection for each other. Reminders, using "I love you" statements are good practices.*	☑ True ☐ False
6. When co-parents are planning to discuss important topics with children, it is best to prepare and even role-play or rehearse. *True. It is important for parents to have a united front to avoid confusion. Sometimes it takes practice and a bit of informal rehearsal. For example, a couple might say, "I'm going to tell her how we are going to do it." You can then chime in, and say "what we think is best...." This informal rehearsal establishes what role each person will play in the discussion.*	☑ True ☐ False
7. Reflection is an important part of taking responsibility and accountability for actions. *True. Reflective thinking may bring about clarity and help individuals take responsibility for their roles and accountability for actions.*	☑ True ☐ False
8. Children should have access to their parents, even if they are in prison or living outside of the home. However, never force children into compliance. *True—but situational. Consider the child's best interest.*	☑ True ☐ False
9. Try to implement safeguards to protect children from guilt over adult relationship issues. *True. Remind children that adult situations are not their fault and that they are loved regardless of the circumstances.*	☑ True ☐ False
10. Only parents with professional backgrounds can use trauma-sensitive, strength-based parenting skills. *False. Caregivers of all types and backgrounds can learn the basics about trauma-inducing situations. Safeguarding children from violence, abuse, abandonment, conflict, neglect, and multiple other risks can be the aspirations of all parents and caregivers. Strength-based parenting involves focusing on the child's strengths and uplifting the caregiver's strength to serve the child or children best.*	☐ True ☑ False

MODULE 11

ACEs, Triggers, and Trauma

MODULE FOCUS

- Section 11.0. Healing Trauma. Introduce trauma risks related to trauma producing experiences in children by age groups.
- Section 11.1. ACEs and Child Well-Being. Introduce the concepts: Adverse Childhood Experiences (ACEs) and Traumatic Stress.
- Section 11.2. Toxic Stressors. Compare and contrast stress, toxic stress, and identify stress reduction strategies.
- Section 11.3. We Have Superpowers. Identify and understand the application of trait-based strengths.

Resources

Read Guidebook: Hart-Johnson and Johnson (2025) | Chapter 11, "ACES, Triggers, and Trauma"

Additional Resources

Optional Resources: The Center for Disease Control and Prevention. (2019). *Preventing Adverse Childhood Experiences (ACEs): Leveraging the best available evidence.* Retrieved from https://stacks.cdc.gov/view/cdc/82316

Williams, D. (n.d.). *Social and behavioral determinants of Toxic Stress* [Video file]. YouTube. https://www.youtube.com/watch?v=eCeAzhKobk8.

Introduction

The journey of life can be exciting and at times a mystery. Life comes with both good times and challenging experiences. It is likely that everyone reading this workbook has faced exposure to some form of adversity when growing up, even under the best of conditions. About 40 years ago, a team of researchers endeavored to understand what happens when children are exposed to cumulative adversities. This section explains the study and offers insights.

ACEs BACKGROUND

During the 1990s, Kaiser Permanente and the Centers for Disease Control and Prevention (CDC) conducted a landmark study that revealed the connection between early life (childhood) stressors and long-term negative health outcomes (Danese & McEwen, 2012). This study is commonly referred to as the "ACE Study." The Center on the

Developing Child, Harvard University (n.d.) indicated that Adverse Childhood Experiences (ACEs) are considered children's early exposure to physical, sexual, or emotional abuse, neglect, a primary caregiver's mental illness, parental incarceration, and household conflict/violence.

ACEs are generally tallied and aggregated as a score. The more ACEs a child experiences, the greater the child is prone to future adverse conditions such as heart disease, diabetes, poor academic performance, and even substance use later in life. In a research study to determine life expectancy related to Adverse Childhood Experiences, Jia and Lubetkin (2020) indicated that participants who experienced three or more ACEs were at high risk for future chronic disease and trauma, behavioral problems, and other adverse health outcomes.

Perhaps, one of the most overused but least understood terms associated with parental incarceration is "trauma." The Merriam-Webster online dictionary describes this condition as:

- an injury (such as a wound) to living tissue caused by an extrinsic agent;
- a disordered psychic or behavioral state resulting from severe mental or emotional stress or physical injury;
- an emotional upset.

While there are many variations of the descriptors for trauma, we adapt the following from (Malchiodi 2015, p. xiv):

> "Depending on the child, the degree of exposure to distressing events, trauma can be an experience that is mentally, emotionally, and physically exhausting, as well as terrifying, and confusing."

Addressing traumatic experiences in children may require the attention of caring parents who establish elements of safety, trust, and support with a consistent degree of attunement and continuity.

This module covers Adverse Childhood Experiences (ACEs), triggers, and trauma. Through the exercises, learners will examine ways to better understand how children experience and potentially heal from trauma. Concepts of toxic stress and interventions/preventions also are introduced.

Section 11.0. Healing Trauma

Section Focus | Case Example

It Is Similar to Death

Some children experience parental incarceration as a horrifying non-death loss. The sudden or even gradual degradation of the family can feel shocking, frightening, and confusing—This is trauma.

—Focus Group Caregiver

Section Objectives

☐ Learn about trauma-producing risks associated with parental incarceration
☐ Identify signs of trauma in children
☐ Learn about caregivers' safeguards through prevention
☐ Reflect critically and journal thoughts on trauma risk prevention and reducion of risk exposure

Overview

It is often heartbreaking to see young children grieving. Perhaps our hearts break the most when we come to realize, children generally do not have long histories that affirm, they indeed will get over the separation and loss of childhood experiences when their parents are incarcerated. However, we as adults can help to ease their discomfort and pain. There are thousands if not millions of children who have learned to cope and recover from loss. This doesn't make the process easier, but it should give us hope that recovery is possible.

More than two-thirds of minor children (under 16 years of age) in the United States have experienced at least one traumatic event in their young lives (Substance Abuse and Mental Health Administration [SAMHA], 2022). One in seven children have experienced abuse and more than one thousand young people are treated every day for mental health emergencies (SAMHA, 2022). One in four children attending school in the United States has experienced trauma (with potentially co-occurring adversities taking place in their lives).

Trauma producing risks (events may include):

Any form of psychological abuse
Neighborhood violence
Sex trafficking
Witnessing violent treatment or arrest, or fatality of a loved one
War experiences or natural disasters
Life-threatening illness

Trauma seems to have similar characteristics across different adverse social contexts and emergencies. For example, a child witnessing a parent's arrest could experience trauma. An accident or a life-threatening situation could also cause trauma. Additionally, contiguous threatening and distressful events to children can cause trauma. Research reveals that trauma can have immediate and sometimes lasting impacts in general (Malchiodi, 2015).

The early onset of trauma occurring during children's formative years can affect memory, attention, and cognition. The National Child Traumatic Stress Network (2008) highlights the following specific signs of trauma and potential impacts:

- Feelings of anxiety and frustration may dominate a child's emotions
- May cause impairment to problem-solving and logic
- Somatic or physical responses to trauma might include stomach aches and headaches
- Triggers might include intense responses to tight spaces; experiencing similarities to the traumatizing event (when feeling vulnerable, such as experiencing bullying, teasing, or labeling as incompetent)

While children may experience trauma, there are steps that caring adults can take to prevent traumatic events from causing additional adverse conditions.

Foundational Learning

First, identify signs of trauma in children. Parents can advocate for their children to reduce the likelihood of trauma exposure. First, in addition to the above general appearances of trauma, parents should familiarize themselves with what trauma looks like in children in different age groups. According to SAMHA (2022):

PRESCHOOL CHILDREN

Fear of being away or separated from caregivers
Eating problems (e.g., loss of appetite)
Bouts of crying
Frequent nightmares

ELEMENTARY CHILDREN

Anxious and afraid
Feeling guilty or shameful
Fuzzy cognition or inability to concentrate
Hard time falling asleep and remaining asleep

MIDDLE CHILDHOOD AND OLDER CHILDREN

Eating patterns may manifest into eating disorders
May use substances (drugs) as coping
Become promiscuous and engage in sexual behaviors
Feelings of depression and loneliness

While trauma imposes risks, caregivers and other stakeholders (e.g., teachers, advocates, social workers, law enforcement, and helping professionals) can use collective responses to ensure the well-being of children through prevention practices.

CAREGIVERS' SAFEGUARDS THROUGH PREVENTION:
  WHAT ADULTS CAN DO TO MANAGE TRAUMA

- Make sure that children at risk for traumatic exposures have at least one reliable, caring, supportive caregiver
- Ensure that programs and environments for children have intrinsic safeguards, protections, and protocols against abuse
- Develop awareness campaigns in schools, families, communities, and other touchpoints of child engagement, where trauma is understood
- Lead with strength-based decision-making. Do not assume that acting out and rules violations in young children are signs of aggressiveness. The behavior could be an indicator of trauma. Children who encounter abuse or violence may model those behaviors.
- Create safe spaces and supports for children at all levels of society—hold legislators, policymakers, and law enforcement accountable for treating all children with dignity, respect, and trauma-informed care.
- Monitor children's behaviors, look for signs of trauma and contact helping professionals to validate or get first and second opinions.

ACTIVITY 41

ACEs, Triggers, & Trauma

Review Module 11 and Section 11.0. Reflect upon the content specific to trauma risk and prevention, and list at least *three* substantive steps that can be taken to reduce trauma in children.

Reflect upon what stands out as important for caregivers to know. Please list these findings under Reflections. Please note that there is no answer key for this critical thinking exercise.

Facilitators: *Using this activity as a group exercise; engage learners in a forum, inquiring about "What Adults Can Do to Manage Trauma." Use a flip chart or whiteboard (digital or hard copy) and note how everyone can contribute to reducing the risk of trauma in children.*

Reflections

Section 11.1. ACEs and Child Well-being

Section Focus | Case Example

ACEs

People at the individual, relational, community, and societal levels of responsibility and accountability can implement, protect, and support child well-being.

Section Objectives

- ☐ Deepen knowledge about Adverse Childhood Experiences (ACEs)
- ☐ Understand the relationship between ACEs and stress response
- ☐ Critically assess ACEs and trauma prevention/protective strategies

Overview

Continuing from the module overview, Adverse Childhood Experiences (ACEs) are commonplace in the United States. About 61 percent of the population has experienced traumatic events during childhood (The Centers for Disease Control and Prevention, 2019; 2022). Typically, ACEs describe risks associated with highly stressful events before a child becomes an adult (18 years of age). If the risks are left unaddressed, it can result in adverse physical health conditions and poor emotional outcomes. The following is an extended list of ACES:

- Parental incarceration
- Abuse
- Neglect
- Household challenges (conflict, negligent parenting, lack of structure)
- Poverty
- Parentification (caregiver-child role reversal)
- Violence exposure
- Separation
- Bereavement
- Discrimination
- Intergenerational trauma (genocide, slavery, displacement)
- Life transitions

These risks are thought to undermine the health and well-being of young people. Many more negative exposures can add to the childhood risks mentioned above.

Foundational Learning

The relationship between ACES and stress response. Adverse Childhood Experiences (ACEs) and trauma are conditions that threaten child well-being. According to the

National Child Traumatic Stress Network [NCTSN] (n.d.) when children have repeated exposure to trauma, they develop responses that are persistent and may result in ongoing emotional upsets. In other words, the trauma remains with the child if untreated. NCTSN calls this condition, *Traumatic Stress*. They indicated that this condition could interfere with children's lives to the degree it affects their academic, social, and familial engagement. All children, whether infants or 17 years of age, are subjected to the ill effects of trauma. Untreated or unaddressed trauma can adversely affect the brain and central nervous system.

ACEs and trauma prevention /protection strategies. The following are tips to help children with trauma and ACEs exposure:

- Provide unconditional love and support
- Get professional help, if warranted
- Establish and maintain routines
- Ask permission to touch/make physical contact with traumatized/abused children (noting that trauma experiences may have been through physical contact)
- Provide a safe space for children to share their feelings and check in
- Increase supports, especially during crises
- Be clear in setting family guidelines for behavior (practice positive rather than punitive discipline)
- Be sensitive to triggers that may re-traumatize (practice attunement)
- Anticipate and consider upcoming events that might be traumatizing and find ways to safeguard children in a manner consistent with supporting their emotional well-being
- Understand the nature of trauma and when and how to seek support
- Realize that children's adverse behavior could be associated with ACEs and traumatic events

Finally, caregivers and adults can offer children their unwavering protection and guidance. Children exposed to intense situations require compassion and purposeful attention to reducing stress. Young children who encounter daily stressors may not know how to respond to all events they experience. Caregivers can find ways to examine continuously the natural support systems that help restore calm and establish safety in children's lives.

ACTIVITY 42

ACEs, Triggers, & Trauma

Consider the following scenarios in Table 11.1.0. Protective Response. This activity enhances critical thinking skills. Describe how parents or adults might respond to each situation by taking protective actions. An illustrated example follows. While these are potentially difficult circumstances to ponder, note that each year thousands of children do encounter these situations. These exercises are designed for learners to think about preventive strategies as a counteraction.

Facilitators of Group Sessions: Follow the instructions for the individualized tasks but open the discussion up to the entire group of learners. Be sure to prompt and engage learners who tend to be quiet in group discussions to ensure all voices are heard.

INDIVIDUAL /GROUP:

Step 1: First, determine if "family intervention" or "formal intervention" is needed. Family intervention includes the parent/caregiver(s) taking action. Formal Intervention requires a helping professional's support (clinician, psychologist, therapist, counselor, social worker, or other practitioners).

Step 2: Mark the entry "Family Intervention," "Formal Intervention," or both.

Remember, each child and situation is different. Justify your answer.

Step 3: Justify your answer.

Table 11.1.0 Protective Response: Family Intervention, Formal Intervention, or Both?	
Issue/Scenario	*Family Intervention or Formal Intervention*

Example:
  A child witnessed a police officer arrest his mother.
	Protective Action:
	  A child needs age-appropriate information to help them understand that their parent will be okay and that they are not hurt by the police. Second, the caregiver should explain the role of police officers in the community. An example includes saying: "I know you are afraid for Mom/Dad. They have to talk with the police about something important. Grandma is here to make sure you are taken care of."

#1. A child showed signs of emotional distress after the incarceration of the parent. Then, days later, they resumed their normal play activities.	Family Intervention or Formal Intervention? Protective Action:
#2. A child does not want to go to school. He is afraid of being bullied because his dad is in prison.	Family Intervention or Formal Intervention? Protective Action:
#3. A child appears to stare off into space. She does not smile and has been quiet, playing with her doll. While she eats dinner, she often leaves most of her food untouched. She sleeps a great deal.	Family Intervention or Formal Intervention? Protective Action:

See Answer Key for Section 11.1, Activity 42 after Module 11 Reference list.

Section 11.2. Toxic Stressors

Section Focus | Case Example

Toxic Stress

"I feel like I let him down. I'd feel responsible for him not having the life he was owed. I feel that I need to overcompensate for the deficiencies. I felt like I was a failure when it came to providing him with the family dynamic he deserved."

—Focus Group Caregiver

Section Objectives

☐ Deepen knowledge about toxic stress and the stress response in the body
☐ Identify elements of positive, tolerable, and toxic stress
☐ Learn about toxic stress reduction and preventative strategies
☐ Critically assess and analyze protective responses to counter the adverse conditions of toxic stress

Overview

Toxic Stress

The term "toxic stress" refers to a wide array of biological changes that occur at the molecular, cellular, and behavioral levels when there is prolonged or significant adversity in the absence of mitigating social-emotional buffers.

—Garner & Yogman, 2021, p.1.

It is generally a caregiver's role to care for others. When reading the above quote in the case example, one might empathize or understand how caregivers might reflect deeply on falling short of their ideals. Caregivers such as in the quoted text understood their child's exposure to ongoing stress, where she felt her child did not get the care the child needed.

In this section, we return our focus to stress to explain how stress varies and we offer methods to regulate and co-regulate stress in children.

Stress response in the body. Everyone will experience stress at some point in their life. Some stress is good. It can be motivational or save lives. Stress can prompt the body to deal with frightening, scary, or adverse conditions. Continued exposure to the body's stress response system, however, can lead to toxic stress. Unregulated stress is known as a *continuous fight-or-flight response*. According to the Center on the Developing Child at Harvard, excessive stressors can disrupt the brain's architecture. This conditioning makes the child more prone to be hypervigilant even when *not* faced with a threat. Under normal responses to stress, several physical and emotional conditions occur.

When a child is stressed, their biological systems are activated (e.g., their heart rate may increase under stressful conditions). They may experience an elevation of stress hormones. However, with healthy emotional regulation or co-regulation assistance from the caregiver, the child's body can restore its sense of balance and adjusts to normal functioning.

Foundational Learning

There are three types of stress introduced in this section: *positive stress, tolerable stress*, and *toxic stress*. Positive stress is a condition that may motivate individuals. An example of positive stress is the stress brought on when first speaking to a large audience. Or, positive stress might entail preparing for a competition and getting butterflies in one's stomach. Next in the continuum is severe conditions of stress that may become serious but are *tolerable*. Tolerable stress is exposure to more significant emotional impacts that may induce prolonged stress, such as the death of a loved one, an accident, or the incarceration of a securely attached parent. However, this stress can be tolerated, and children generally recover without therapeutic intervention. While there is an escalation from positive stress to tolerable stress, children can learn to cope with these conditions and return to their baseline when a supportive relationship buffers the condition(s). *Toxic Stress* results from prolonged and significant adversity with the absence of intervention. In this state, a child could be exposed to chronic neglect, abuse, family violence, and/or stressors that exceed the child's capacity to cope. The result could be an overextended stress response system. The long-term implications could result in compromised health and well-being.

Before providing the counteractions to stress, we first focus on causes of stress, especially for children of color. Children of color are impacted by parental incarceration greater than their peers without parents in prison. David R. Williams, Ph.D. (n.d.) indicated that all racial groups of Americans face toxic risk factors. Socioeconomic status can increase the risks (household income, education, occupational status, and wealth). However, children of color tend to experience greater exposure to adversities, such as:

- Households with mental illness and or substance use
- Divorce/separation
- Poverty
- Intimate partner violence
- Community violence
- Racism
- Parental death
- Parental incarceration

Toxic Stress Reduction and Prevention Strategies

Ways to address toxic stress using systemic strategies:

- Support attendance at Head Start and early childhood education
- Support families by informing them of preventative strategies
- Promote protective factors
- Build resilience in families and children

As repeated throughout this workbook, having a loving and supportive caregiver-child relationship can help to offset the risks and potential damage of ACEs and trauma. Caregivers can help their children to:

- Minimize exposure to ongoing stress
- Build self-confidence and self-esteem
- Help children co-regulate and respond to emotions in adaptive ways (i.e., deep breathing and/or learning coping though communication about their emotions)
- Integrate natural support systems before, during, and after crisis or stress exposure

Each of the recommendations mentioned above can be applied to the caregiver. Minimizing exposure to stress, building self-confidence, regulating emotions, learning coping, and using natural support systems all are fitting for caregivers, too.

ACTIVITY 43

ACEs, Triggers, & Trauma

Review and scan Module 11, paying particular attention to Section 11.2. Using critical thinking skills, develop a protective response to counter the adverse conditions, as shown in activity 43. This activity is an individual or group activity. *Facilitators of Group Activities:* Elicit ideas on administering protective factors from the group. Please note that there is no answer key for this critical thinking exercise.

Note: Each learner is asked to complete the exercise and justify their views.

Table 11.2.0 Risk and Protective Responses	
Risk Conditions	*Protective Response*
A child's pet died.	
The child has moved twice in one year.	
The mother is not at home to make breakfast for the child before attending elementary school.	
A relative in the home has been using alcohol, and there is substance abuse.	
The mother is planning to divorce the children's father.	

Section 11.3. We Have Superpowers

Section Focus | Case Example

SUPERPOWERS

I was in jail and became like a nun. I wrote a book. I felt like giving up and had a lot of despair. I went through a lot of emotion, and it was time to heal. I tried to teach everyone about God. I tried to transform my life in 30 days. I figured they would let me out of jail. I immediately decided that I would never put my child in that situation again.

—Focus Group Caregiver

Section Objectives

☐ Identify trait-based and personality strengths
☐ Critically reflect on the application of personal strengths analysis
☐ Deepen knowledge and vocabulary related to strength-based parenting.

Overview

Families generally have a history of successes and challenges, triumphs, and defeats. Some people go through experiences where enlightenment and spirituality can become their saving grace (as noted in the case example). Recognizing their uniqueness and history of overcoming challenges can help families harness internal strength and fortitude during times of need.

Every family member may have something positive to contribute to the well-being of the family system. Sometimes, it takes a deliberate focus to determine the strengths and positive qualities of family members, especially when reflecting upon events in life where change is desired.

Foundational Learning

Trait- and personality-based strengths and characteristics can enhance a family's quality of life and contribute to healthy interpersonal relationships. By using a strength-based approach, families focus on the positive qualities rather than the negative aspects of the family system. Many strengths are taken for granted, yet they serve as qualities that can enhance family system support and bonding. For example, a mother could be a skilled craftsperson (who creates arts and crafts). This talent could contribute to family-based activities where arts and crafts night is used as for family bonding, recreation, and learning experiences.

Trait-based strengths. The defining qualities of *trait-based strength*, concerns the positive attributes of an individual, where they apply positive qualities to accomplish goals, life endeavors, and align these strengths with their personal perspectives. Generally, people who are self-aware of their gifts, talents, and skills also tend to use trait-based personality strengths when creativity and innovative out-of-the-box thinking is required. When people understand their strengths and use them during times of stress, the process tends to foster:

- Greater resilience
- Positive energy
- Less stress
- Higher levels of self-confidence and self-esteem
- More happiness in their lives

Recently, strength-based literature has emerged, highlighting its application in multiple areas, including community organizations, counseling, pediatrics, human services, and social work (e.g., Zaccaro et al., 2004). Individuals from all walks of life are using this approach for personal empowerment and achieving self-actualization. Caregivers might consider which trait-based qualities align with their parental goals for themselves and family.

Trait-based approaches emerged from trait theory, mainly used in management and leadership domains. However, caregivers are leaders, and they may benefit from using these cross-functional skills that appear to be in alignment with strength-based parenting practices. The theory holds that the following attributes are qualities of a good leader (Zaccaro et al., 2004):

- Consciousness/Mindfulness
- Cognitive abilities
- Openness
- Motivation
- Social intelligence
- Emotional intelligence
- Emotional stability
- Self-monitoring
- Problem-solving
- Agreeableness

In addition to trait-based approaches, personal strengths analysis is also helpful in understanding the unique qualities that caregivers and their children bring to the healing relationship.

PERSONALITY STRENGTHS

Personality traits are the characteristics that make people unique while identifying core strengths, talents, and skills. The following attributes listed in Table 11.3.0, define skills-based strengths.

Table 11.3.0 Personal Strengths Analysis		
Communicator	Courageous	Dependable
Organized	Planner	Detailed oriented
Analytical	Technical	Problem solver
Team player	Collaborator	Interpersonal skills
Good writer	Precise	Motivator

Personal and Parenting skills

Honest	Integrity	Trustworthy
Affectionate	Genuine	Authentic
Attuned	Energetic	Loving
Creative	Patient	Optimistic
Responsible	Role Model	Flexible
Dedicated	Hopeful	Truthful

Building a vocabulary of strengths helps individuals appreciate their capacities as human beings. Many more attributes could expand this list. Strength-based parenting calls for seeing the best in children (and oneself) and having self-compassion, self-love, and personal appreciation. With this strength and unconditional high regard, families stand a fair chance to regain footing after a crisis.

Sometimes, it is helpful to reflect on positive qualities, especially after experiencing disempowering life challenges. A strength-based focus can change perceptions of hopelessness into hopefulness. Qualities such as motivation, and openness to new ideas and possibilities are uplifting concepts. Moreover, a person with problem-solving skills can put these talents to work rather than focusing on the negative aspects. Positive attitudes also teach children to build resilience and grit.

Strength-based parenting. Remember, parenting children is not easy. Each person has unique skills and strengths, and there are always opportunities to improve personal behavior and family relations. Sometimes, a problem can be resolved through the support of a family member, friend, or outside resources. Try to find the silver lining in these situations. Some of life's biggest challenges contribute to resilience, growth, and positive outcomes.

ACTIVITY 44

ACEs, Triggers, & Trauma

This activity is titled "My Superpowers—My Strengths." This exercise can be performed as a group, or individualized. *Please note that there is no answer key for this critical thinking exercise.*

1. Reflect on the list of attributes listed in the Table 11.3.0 Personal Strengths Analysis. Consider your strengths. Imagine yourself having the leading role as a character in a storybook. As this character, name your most incredible superpowers based on the list of attributes in in the space below. (Group exercise: have each learner name their leading character role and associated strength[s].) Feel free to add to the list using your own ideas of character strengths.

2. As a caregiver, what strengths do your children see in you? Try to list your strongest attributes. You may describe these attributes from the Personal Strengths Analysis. Consider strengths outside of the list. (Group exercise: have everyone contribute an attribute.)

3. Now, consider strengths that are not always apparent when people look at you. These are the talents, skills, and personality traits that you have that others may not see when they are around you. Perhaps, they only emerge during certain times. Name at least three attributes or characteristics that are positive. (Group exercise: have each individual name at least one positive attribute that they possess.)

4. Consider children as individuals with their own strengths. If you have children, think of them and list five strengths that each child possesses. They may have similar strengths. **Group exercise:** have each individual contribute a strength that they see in their child(ren). If you are not a caregiver/parent, think of a child you know when addressing the question.

OPTIONAL ACTIVITIES:

As you think about raising a family using a strength-based approach, what should be the family's collective strengths? Group exercise: have each individual contribute a strength they imagine as important for building a strong family. If learners are not caregivers, they can provide an aspirational answer below.

References

The Center on the Developing Child Harvard University. (n.d.) How early childhood affects lifelong health and learning. Retrieved from https://developingchild.harvard.edu/resources/how-early-childhood-experiences-affect-lifelong-health-and-learning.

The Centers for Disease Control and Prevention. (2019). Preventing adverse childhood experiences (ACEs): Leveraging the best available evidence. Retrieved from https://stacks.cdc.gov/view/cdc/82316.

The Centers for Disease Control and Prevention. (2022). Fast facts: Preventing adverse childhood experiences. Retrieved from https://www.cdc.gov/violenceprevention/aces/fastfact.html?msclkid=69cbb3acd13911ec867fb202c5b03892.

Danese, A., & McEwen, B.S. (2012). Adverse childhood experiences, allostasis, allostatic load, and age-related disease. *Physiology & behavior*, 106(1), 29–39.

Garner, A., & Yogman, M. (2021). Committee on psychosocial aspects of child and family health, section on developmental and behavioral pediatrics, council on early childhood. Preventing childhood toxic stress: Partnering with families and communities to promote relational health. *Pediatrics*, 148 (2): e2021052582. 10.1542/peds.2021-052582

Hart-Johnson, A. & Johnson, G. (2022). Caregivers' family relations assessment and communication strategies. *Science Publishing Group*, 11(5), 157–168. https://www.sciencepublishinggroup.com/article/10.11648/j.pbs.20221105.12.

Jia, H., & Lubetkin, E.I. (2020). Impact of adverse childhood experiences on quality-adjusted life expectancy in the US population. *Child abuse & neglect*, 102, 104418.

Malchiodi, C.A. (2008, 2015). A group art and play therapy program for children from violent homes. In C.A. Malchiodi, *Creative interventions with traumatized children* (pp. 247–263). Guilford Press.

The National Child Traumatic Stress Network (NCTSN.org). (2008). Home. Retrieved from https://www.nctsn.org/?msclkid=abb69c0ad13711ec8c9abb88d19a2166.

Substance Abuse and Mental Health Services Administration. (2022). National child traumatic stress initiative (NCTSI). Retrieved https://www.samhsa.gov/child-trauma.

Williams, D. (n.d.). Social and behavioral determinants of toxic stress [Video file]. YouTube. https://www.youtube.com/watch?v=eCeAzhKobk8.

Zaccaro, S., Kemp, C., & Bader, P. (2004) Leader traits and attributes. In J. Antonakis, A. Cianciolo, & R. Sternberg (Eds.), *The Nature of Leadership*. Sage Publications.

Answer Key for Section 11.1, Activity 42

#1. A child shows signs of emotional distress after the incarceration of the parent. Then, days later, they resume their normal play activities. *Family Intervention:* This response might suffice. Just because the child is playing does not mean she has not suffered trauma. Parents can monitor the children for signs of distress. If needed, check in with a helping professional to ask for guidance and support.

#2. A child does not want to go to school. He is afraid of being bullied because his dad is in prison. *Family Intervention and Formal Intervention (Both):* Children will need the support of the family, advocating for them, but also the support of the school to ensure that they are managing situations around bullying. The child might need help in building self-confidence and also learn how to avoid situations where they are vulnerable (walking with pairs or groups rather than alone).

#3. A child appears to stare off into space. She does not smile and has been quiet, playing with her doll. While she eats dinner, she often leaves most of her food untouched. She sleeps a great deal.

Formal Intervention: Consider seeking support beyond the family's resources. The child might disassociate or experience emotional numbness, which typifies trauma responses. Do not force the child to talk or have expression. A therapist may help the child work through this situation. A professional may also provide parents with tips and tools to use.

Tough Topics:
Suicide and Creating
Safe Spaces

MODULE FOCUS

- Section 12.0. Sudden Loss and Trauma Revisited. Extend the focus on trauma concepts, self-harm, and mitigation of suicide risk.
- Section 12.1. Suicide Risks. Assess the prevalence of suicide in the United States.
- Section 12.2. Home and Safety. Identify and prepare home safety and emergence checklists.
- Section 12.3. Anti-Bullying Perspectives. Understand bullying and suicide risks and learn about bullying prevention.

Resources

Read Guidebook: Hart-Johnson and Johnson (2025) | Chapter 12, "How can a child this young even think about suicide?"

Additional Resources

Mayo Clinic. (n.d.). *What to do when someone is suicidal.* https://www.mayoclinic.org/diseases-conditions/suicide/in-depth/suicide/art-20044707.
PACER's National Bullying Prevention Center: https://www.pacer.org/bullying.

Introduction

This module deals with tough topics. It is important that while they may appear to be tough, parents who understand how to directly address these situations can gain clarity on how to reduce associated risks and ultimately prevent them. Therefore, this module continues the focus on strengthening the caregiver role and uplifting the well-being of children through building awareness on risk reduction and prevention.

CREATING SAFE SPACES

Children need safe spaces after enduring such life situations that involve sudden loss and trauma. A caregiver who recognizes the signs of physical and emotional trauma should respond accordingly. Starr (2022) indicated that the following are characteristics of a safe space (adopted from elementary school use but can be effective in the home as well):

- Physical: Set up a designated area for little people (consider size, color, and privacy). Use this space as a place to sit and discuss important issues.
- Calming Tools: Have essential items such as tissues, a squeeze/stress ball, and other items, notepad /sketch pad and crayons or markers for drawing or pointing out emotions or ideas that are discussed. Also, an emotional wheel is a great way to give feelings a name (see Module. 5, Figure 5.1).
- Modeling: Work together to cultivate a safe place as a nook where children feel empowered to express themselves and be heard.

This module covers difficult topics such as suicide prevention and introduces ideas to improve home safety. The section concludes with a focus on anti-bullying.

Section 12.0. Sudden Loss and Trauma Revisited

Section Focus | Case Example

THE POLICE MADE HER DAD CRY

It's important that the child hears from the incarcerated parent that they, the parent, made a mistake. My child was very upset with the police for a long time. She was very, very angry because the police took her daddy away. The police made her dad cry and she really needed to hear from her dad—that this situation was his fault, and it was not her fault. She's been in counseling. And she was three at the time and her therapist sounds like she has some post-traumatic stress. She can vividly describe to this day what it felt like to see her dad taken away.

—Focus Group Caregiver

Section Objectives

- ☐ Deepen knowledge about sudden loss and trauma producing events
- ☐ Identify trauma management techniques
- ☐ Reflect critically upon and develop home safety options

Overview

Home safety and reducing risks take into consideration the most extreme of circumstances. First, it is important to understand that many children will recover from parental incarceration and become resilient individuals. However, it is also important to acknowledge the risks that may unfold. This section introduces loss and trauma and risk mitigation strategies specific to sudden loss, trauma producing events and suicide prevention.

Sudden loss (such as the scenario described in the case example) can traumatize children and trigger depression, suicidal thoughts, and other feelings associated with separation. Caregivers are instrumental in helping children to better understand life skills that can reduce suicidal risks. The Suicide Prevention Resource Center (2023) holds that supportive relationships are the key to risk mitigation. While stories of young people do not often make the daily news, about 12 children each day follow through on self-harm leading to death. Prevention is the key to reduce these occurrences.

Foundational Learning

This section helps families and practitioners learn about risks related to suicide. Becoming aware of the signs can help identify when children are struggling with this condition. Caregivers can also learn of resources and support to help support both the child and parent.

Suicide could be a cry for help. Thus, the first step involves looking for changes in behavior (SPR, 2023). Additionally, look for the following warning signs (SPR, 2023):

- The child displays a sense of hopelessness
- The child isolates or withdraws
- The child shows bouts of irritability or aggressiveness
- The child is found to have lethal means (weapons or substances)
- The child has a negative self-appraisal
- The child talks about death
- The child engages in self-harm
- The child engages in high-risk activities
- The child starts giving meaningful objects away
- The child feels like they are a burden
- The child has conveyed suicide attempts

If any child under your care is in immediate danger, call 1-800-273-8255 (United States) or your local emergency number. Take all threats seriously, remove dangerous weapons and substances from your home, and stay with the child until help is present.

Talk with your child:

> "I am concerned that you have been sad for a long time. I would like to talk with you about how you are feeling."

Do not be judgmental; listen; do not overreact or get angry; let the child know you care; help to restore hope—that there is almost always an answer to problems.

ACTIVITY 45

Tough Topics

Reflect on Section 12.0 on Suicide. Consider what stands out as critical information. Make note below of three significant takeaways as Reflections. Facilitators of Group Learners: elicit from learners their ideas about the significant takeaways and share their insights and reasoning. Visit Https://sprc.org for multiple resources on suicide prevention. Please note that there is no answer key for this critical thinking exercise.

Reflections

1.

2.

3.

Section 12.1. Suicide Risks

Section Focus | Case Example

Young Children and Suicide

A person at any age can commit or attempt suicide.
All discussions regarding suicide are serious.

Section Objectives

☐ Understand the importance of asking children about self-harm
☐ Gain an understanding relating to parental incarceration and suicide risks
☐ Obtain knowledge about suicide terminology
☐ Critically reflect on concepts and terms aligned with suicide and suicide prevention

Overview

"Hope can prevent Suicide" (SPR, 2023, p. 9). While situations involving suicide, generally refer to individuals facing a state of hopelessness, hope can be a source of changing outlooks on life. Information is powerful in that parents can develop a keen awareness of what to look for and how to offer prevention.

Ask Children About Self-harm

While having a talk about children's self-harm may be difficult, SPR offers that parents should ask direct questions and not hesitate to discuss their concerns with children. Some parents may fear holding a discussion with their children, fearing that they will influence ideas that contribute to thinking about self-harm. However, SPR indicated that these discussions do not increase suicide risks.

By talking with children, parents can determine the level of risk. Using such phrases as:

- I see that you are down. Are you having thoughts of hurting yourself?
- Are you feeling as though you want to escape?
- How are you feeling about life?

Always seek help if the child is responding in a manner that indicates they are/will attempt self-harm. Remind children that you are there for them and that you will not judge them. Give them hope through letting them know that there are sources and resources available to help them. Listen kindly and lovingly and take them seriously.

A Note About Parental Incarceration and Suicide Risk

There are many risks associated with parental incarceration. One of those risks is children having thoughts about suicide or self-harm. Many of the risk factors for suicide are also consistent with risks identified with parental incarceration. In one study, almost one-fourth of youth identified in a sample of children had an incarcerated parent Gifford, et al. (2019). These children also had higher risks for psychiatric conditions (Gifford et al., 2019). Recent reports indicated that suicide rates for children from ages 5 to 11 have increased dramatically (Ruch et al., 2021).

In our own research study, thirteen percent (13%) of participating caregivers indicated that their children discussed suicide or attempted to take their lives (Hart-Johnson & Johnson, 2022). When a child talks about self-harm and or suicide, take the matter seriously.

Foundational Learning

The National Institute of Mental Health (2021) indicated that a child's suicide can impact the entire family as well as those networks closely linked to its members. When children have ideas about suicide, they experience acute distress (NIMH, 2021). This phenomenon is the eighth leading cause of children's death: where about 95 percent of these deaths occurred in the family home; 52 percent died from using a handgun and almost 19 percent died by other firearms (e.g., rifle, ghost gun), About one-third of these children had unaddressed mental health conditions.

The terms below help to differentiate between what is an attempt versus the intent to carry out the act.

Terminology
The following differentiate: suicide, suicide attempts, suicide ideation, and non-suicidal self-injury.
Suicide: Suicide is death caused by deliberate self-injury with the intent to end one's life. Suicide is the leading cause of death for children and adults ages 10 to 64 (The Centers for Disease Control and Prevention, 2022), respectively.   **Suicide attempts:** A suicide attempt is when a person has the goal of ending one's own life but fails in carrying out the act.   **Suicide ideation:** Thoughts, ideas, contemplation, or rumination about suicide.   **Non-suicidal self-injury:** This term refers to self-injury. Generally, the attempt does not correlate with a deliberate attempt to commit suicide. Signs of non-suicidal self-injury could include scars, cuts, bruises, wounding, harboring a collection of sharp objects, and covering up the scars with clothing (Mayo Clinic, n.d.).
Suicide Risks: Thoughts or the notion of committing suicide could be influenced by: **Grief**   **Feeling abandoned or rejected**   **Relationship issues**   **Substance use**   **Children who have experienced bullying, violence, abuse, and sexual abuse**

Once a child attempts to commit suicide, it is likely they will also make future attempts later in life unless intervention is achieved (NIMH, 2021). Feelings of hopelessness and helplessness can result from triggered emotions where children feel disempowered. The following are additional risks for children's suicide:

- Inability to cope with life stressors
- Having friends who self-harm
- Unstable family environment
- Neglected as a child
- Experienced traumatic events
- Mental health issues

What to Do for Children

If a child is self-injuring, seek help. This behavior is not a situation that will just go away if ignored. If the person is a child, contact a pediatrician or medical doctor. While it may be tempting to get angry, do not be abrasive to your child because of his/her behavior (Mayo Clinic, 2020).

Additionally, the Mayo Clinic (n.d., p. 1) suggests:

- Call your mental health professional if you're seeing one.
- Call a suicide hotline. In the U.S., call the National Suicide Prevention Lifeline at 1-800-273-TALK (1-800-273-8255) or use their webchat on suicidepreventionlifeline.org/chat.
- Seek help from your school nurse or counselor, teacher, doctor, or other health care provider.
- Reach out to a close friend or loved one.
- Contact a spiritual leader or someone else in your faith community.

Offsetting the risks: suicide prevention

- Strengthen familial support systems
- Manage finances to prevent poverty or financial insecurities
- Make the home environment stable
- Create a safe home: Remove lethal weapons, lock up dangerous weapons, restrict access to alcohol

Seek out formal support of a doctor, mental health practitioner, or helping professionals when necessary. Take all suicide threats seriously.

ACTIVITY 46

Tough Topics

Review the content in Section 12.1. Reflect upon the seriousness and significance.
Read: https://www.cdc.gov/suicide/index.html
Please answer the following questions by filling in the blank.

1. Feelings of hopelessness and helplessness can result from triggered emotions where children feel _____.

2. Recent reports indicated that _____ rates for children from ages 5 to 11 have increased dramatically.

3. Children who have experienced _____, violence, abuse, and sexual abuse [fit the category for suicide risks]

4. Suicide is death caused by deliberate self-injury with the _____. Suicide is the leading cause of death for ages 10 to 64.

5. Signs of _____ could include scars, cuts, bruises, wounding, harboring a collection of sharp objects, and covering up the scars with clothing.

See Answer Key for Section 12.1, Activity 46, after the Module 12 Reference list.

Section 12.2. Home Safety

Section Focus | Case Example

SAFETY BEGINS WITH PREVENTION

Every home should have a safety plan and emergency contact list

Section Objectives

- ☐ Reflect critically on ideas about household safety
- ☐ Assess and devise a family emergency planning checklist
- ☐ Create an emergency plan/checklist

Overview

Families may experience a number of unanticipated emergency situations where the potential for stress and chaos can be reduced with proper planning. Such emergencies might involve home damage, familial conflict and/or violence, civil unrest, and other untimely events.

Ways to Make the Home Safe

The current chapter focused on suicide prevention. Here are a few ways to increase safety in the home (especially if you suspect your child is high risk) as a preventative strategy:

- Keep all weapons and prescription medicines locked away
- Remove lethal tools from access (knives, ropes, guns)
- Provide a support system where the child is not left alone—show them you care
- Promote healthy living, positive focus, and goal setting
- Use strength-based parenting practices

EMERGENCY PLANNING

Generally, a family emergency plan comprises steps and communication strategies should a disaster or a sudden emergency call for an evacuation. However, the strategy could include a safety plan for the aforementioned personal emergencies. For example, what must the family consider if they had to leave home in the middle of the night? Who would the children call if the parents were taken away suddenly? What is the plan for contacting people for support or advice? Who is the designated adult for children, should the parents be unavailable? Other emergencies could include:

- ☐ Neighborhood violence or severe conflict or threat
- ☐ Hospitalization of significant household members where sudden child-care is warranted

☐ Parental or family member arrest
☐ Physical injury or death
☐ A mental health condition
☐ A weather emergency

Foundational Learning

Several government websites provide tips and tools to help families prepare for emergencies. However, unanticipated life situations might call for emergency strategies and improvising on the spot, as well. It is best to hold an initial planning discussion with family members, even if it feels uncomfortable. Having a safety plan in place is like preparing a Living Will—conduct the task as an "annual event" and update it at least yearly.

WHAT IS THE PURPOSE FOR EMERGENCY PLANS?

All family members should be aware of essential information to execute when little time exists for planning and strategizing for emergencies. The plan can include:

- Whom to contact
- Where to go or where to meet
- What to take
- Who are important contacts

There are a number of resources that can be used to help prepare a plan. The following activity provides resource sheets to identify and implement a family plan. The plan includes evacuation routes, disaster response, safety response, etc.

ACTIVITY 47

Tough Topics

Critically reflect upon the information presented in Section 12.2. Create a family emergency plan using the checklist below, add other information that may be supportive for your personal checklist. Keep in mind that emergencies could be in or outside of the home. List emergency numbers, childcare providers, and other important phone numbers.

Family Personal Emergency Checklist		
Update Annually		
Emergency Contact Name or Organization	Contact Information	Notes| Family Member Coordination: When to meet during an emergency. When to call. Cross street locations in the event of an emergency.
Suicide Hotline		
Local Hospital(s)		
Police Department		
Mental Health Provider		
Poison Control Center		
Local Shelter(s)		
Fire Department		
Red Cross		

Other Important Contacts (attorneys, social workers, mental health providers, teachers, school.	Important Notes

Please note that there is no answer key for this critical thinking exercise.

Section 12.3. Anti-bullying Perspectives

Section Focus | Case Example

ANTI-BULLYING

Households with children should consider identifying bullying behaviors and develop protocols as a response for family member prevention and protection.

Section Objectives

- ☐ Learn what constitutes bullying
- ☐ Learn how children can reduce the risk of being bullied
- ☐ Explore prevention strategies for children

Overview

Because parental incarceration is a condition often linked with social stigma, children and their parents may be targets of shaming and forms of bullying. Parents who recognize the signs and execute prevention strategies may help to reduce the risks to their children.

Bullying can be verbal, emotional, physical, or technological. It can be carried out in person or through technology (cyber-bullying). The levels and severity of bullying can range from intimidation to physical threats and violence. Within a bullying situation, the target are often perceived as weak and vulnerable.

Foundational Learning

According to the Centers for Disease Control, 1 in 5 children are bullied in the school environment (on the way to school, during, or after). Inappropriate teasing, hitting, kicking, punching, teasing, sexual innuendos, verbal abuse, and embarrassment are all tactics of people with bully behaviors. However, Pacer's National Bullying Center (PNBC) (2021) indicated that this form of intimidation can be prevented through family advocacy, self-advocating, and empowering youth with strategies to build confidence.

Bullying usually is reported by children and parents to law enforcement or school administrators. However, parents tend not to see acts of bullying until a teacher or other adults get involved, disclosing the incidents. Children can learn to reduce the risk of bullying treatment and advocate for their own safety (PNBC, 2021).

Children who experience bullying may experience stress and distress. Bullying is considered an Adverse Childhood Experience (ACE). Some (40%) children are more likely to experience bullying than others. For example, LGBTQ children (lesbian, gay, bisexual, transgender, or queer), face a higher risk than non–LGBTQ individuals. Incidents of bullying among children tend to be highest in middle school (CDC, 2022). The following are tips on how children can reduce the risk for being bullied.

Youth can become empowered to prevent bullying occurrences by:

- Feeling empowered to take a stance
- Join or create a school's anti-bullying campaign
- Learn to respectfully disagree and negotiate
- Become confident
- Be positive

There are additional tips that can be gleaned from fact sheets listed on the following website: *Bullying Prevention 101*: https://www.pacer.org/bullying/info/pdf/BP-101-parents.pdf

Prevention of bullying is possible. Additional strategies for preventing bullying behavior includes utilizing the following ideas/strategies:

- Institute faith or religious belief anti bullying campaigns
- Advocate for intolerance toward violence
- Maintain a high GPA
- Hone positive social interpersonal skills
- Develop social competence and acceptance

ACTIVITY 48

> ## Tough Topics
>
> Review Sections 12.3. For this critical thinking activity, reflect upon the serious-ness of bullying. This condition can result in severe injury or death. However, care-givers can take precautions towards prevention.
>
> *Individual or Group Exercises:* Imagine meeting with a children's group of 5- to 10-year-olds. Based on the foundational learning, document the talking points that would be shared with the group of children about bullying and prevention strategies. Note any substantive ideas in the section labeled Reflections. There is no answer key for this critical thinking exercise.

Reflections:

References

The Centers for Disease Control and Prevention. (2022). *Facts about suicide*. Retrieved from https://www.cdc.gov/suicide/facts/index.html.

Gifford, E.J., Kozecke, L.E., Golonka, M., Hill, S.N., Costello, E.J., Shanahan, L., et al. (2019). Association of parental incarceration with psychiatric and functional outcomes of young adults. *JAMA Network Open*, 2(8):e1910005.

Hart-Johnson, A., & Johnson, G. (2022). Caregivers' family relations assessment and communication strategies. *Science Publishing Group*, 11(5), 157–168. https://www.sciencepublishinggroup.com/article/10.11648/j.pbs.20221105.12.

Mayo Clinic. (2020). *Mindfulness exercises*. Retrieved from https://www.mayoclinic.org/healthy-lifestyle/consumer-health/in-depth/mindfulness-exercises/art-20046356.

Mayo Clinic. (n.d.). *Suicide: what to do when someone is suicidal*. Retrieved from https://www.mayoclinic.org/diseases-conditions/suicide/in-depth/suicide/art-20044707.

The National Institute of Mental Health. (2021). *Understanding the characteristics of suicide in young children*. Retrieved from https://www.nimh.nih.gov/news/research-highlights/2021/understanding-the-characteristics-of-suicide-in-young-children.

Pacer National Bullying Prevention Center. (2021). *Bullying prevention 101*. Retrieved from https://www.pacer.org/bullying/info/pdf/BP-101-parents.pdf.

Ruch, D.A., Heck, K.M., Sheftall, A.H., Fontanella, C.A., Stevens, J., Zhu, M., Horowitz, L.M., Campo, J.V., & Bridge, J.A. (2021). Characteristics and precipitating circumstances of suicide among children aged 5 to 11 years in the United States, 2013–2017. *JAMA Network Open*, 4(7), e2115683-e2115683.

Starr, J. (2022). *A safe space for small children with big feelings. Teaching with Jillian Starr*. Retrieved from https://jillianstarrteaching.com/safe-space-classroom/.

The Suicide Prevention Resource Center. (n.d.). https://www.samhsa.gov/suicide-prevention-resource-center-sprc.

Answer key for Section 12.1, Activity 46

1. Disempowered
2. Suicide rates
3. Bullying
4. Intent to end one's life
5. Non-suicidal self-injury

Anger Management

MODULE FOCUS

- Section 13.0. This Makes Me Angry. *Review characteristics of anger.*
- Section 13.1. Children Experiencing Anger. *Discuss primary and secondary emotions related to anger.*
- Section 13.2. Anger and Unmet Needs. *Identify ways that anger can be an expression that children's needs are not met.*
- Section 13.3. The Body Reacts to Anger. *Learn about the body's response to anger.*

Resources

Optional Resources: Bailey (2019). *Episode 48: How to help children manage rage.* Search on title on YouTube or use URL: https://www.youtube.com/watch?v=svgqsmRE5Us.
Read Guidebook: Hart-Johnson and Johnson (2025) | Chapter 13, "The Underpinning of Anger."

Introduction

To many people, anger is a form of self-protection, an emotion that guards against disrespected boundaries. The idea that someone would disregard a person's need to be heard, understood, or considered might be the culprit of angered emotions. Sometimes shame, disgrace, or guilt results in anger, as well. Closely linked emotions also include feelings of loss, which sometimes feels like being cheated of something that is rightfully ours—resulting in anger.

Children may face multiple losses in their lifetime that may leave them angry, confused, and frustrated. Young children may encounter losses of friendships, the family pet, transition away from childhood neighborhood, and numerous other scenarios.

Loss is a denial and detachment from something. For example, in death-related incidents, the denial is a continued relationship. When a child loses a familiar childhood staple such as a favorite teacher, school, or friendship, this transition is a denial and detachment from their relationship networks. Consequently, loss can manifest into anger.

Bailey (2019) characterizes the cycle of anger related to loss as follows:

- When adults do not attune themselves to a child's feeling of loss, it can morph into anger.
- When anger is not managed, it can manifest as inappropriate behavior, escalating to rage
- Unregulated and unaddressed rage can result in violence.

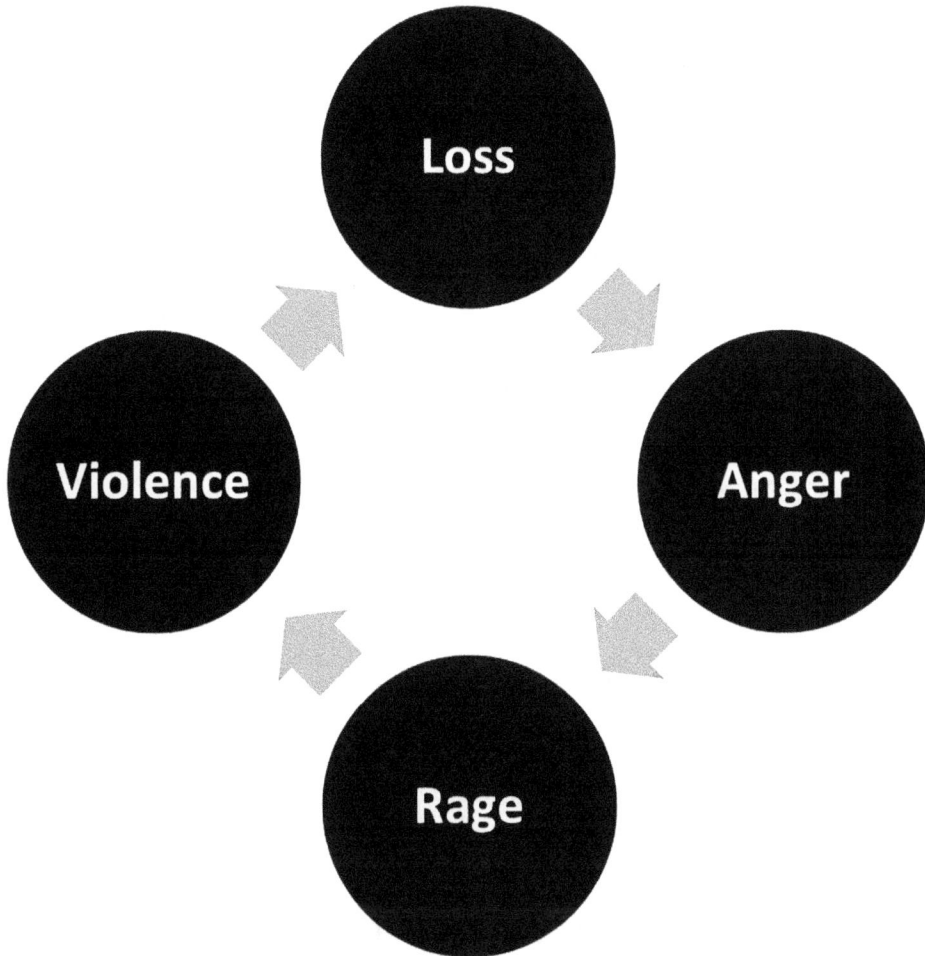

Figure 13.0. Loss-Violence Continuum.

The diagram in Figure 13.0 shows loss as the escalating event. The anger emerges, resulting from the denial of access. Rage may manifest in the same or different contexts. For example, unaddressed anger could result in behaviors of aggression toward others that result in rage. An example may be a child who is angry and turns his anger to breaking objects in a rage. In the research study Hart-Johnson and Johnson (2022), a caregiver described how her child channeled his anger by breaking outdoor furniture. While his rage did not manifest into violence against the caregiver, repeated unchecked behavior could escalate to adverse physical outcomes.

Parents are encouraged to help children address conflicting feelings before they result in anger and potentially, physical aggression. This section provides scenarios, recommendations, and considerations in understanding anger and interventions.

This module covers interventions related to anger management. The topic is applicable to the caregivers as well as the children. The sections cover how anger can be a motivational tool as well as a maladaptive response. The module closes with techniques to cope with anger.

Section 13.0. This Makes Me Angry

Section Focus | Case Example

Dealing with Anger

Sometimes, anger masks emotional pain. This feeling can lead to exposure of the real underlying issues that need healing. The process generally entails reflecting, building self-awareness, accountability, and taking self-inventory.

Section Objectives

- ☐ Learn the characteristics of anger
- ☐ Learn the definition of anger
- ☐ Critically reflect on the myths versus facts associated with anger

Overview

Characteristics of Anger

Becoming angry and frustrated is a human experience. Sometimes, anger can be healthy as it serves to motivate people to make change. For example, people may become angry because of long standing habits, and they decide to set goals to change.

Sometimes, children and their families become angry because they feel disempowered. At other times, individuals may become angry because they feel abandoned or neglected. These feelings often align with parental incarceration. Children may become angry when they no longer have access to their parents. This point alone makes this section important knowledge for caregivers of affected children.

While universal as an emotion, anger is a complex phenomenon that is often misunderstood. With reflection, individuals usually can get to the root of their feelings and the origin of their anger. Anger typically comprises feelings and behavior that appear to be primary but are generally secondary emotion. For example, a person who feels cheated may appear angry, but the underlying primary feeling is that of being undervalued or slighted. In this section, we explore the characteristics of anger and the management of this emotion.

Foundational Learning

Anger appears to be a default behavior where the individual fails to look below the surface and scrutinize what they are actually feeling. Anger musters physical and emotional responses that are often challenging to navigate. Anger undergirds primary feelings such as distrust, inadequacy, hurt, or neglect.

Anger: Definition

The Substance Abuse and Mental Health Services Administration [SAMSHA] (2019) defines *anger* as an emotion with multiple tiers or levels. Anger can range from mild irritation to full-blown uncontrollable rage (SAMSHA, 2019). The following characteristics typify anger:

- Anger can be positive or negative
- Some anger is self-motivating, where people are inclined to make decisions and take action.
- Inappropriate anger can be harmful and threatening
- The expression of anger can be inward (toward self) or outward-directed (toward others)
- Displays of angered behavior are inappropriate when it does not match the severity, the level of offense or offending act
- Closely aligned with anger, aggression is an outward display of behavior directed toward people, places, and things (or self)
- Aggression generally is intentional harm toward others (verbally or physically).

The following myths are associated with ideas and concepts related to anger (SAMSHA, 2019):

Myths About Anger
Myth: Once a person has a "bad temper," it never changes. **Reality:** People can learn to control their tempers and calm themselves through practiced self-regulation
Myth: Anger always leads to aggressive outcomes **Reality:** This is not true. People can learn to identify their triggers and conditions that perpetuate angered responses.
Myth: It is good to vent **Reality:** This concept is outdated science. People who vent using tactics such as punching pillows get better at punching pillows and being angry.
Myth: Children inherit their parent's behavior **Reality:** According to SAMSHA (2019), children might inherit facial expressions and gestures from their parents. However, learned anger management practices can alter behavioral outcome of having a trait for anger.

Facts: Anger
People can learn to habitually address trigger responses by using strategies that counter and break the cycle of automatic behaviors. When individuals learn how to recognize their triggers and become self-aware, they can use these techniques to change their responses.
Angered feelings can include mild irritation. About 70 percent of people who responded to a survey indicated they felt irritable at least once a day (Mental Health America [MHA], 2021).
In 2020, about 80 percent of the surveyed people reported having anger to the point of arguments (MHA, 2021). The study also found that social media is quickly growing as a platform for expressions of anger.
Taking steps towards anger-management can reduce frustrations and irritations that lead to anger.
Developing a plan to address culprits of anger might involve getting organized (reducing chaos); changing surroundings (positive environments versus negative); releasing feelings and talking through issues in a rational manner; and reducing known stressors.

ACTIVITY 49

Anger Management

Reflect on sections 13.0 *Overview* through *Foundational Learning*. Make a mental note of what stands out. Now, consider the myths associated with anger. Ponder your beliefs about anger. As individuals or as a group exercise, please address the following questions.

- ° When a person becomes angry, they may feel sensations in their body, such as flushed cheeks, nervousness, increased heartbeat, and possibly rigid posture. Everyone gets angry. What does anger feel like to you? Be specific in naming what the sensation feels like in your body.
- ° Recall an event that made you angry. Note what it felt like to experience anger. Now, using the "Anger meter" below (Figure 13.0.1), identify the anger level number felt before the named event: _____ and during the angering event: _____. Finally, idetify the number or level after the event _____.

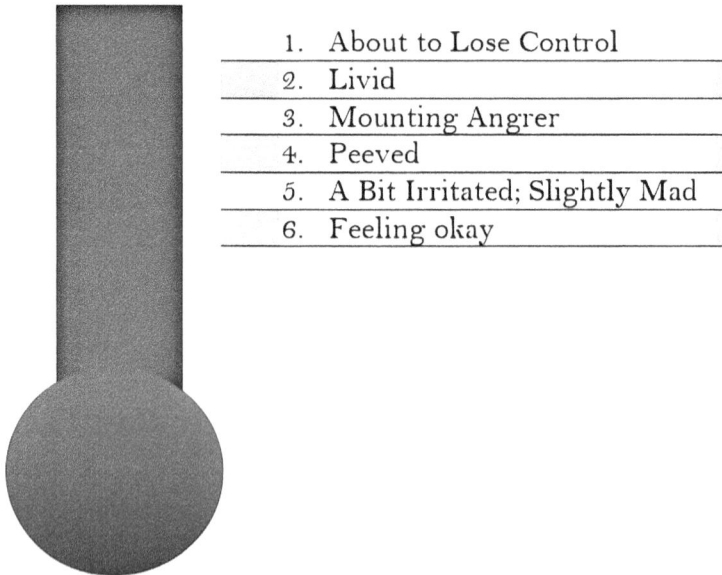

1.	About to Lose Control
2.	Livid
3.	Mounting Angrer
4.	Peeved
5.	A Bit Irritated; Slightly Mad
6.	Feeling okay

Figure 13.0.1. Anger Meter.

Note: What are the choices or options that could be implemented to reduce anger on the spectrum of results?
Please note that there is no answer key for this critical thinking exercise.

Section 13.1. Children Experiencing Anger

Section Focus | Case Example

CHILDREN EXPERIENCING ANGER

Anger is a survival skill. When prolonged and repressed, anger can impact health and well-being.

Section Objectives

☐ Critically reflect on the thoughts, triggers, feelings, and actions associated with anger
☐ Understand how anger is a normal human response
☐ Identify ways that children and adults can manage anger
☐ Advance knowledge and understanding of words that describe underlying anger.

Overview

Reflection is a great way to understand thoughts, triggers, feelings, and actions associated with anger. Everyone experiences anger even though some may think that anger is wrong or inappropriate. This emotion is at times a survival skill that can propel individuals to sustain a life crisis or experience. Sometimes, parents interpret children's display of angered emotions as inappropriate behavior as well. Fortunately, by understanding the various degrees of anger, caregivers may prevent negative messaging where children believe they are somehow bad or flawed. This section focuses on identifying anger and its various forms and offers suggestions for management through awareness and regulation.

Foundational Learning

Even babies appear to show behaviors that look like anger. This emotion is a normal human response to certain conditions. To better understand anger and its properties, the Behavioral Institute for Children and Adolescents (n.d.) offers the following characteristics describing anger:

- Can energize and motivate
- A pain response
- When a person experiences anger, the brain shifts to survival mode (as opposed to the planning and reasoning functions)
- Long lasting, protracted, stifled, unacknowledged, and suppressed anger is unhealthy

There are strategies that children and adults can use to manage anger and to self-regulate responses. The first step is to build self-awareness. Consider the following ways to increase self-awareness:

Ways to Manage Anger: Children

☐ Parents can help children to take note of how they are feeling by using an emotional meter

☐ Teach children to recognize anger's physical characteristics such as tension, warm or flushed cheeks, tightness in the body

☐ Inform children that anger originates from thoughts, followed by feelings, then actions [Thoughts → Feelings → Actions]

☐ Sometimes, children have patterns associated with anger responses. For example, if a child feels they are ill-equipped to accomplish a task, they may get angry and may throw objects. Looking at this scenario more closely, ask the child what is happening inside. The caregiver might learn that the child feels pressure to excel but has not had adequate practice. Additionally, the child may need help in learning how to better cope with challenges before them.

☐ Anger is often associated with self-evaluation and appraisal. Help children to recognize their strengths.

Ways to Manage Anger: Caregivers/Parents

☐ Reflection, or reflexivity, is a great way to understand and take responsibility for thoughts, triggers, feelings, and actions associated with anger. Often, misperceptions are the culprit for not understanding acts that result in anger.

☐ Reflecting honestly on identifying the underlying feelings and thoughts may help to reveal the true essence of the anger. Any perception held in mind and believed can be challenged for its validity.

☐ Consider what long-held beliefs are not accurate.

☐ Seek knowledge; investigate the ideas, thoughts, and beliefs associated with the issue of concern.

☐ Practice pausing, and asking: Are their alternatives to my initial thoughts that might be plausible? What is really going on? What am I feeling and why am I feeling this way?

☐ Set goals to acknowledge and respond differently.

☐ Develop empathy to understand what motivates others to respond the way they do.

☐ Start to listen more closely; examine, and take accountability for personal feelings and interpretations. Give others the benefit of expressing their truth.

ACTIVITY 50

<table>
<tr><td colspan="3">Anger Management</td></tr>
<tr><td colspan="3">Review Section 13.1. Critically reflect on the content and the ideas presented. Anger could be the external wrapping of a box full of unaddressed and repressed thoughts that never see the light of day. This description helps to understand how anger seems to show up as the exterior emotion when the real issues go unaddressed. These conditions can be unhealthy for children as well as their caregivers when experienced for an extended period.</td></tr>
<tr><td colspan="3">Step 1: In this exercise, consider the role of a caregiver first; then, consider the role as a child. Generally, people respond with anger when their needs go unmet. Perhaps the need is not met or acknowledged. View the list below to explore words that convey feelings that might underpin anger.</td></tr>
</table>

Unappreciated	Fear	Deflated
Invalidated	Stuck	Disenfranchised
Unloved	Unhappy	Marginalized
Unimportant	Frustrated	Oppressed
Unacknowledged	Unlucky	Stigmatized
Not considered	Inadequate	Shamed
Not heard	Cheated	Abused
Ashamed	Ill-equipped	Failure

Step 2: Now, consider your own experiences with anger. Reflect upon experiences where anger was involved. What are descriptive words that articulate what "pushes your buttons"? Name at least 5 scenarios that can bring about thoughts, feelings, and actions related to angered responses. List these thoughts under: Reflection (for extensive reflection, use a journal or separate paper). Next, consider ways to identify and address any triggers before they escalate (review the box, *Ways to Manage Anger*). Please note that there is no answer key for this critical thinking exercise.

Reflections

(List reflections here)

Section 13.2. Anger and Unmet Needs

Section Focus | Case Example

ANGER

Anger can be unhealthy for children when it causes disruption in their daily lives. The inability to manage emotions can impair quality of life for children and their families. Unchecked anger can manifest in habitual reactions that mask more profound emotional discomfort and distress, such as grief, depression, and a host of feelings related to loss.

Section Objectives

- ☐ Lear how unmet needs and anger are related
- ☐ Learn how anger is a form of communication
- ☐ Increase knowledge about the cycle of anger
- ☐ Critically reflect on the caregiver role related to helping children manage angry emotions.

Overview

When a child's needs are not met, they respond in many ways. Anger is just one of many possible responses. Anger is a form of communication to the parent or caregiver. This communication requires attunement of the caregiver to understand the child and the circumstances to get to the crux of the matter. As a result, caregivers may learn that not all communication related to anger has to do with adversity. Children might simply be communicating self-expression, autonomy, or rebellion. Additionally, if children are frustrated and irritated, they may show anger through pouting, sulking, or showing their anger either through nonverbal body language or verbalizing that they are mad. Lastly, not all anger-related behavior in children is problematic. Remember, young children under 10 years old are still growing and learning about emotions and their reactions to life. At this state, they may be too immature to understand how to process the many feelings unfolding. Anger may be a result.

Foundational Learning

Anger does not immediately escalate to full-blown aggression; there is a cycle of progression. This cycle of progression in children often mirrors that of adults. The progression generally begins with a triggering event, followed by negative self-talk or thoughts. Following the thoughts, an emotional response generally follows—likely fueled with a piling on of guilt, shame, or other underlying feelings that intensify the anger. During an anger event, the body goes through a physical reaction (flushed face, increased pulse rate, sweating, etc.), followed by a behavioral response. Figure 13.2.0 illustrates the Cycle of Anger. Repressed anger is held inside and may be related to a passive response (Langelier & Connell, 2005; Therapist Aid, LLC, 2016).

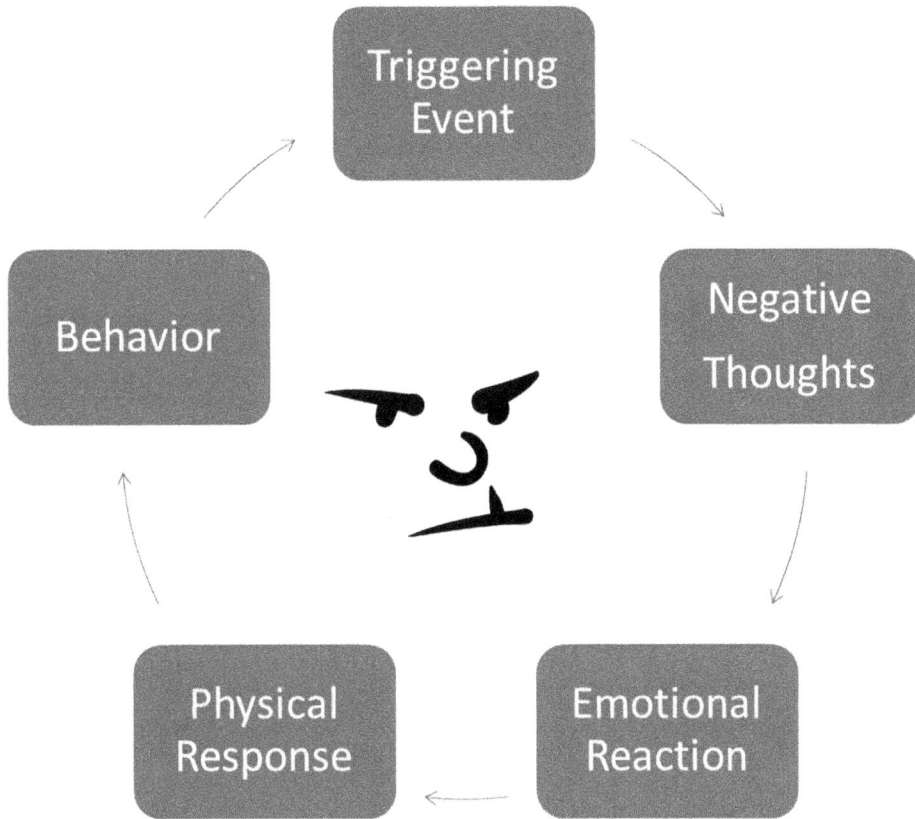

Figure 13.2.0. The Cycle of Anger (Adapted from Therapist Aid, LLC, 2016).

TRIGGERS

In addition to anger being a form of communication, there are triggers for children's anger. Children may have many *triggers* that cause them to react. Triggers are unique to the child. For instance, children may be triggered by reminders of failing at a task. They may be triggered by feeling unappreciated or left out.

As children grow and develop, they may experiment with new soft skills/interpersonal skillsets. Children can benefit from having a caregiver who helps them learn to deal with their primary emotions related to triggers. Examples of triggers are:

- A parent issued a command that is in opposition to the children's wishes
- A child feels their opinions do not matter
- A child feels neglected
- A child feels abandoned

NEGATIVE THOUGHTS

Negative self-talk is generally exaggerated, distorted, even based on inaccurate perceptions. For example, if a parent was arrested and did not have a chance to say goodbye or offer assurance to the child, that may serve as a triggering event. Consider the following triggering event and a child's possible negative thoughts:

☐ "My mom just left me. I am not a good enough child."
☐ "Everyone else has a father, except me!"
☐ "Why can't I speak to Mom on the phone. I must be the cause of her going to jail."

Children might perceive each of these thoughts as valid. When their perceptions are inaccurate, caregivers have the opportunity to teach children about their feelings and offer clarity. These events offer an opportunity to explain and set the record straight.

EMOTIONAL REACTION

According to TherapistAid.com, LLC (2016), negative self-talk is followed by heightened emotions. However, thoughts may only be perceptions and not match the actual intention of others. The beliefs related to the perceptions could be irrational or unrealistic. Hence, a person's emotional response could range from mild to aggressive.

PHYSICAL RESPONSE

There are a number of physical responses that children have when they get angry. The following might typify a child whose anger has escalated:

- Sweating
- Tense muscles
- Elevated heartbeat
- Tightened jaws
- Clenched fists
- Furrowed brow
- Shaking

BEHAVIOR

The behavior associated with anger may vary depending on a child's uniqueness and temperament. The behavior may also depend upon a child's mastery of self-regulation. An example would include a child who has learned that performing certain acts or raising their voice when angered in school is inappropriate. Emotion regulation is the ability to exert control over one's own emotional state. The emotionally regulated child may reason with themselves that it is wrong to act out because there is a consequence. Those who are not as self-aware of how to intercede and use anger management and de-escalation of emotions may not be able to regulate their temper.

Inappropriate behaviors might include:

- Physical aggression
- Kicking
- Arguing
- Screaming
- Throwing objects
- Criticizing
- Yelling
- Fighting

ACTIVITY 51

Anger Management

Review Section 13.2. The following tips are offered to help children who are angry and require the support of their caregivers. Please note that there is no answer key for this critical thinking exercise.

- Do not try to suppress the anger—seek instead to understand its origin
- Connecting Families indicated that judging children keeps them stuck; sensory overload fuels anger; payoffs related to anger reinforces it, and children need to learn to manage their anger.
- Consider what the child is feeling and see their actions and feelings through the lens of empathy
- Consider the knowledge gained from the fight-or-flight response of traumatized children.
- Children who are sensitive to trauma might also experience anger differently. A caregiver might ask how being in hypervigilant mode factors into a child's behavior?
- Teach children about emotions.
- Help children to develop an emotional vocabulary. Sit with them and explain the source of their emotions and how to work through those emotions, using techniques. For example, consider the following scenario:

Case Scenario: Janie

Janie enjoyed the prison visit with her father, but she was restless and tired from the long trip. Towards the last 10 minutes of the visit, she became cranky and restless. The corrections officer abruptly announced that it was time for the visit to end. Her mother quickly got up and prepared to gather Janie to leave. Janie cried and clung to her incarcerated father, begging not to let him go. By the time she reached their car for the drive home, she was having a full-blown tantrum, kicking the back of the driver's seat.

STEP 1: CONSIDER WHAT JANIE MIGHT BE COMMUNICATING THROUGH HER BEHAVIOR:

- Janie likely enjoyed the time with her father.
- The abrupt end to the visit likely startled her.
- Janie was already tired and cranky because of the long drive to the prison.
- Janie may have been afraid and angry because she could not stay with her dad.
- She may have felt that she did not have time to say good-bye.

STEP 2. CONSIDER HOW JANIE'S MOM MIGHT OFFER SUPPORT:

- Janie's mom could first ask Janie what she is feeling inside and help her to understand that emotion.
- Janie likely needs a big hug and reassurance that she is loved by her mom and her dad.

- Make sure that the mom does not match the intensity level of Janie's emotions.
- Ask Janie to take deep breaths, allowing her to calm down. Intentional breathing could be done in the car or even walking toward the car.

ACTIVITY:

Critically reflect upon the scenario about Janie and the options presented for the mom to consider. Now, scan the Module, making note of strategies to identify and manage anger. Next, write down three different options (different from what was offered above) that a caregiver might use to help Janie manage her emotions.

1.

2.

3.

Section 13.3. The Body Reacts to Anger

Section Focus | Case Example

Anger: The Body and Emotions

Anger can suspend or numb emotional pain in the body. Anger can mask a more profound emotion that is shameful. Anger can be an emotional gatekeeper—barring intimacy—yet, there is a physical component, as well.

Section Objectives

- ☐ Deepen knowledge related to fight-or-flight responses (specific to anger)
- ☐ Understand how children display anger
- ☐ Learn how anger, trauma, and loss may co-exist

Overview

Anger has both physical and psychological properties. In general, when a child becomes angry, the heart pumps more or, said differently, the cardiac response means more blood is pumping through the body, delivering oxygen and other essential nutrients. The response is the body's way to protect itself. Using techniques of self-awareness and self-regulation, the body can restore itself to a state of calm.

Foundational Learning

Note that physical reactions associated with anger may occur regardless of the level of threat. For example, whether running from a fearful situation or becoming angry at someone for taking a toy, the body's general physiological response might include:

Anger: Fight-or-flight response.

- The release of the stress hormone cortisol gives the body a boost of power to defend itself.
- The body releases adrenaline to cue the sympathetic nervous system to gear up for "fight or flight." This fight-or-flight response could include:
  - ° Trembling
  - ° Sweating
  - ° Rigid posture or drawing the body inward for protection
  - ° Running away from the threat
  - ° Clinging to the caregiver for protection
  - ° Fighting back
  - ° Displaying flushed cheeks
  - ° Tensing muscles

Recall from Module 4 (Section 4.1., *Foundational Learning*), the aforementioned physical reactions are a part of the **sympathetic nervous system** when the body perceives danger, generating the fight-or-flight response.

Rest and digest. Now, examine what happens with the body during self-regulation:

When the body attempts to restore calm, for instance, aided by a caregiver's protection or reassurance (hug or comforting touches), the body tries to regain balance. **The parasympathetic nervous system** reacts to the caregiver's calming. This process describes the *rest and digest* state of the body. The following occurs as a parasympathetic response:

- heartbeat returns to normal
- the muscles in the body relax
- pupils contract
- the bladder contracts
- the airways constrict.

What brings children to the point of anger? Children may display anger at various ages and stages of life. Toddlers might use assertive behavior that escalates into aggression. *However, not all aggressive behavior is intended for harm.* A toddler may not understand the consequences, for example, that pushing another toddler out of the way to grab food, or a toy, is wrong. Children need their caregivers to point out the correct way to behave. Teaching a toddler manners and social skills that show them how to ask for toys by saying, "I'm sorry" or saying, "Excuse me" are helpful strategies.

Young children learn how to react to situations when adults model behaviors and help them to understand that

- caregivers value various concepts of morality, team play and sharing
- family values include being helpful
- family values include treating others with respect
- caregivers demonstrate and appreciate displays of empathy
- family values are prosocial and interpersonal skills and ideals (communication, clear boundaries, and rules)

Anger, trauma, and loss may coexist. The body responds to traumatic situations similarly to anger responses. The National Center for PTSD indicated that anger is the body's defense and survival instinct when people face "extreme" threats. When people feel wronged, abused, neglected, and betrayed, they may become angry (U.S. Department of Veterans Affairs. Anger and Trauma. PTSD: National Center for PTSD, n.d.).

When the National Child Traumatic Network measures trauma, using the "Trauma Symptom Checklist for Children," they consider elements similar to those that align with separation and loss (Briere, 1996). For example, when a helping professional or clinical therapist uses the instrument to determine a child's trauma, the following domains are assessed for children in the age range of from 8 to 16 years old:

- Traumatic Stress
- Grief/Loss
- Anxiety/Mood (Internalizing Symptoms)
- Neglect

After working through the exercises and activities in this workbook, it should be apparent that several overlaps occur with ACEs, triggers, trauma, risks of parental incarceration, and anger responses.

Remember: Parental incarceration for families and children can be traumatic in itself. This condition is also one of the many ACEs children may experience:

- neglect (due to parental incarceration)
- anxiety and mood swings
- feeling grief, loss, and stress

A child can experience all these feelings and responses simultaneously or at different stages. With clear and sound communication, caregivers can help children adjust to the aforementioned emotions using age-appropriate language.

Caregiver Superpowers

Even though the risks associated with trauma, grief, anxiety, neglect, and anger seem to mirror similar responses in the mind and body, caregivers should remain hopeful. Children can rebound from difficult circumstances. As reinforced throughout this workbook, children need the love and support of their caregivers. Caregivers can use their superpowers of teaching to help children regulate, cope, and believe that they can once again regain normalcy after a traumatic event. Helping children to feel safe, valued, loved, and supported, and creating a stable, predictable, consistent, and safe environment can provide the foundation for healing.

ACTIVITY 52

Anger Management

In preparation for this activity, review Section 13.3. Overview through *Foundational Learning*. Now, complete the fill-in-the-blank exercises.

1. The body responds to traumatic situations similarly to

_____ .

2. Children need their _____ to point out the correct way to behave.

3. Caregivers can use their superpowers of _____ to help children regulate, cope, and believe that they can once again regain normalcy after a traumatic event.

4. The stress hormone _____: gives the body a boost of power to defend itself.

See Answer Key for Section 13.3, Activity 52 after Module 13 Reference list.

References

Bailey. (2019). *Episode 48: How to help children manage rage.* YouTube. Retrieved from https://www.youtube.com/watch?v=svgqsmRE5Us.

The Behavioral Institute for Children and Adolescents. (n.d.) Retrieved from https://behavioralinstitute.org/.

Briere, J. (1996). *Trauma Symptom Checklist for Children (TSCC), Professional Manual.* Odessa, FL: Psychological Assessment Resources. Retrieved from http://www4.parinc.com.

Hart-Johnson, A., & Johnson, G. (2022). Caregivers' family relations assessment and communication strategies. *Science Publishing Group,* 11(5), 157–168. https://www.sciencepublishinggroup.com/article/10.11648/j.pbs.20221105.12.

Langelier, C.A., & Connell, J.D. (2005). Emotions and learning: Where brain based research and cognitive-behavioral counseling strategies meet the road. *River College Online Academic Journal,* 1(1), 1–13.

Mental Health America. *Dealing with anger and frustration.* Retrieved from https://mhanational.org/dealing-anger-and-frustration.

The National Child Traumatic Stress Network. (2008). *Child Trauma Toolkit for Educators.* Retrieved from https://rems.ed.gov/docs/NCTSN_ChildTraumaToolkitForEducators.pdf.

Substance Abuse and Mental Health Services Administration. (2019). *Anger Management for substance use disorder and mental health clients.* Retrieved from https://store.samhsa.gov/sites/default/files/d7/images/-pep19-02-01-002-thumbnail.jpg.

TheTherapistaid.com (2016). *The cycle of anger.* Retrieved from https://www.therapistaid.com/worksheets/-cycle-of-anger.pdf.

U.S. Department of Veterans Affairs. (n.d.) *Anger and trauma.* PTSD: National Center for PTSD. Retrieved from https://www.ptsd.va.gov/understand/related/anger.asp.

Answer Key for Section 13.3, Activity 52.

1. anger
2. caregivers
3. teaching
4. cortisol

No Shame

MODULE FOCUS

- Section 14.0. Shame: The Wise Chicken. Identify the linkage between negative perceptions, self-image, and shame.
- Section 14.1. Now Tell Me the Good News. Learn how self-talk can neutralize disempowering thoughts of shame.
- Section 14.2. Shaping Self-Worth and Self-Acceptance. Identify how children's opinions of self-worth are formed and how they can re-write the narrative.
- Section 14.3. Crying Shame. Learn methods to teach children on addressing and responding to stigma while building self-confidence.

Resources

Read Guidebook: Hart-Johnson and Johnson (2025) | Chapter 14, "Stigma, Shame, and Parental Incarceration"

Introduction

Almost everyone has experienced shame at some point in their lives. Shame appears to be a complex emotion felt internally and associated with external conditions, people, and situations. This module explores shame from the social context of having an incarcerated family member or other conditions that challenge caregivers' and children's well-being. This module covers shame, guilt, and accounts for how the emotions related to incarceration can affect the family. The activities are designed to better understand how shame and guilt can drive behaviors. The module closes with activities that are focused on understanding the connection between low self-confidence, shame, and bullying.

Shame describes the feelings associated with an individual's assessment of self. Stephen Pattison, author of *Shame: Theory, Therapy, Theology* (Pattison, 2000), indicated that shame is associated with feeling "diminished and inferior" (p. 85). In his work, Pattison shares insights on behaviors related to shame not typically reported. He indicated that some people relieve themselves and fill the emptiness aligned with shame through serving or being another's helper. This alignment might illustrate remorse associated with the condition. Others may exhibit shame-rage (angered responses) through aggression. Further, people have shame "scripts" that play out in their minds, motivating behaviors expressed when attacking others or as coping behaviors.

Section 14.0. Shame: The Wise Chicken

Section Focus | Case Example

THE WISE CHICKEN

A wise chicken wandered away from the chicken coop. The chicken hurried at lightning speed, searching to discover the world outside his living quarters. Then "Wise Chicken" met a turtle. The chicken told the turtle about his goal to see the world. This excitement made the turtle sad, envious, and also ashamed. The turtle said to himself, "I can never discover the world with my slow pace compared to the chicken's speed." The turtle felt inferior and hopeless. The wise chicken then reminded the turtle, "You have a lifetime to discover the world. A turtle's pace is a gift of longevity. For me, life is short, and I got places to go and a short time to get there."

Section Objectives

☐ Learn about the characteristics of shame
☐ Learn about shame and self-perception
☐ Differentiate between internal and external expressions of shame

Overview

Fortunately, for every negative feeling there is a positive antidote. This section covers shame, yet research reminds us that the antidote to shame is a positive self-image and self-confidence and accurate perceptions. Given the prevalence of stigma and shame associated with incarceration in general, this section provides an understanding of the concept and a discussion on the underlying feelings.

Paul Gilbert provided a framework to understand shame and its comparison to guilt (Gilbert, 2097). Gilbert indicated that shame is generally associated with feelings of:

- Inferiority
- Helplessness
- Disempowerment

Other characteristics of shame include the perceptions of being scorned, ridiculed, humiliated, and feeling small, rejected, disliked, and weaker than others. The feeling is inward directed yet has external impacts. For example, an ashamed person may feel unworthy (inward-directed) as influenced by someone who doubted their abilities or rejected their friendship (external influence).

Guilt is different from shame in that it is a sense of self-blame and personal accountability for actions. Characteristics of *guilt* include the feelings associated with letting people down, failing at something one is responsible for, or even remorse for not achieving.

Foundational Learning

Shame and self-perception. There can be many reasons why a person feels shame. Sometimes, people feel a fear of rejection or not living up to expectations. Others may harbor secrets and experiences that contribute to self-appraisals of feeling inferior. The vignette in *14.0 Shame, The Wise Chicken*, illustrates how perceptions can shape unrealistic ideas. In the story, the turtle's perceptions of himself as inferior illustrate a comparison of his life to the chicken's. Turtles, by nature, have slow metabolisms, which equate to living longer than many other species. The silver lining of being slow allows the turtle to see the world at his own pace. The takeaway from the story is that, sometimes, humans have self-perceptions colored by narrow and unrealistic thoughts. Through reexamining our perceptions and seeing life through a realistic lens, we can reshape our views of life experiences.

When people feel shame, they sometimes withdraw from social connections. Reasons for shame might also include two conditions: internal and external shame. Gilbert (1997) indicated that **external shame** concerns other people's opinions regarding the shamed individual. **Internal shame** entails imagining or thinking how other people value the affected individual.

Examples of these conditions include: (**internal thoughts affecting external behaviors**)

- An adult raised in poverty feeling as though they will never fit in with the "elite"
- A child hiding the secret that their parent is in jail or prison
- A person who cannot read
- The aunt who recovered from substance use consistently avoids family gatherings, believing that the family thinks she is "broken."
- "I am too ugly to fit in with the other children"

The above examples illustrate how perceptions and beliefs can influence feelings of shame and drive behaviors. There are methods to reframe distorted self-perception and thoughts through developing self-awareness and building self-confidence. Please proceed to Section 14.1, after completing Activity 53.

ACTIVITY 53

No Shame		
Review sections 14.0., *Overview* through *Foundational Learning*. With this content in mind, answer the following questions in the True or False exercise. In this self-check, identify if the statement is True or False.		
True or False?		
1. Guilt is different from shame.	☐True	☐ False
2. Gilbert indicated that shame is generally associated with feelings of: • Inferiority • Happiness • Disempowerment	☐True	☐ False
3. A person who thinks others believe they are inferior illustrates an example of external shame.	☐True	☐ False
4. A child who is embarrassed and hides the family secret that their parent is in jail or prison is an example of external shame.	☐True	☐ False
5. The story about *The Wise Chicken* and the turtle illustrates how unrealistic ideas shape perceptions. In the story, the turtle's perceptions of inferiority are an example of internal shame and unrealistic logic.	☐True	☐ False

The Answer key for Section 14.0, Activity 53, follows Module 14 References list.

Section 14.1. Now Tell Me the Good News

Section Focus | Case Example

SELF-CONFIDENCE AND EMPOWERING THOUGHTS

"The thing I am most proud of is…."
"I love myself because I…."
"You are loved."
"I am grateful to have you in my life."

Section Objectives

☐ Learn how self-esteem can neutralize shame
☐ Understand the difference between shame, self-worth, self-esteem, and self-confidence.
☐ Critically reflect on ways to help children build self-confidence

Overview

Families and children may feel greater self-worth and self-confidence when treated by others with dignity and respect. However, self-confidence is not based entirely on external influence. People can identify positive qualities within and use positive self-talk as empowerment tools. Given that feelings of stigma and shame are two prevailing aspects of parental incarceration, it is essential to find ways to build resilience and boost confidence in affected families. Working on self-confidence might increase feelings of acceptance and worth and build self-esteem.

Foundational Learning

Concepts related to self-confidence, positive self-worth, and high self-esteem seem to align and counter a person's expression and feelings of shame. The following reviews present a general definition of the relationship between these concepts.

Shame: generally, entails how people feel about themselves. Specifically, shame involves feeling inferior, less-than, not good enough, and perhaps, helpless to do anything about it. It is a form of self-devaluation. Inaccurate perceptions may primarily drive shame. *To counter feelings of shame, reflect on inaccurate perceptions and reframe thoughts founded upon facts and truth. Dismiss fallacy and inaccurate thoughts of disempowerment. Reflect on your truth and times where you have overcome the odds. Again, focus on your strengths as an individual.*

Self-worth: While aligned with shame, self-worth is a self-assessment of a person's worthiness. This valuation aligned with deep beliefs and perceptions held about oneself is thought to be more severe than shame. *To counter feelings of low self-worth, create daily affirmations of one's positive characteristics and value to the world.*

Self-esteem: Generally, self-esteem describes how people feel about themselves at a point in time. People who have low self-esteem may lack confidence. People with low self-esteem may not engage in activities or have social withdrawal because they do not live up to perceived standards. Low self-esteem can manifest into emotional or behavioral problems if unaddressed. People with low self-esteem may have self-doubt, feel unworthy compared to others, and criticize themselves. *To counter feelings of low self-esteem, try to set incremental goals and affirm personal strengths. Celebrate your victories, no matter how large or small.*

Self-Confidence: Maybe the opposite feeling of shame is self-confidence. Shame describes feeling bad about making mistakes or not being good enough. Self-confidence describes having a high opinion and belief in one's status and self-efficacy. *To counter feelings of low self-confidence, set reasonable goals and practice becoming the best version of yourself. Remind yourself of your personal power. Use SMART goals. (see Section 6.0, S.M.A.R.T. goals)*

Helping Children to Build Confidence and Feel Empowered

Caregivers send verbal and nonverbal messages to children related to their worth and value. For example, caregivers who tell their children, "I love you," yet their body language says to "Stay away," or "I do not have time for you" sends conflicting messages.

Some strategies that caregivers can use to help boost a child's self-confidence are indicated below:

- Show children respect and appreciation to help develop self-worth.
- Allow children leverage to explore, learn, and engage in activities.
- Create a safe space where children's failure is not ridiculed.
- Spend quality time with children, giving them full attention when sharing an activity or discussion
- Help children understand and deal with emotions (especially shame and self-worth).
- Help children to understand they are not to blame. [During adverse childhood experiences and traumatic events, children may feel ashamed of the family situation. They may also feel guilty, as if the incarceration is their fault.]
- Young children are learning, yet they will fail at some tasks and activities. Help them to realize that failure does not equate to self-worth.
- Show children unconditional love. Give praise and words of encouragement when a child makes positive *actions* that show their competence and growth or skills development.
- Focus on the action rather than referring to the child as being good or bad. For instance, rather than say, "Good boy," focus on the specific task, saying, for example, "You did a great job putting your toys away," "I am proud of you!"
- Do not compare your children to each another. This may cause division and siblings may have conflicts.

Caregivers play an essential role in helping children to understand their self-worth and value. Children who are given opportunities to practice skills, make choices, and take on tasks and responsibilities may strengthen self-confidence and self-esteem. While everyone will likely feel some shame at some point associated with setbacks, children who have a positive image of themselves can move past these challenges by focusing on their overall self-worth.

ACTIVITY 54

No Shame

Caregivers have many responsibilities when raising children. These can be fun, productive, loving exchanges, watching children grow and mature. However, there are other conditions such as parental incarceration and other losses that add complexity. At times, incarceration can be challenging and pose conditions of shame, stigma, and even reduced self-confidence if not acknowledged and managed. Caregivers can develop a positive and strength-based behaviors that offers children models as they develop their own abilities and life skills. Additionally, strength-based focus may be helpful in managing such conditions as stigma and shame associated with incarceration.

In this exercise, reflect on individual positive qualities, and name them below.

What areas are you most confident related to your ability to parent?
   1.

   2.

   3.

What positive self-talk do you, or can you, use for personal uplift?
   1.

   2.

   3.

What are the strongest characteristics associated with your core belief system?
   1.

   2.

   3.

These reflections can be empowering and a reminder of how many positive aspects of one's life are truly admirable. This in itself can be uplifting. *Note: This exercise can be used to identify children's strengths as well.*

Section 14.2 Shaping Self-Worth and Self-Acceptance

Section Focus | Case Example

DEVELOPING CONFIDENCE

The way we talk to our children becomes their inner voice.

—Peggy O'Mara

Section Objectives

☐ Learn about the caregiver/parent's influence in shaping child self-image (life stores)
☐ Learn how parents can reverse potentially harmful effects of inadvertent ridicule using corrective actions
☐ Identify characteristics of healthy self-worth in children and caregivers
☐ Critically reflect on ways to help children develop self-acceptance and self-love

Overview

Each day, children write the story of their lives, just as we did when we were children. As the quote by Peggy O'Mara indicates, the voice that lingers in a child's mind well into their adult years is likely something said by a parent. In this metaphor, parents may have the most significant impact in shaping children's life stories.

Children's thoughts about themselves develop early in life. From about a year old and onward, children's identities get shaped by their parent's appraisal as well as in other environments, such as school and social settings. Whether they know it or not, caregivers constantly send children messages (both positive and negative) regarding their worth, thereby shaping a child's self-image. The good news is that it is never too late to change course and develop empowering behaviors that lead to children's self-compassion, self-love, and self-confidence.

Foundational Learning

Many experiences influence a child's opinion of themselves. As children continue on their journey of development, the people in their environments at home, at school, and in other social settings may shape how they view themselves. The Mind Shift Foundation (TMS) indicated that a parent's communication can profoundly impact children's perceptions of themselves (TMS, n.d.). This organization further states that children's self-worth could be affected negatively by caregivers:

- Having a cursory interest and engagement with children
- Showing children disapproval through frowns, expressions (rolling of the eyes, frowning, and other facial expressions), and body language

- Pushing the children to excel beyond their capacity; then ridiculing them for failing
- Yelling at children, labeling them as lazy, disorganized, messy, stupid, a problem child, inadequate, unworthy, and with other names
- Comparing one sibling to another
- Telling children that they are going to be left or put out of the house if they do not meet certain conditions

Many parents may inadvertently show one or more of the aforementioned behaviors. Every parent gets short-tempered or exhausted, sometimes. If a parent does engage in this behavior, apologies go a long way. Acknowledging and working towards change could reverse the intent (related to inadvertent ridicule).

Parents can consider the following corrective actions:

- Apologize when making parenting mistakes
- Provide children with unconditional love
- Let children know that they matter
- Take an interest in children's activities
- Listen to them, make eye contact, and give full attention to their discussions
- Provide children with warmth and caring
- Engage with children and support their interests
- Give children praise and celebrate their successes
- Make the home a place where children feel safe, welcome, and loved
- Help children to set reasonable goals
- Let kids make decisions and contribute to family choices
- Talk to children about significant changes and anticipated transitions
- Believe in your child and let them know that you "have their back"
- Assign age-appropriate responsibilities and allow children to figure out tasks—if they fail at the task, help them to develop grit to try again

Questioning oneself is normal. Everyone will likely have times where they assess their own worth and value. What does healthy self-worth look like in children and caregivers?

- They are happy and generally laugh, giggle, or smile
- They set goals and may be competitive with the belief that they can accomplish the activity
- Setbacks do not define them—they bounce back
- They adjust to frustration and negative feelings
- They are helpers and take on responsibility
- They show excitement in approaching new tasks
- They are social and get along with family and friends
- They have empathy and compassion toward people
- They have confidence and endeavor new tasks and activities

Helping children develop a healthy social competence goes a long way in how they perceive themselves. Modeling behavior of how to engage socially begins in the home. Parents can help children to have positive interpersonal skills. These skills are crucial since children become incredibly conscious of friendships and peer relationships as they grow beyond middle childhood.

ACTIVITY 55

No Shame

Families can use the following tips to help children develop a positive self-image.

- Tell children they are appreciated
- Help children conduct a strength inventory (note all of their positive qualities).
- Play games that require problem-solving skills and draw upon logic and strategy skills
- Engage in activities with children such as painting, crafts, and cooking— offering praise for their accomplishments and helping them to learn where they have not mastered tasks
- Assign chores and tasks that are age-appropriate so that children can develop a sense of mastery and learn by doing

Critical Thinking Activity:

- Consider your child's demeanor and your perception of their self-esteem or self-worth.
- Identify three actions that you can take to bolster your child's self-worth.
- What can you commit to doing every day (towards this positive outcome)?
- What are your related goals for the next day, week, month?

Journal your goals and ideas.

Please note that there is no answer key for this critical thinking exercise.

Section 14.3. Crying Shame

Section Focus | Case Example

Shame and Power

Stigma involves labeling, and potentially excluding people from social networks.

Section Objectives

☐ Learn how incarceration can result in the stigmatizing of children and families
☐ Critically reflect on the importance of helping children build self-confidence

Overview

Incarceration is one of those social conditions that may result in some level of stigma and shaming. Consequently, some people treat the families of the incarcerated harshly—they do not understand the effects. At times, even children are treated poorly by others. When family members buy into the perception that they are somehow flawed, its members, including the children, might question their own identity and worth. This inaccurate idea can be reversed.

Foundational Learning

Standing up against stigma and shaming is similar to taking a stance towards rejecting bullying. Parents can teach children how to become assertive and confident. This requires practice. As children develop confidence, parents can:

- help children to develop healthy identities by modeling good character
- teach children to carry themselves with confidence in their posture and interactions
- help children to develop their intuition (spider senses); be alert and look out for risks
- make the distinction between family privacy and family secrets
- encourage children to engage with friends and family members
- teach children to be assertive and respectful
- teach children to speak up and discuss any attempts or hints of shaming, stigma, or bullying by others (e.g., schoolmates, parents, community center administrators)
- teach children not to bully or shame others

In the end, being stigmatized, bullied, or shamed may feel similar. Children who have developed a strong sense of self, however, will realize that people who bully and point out weaknesses in others are likely unhappy with themselves.

Finally, the incarceration of a loved one might be embarrassing to family members. It may seem natural to internalize some of the circumstances as shameful. However, it does not have to stay that way. Affected families can establish and reinforce their own identities by focusing on the positive aspects of their character. Individuals can reclaim or reinvent their lives where outside circumstances no longer define them.

Activity 56

No Shame

In this activity, critically reflect on the importance of helping children build self-confidence. Recall the potential impacts of stigma and shame on children. Next, scan Module 14, consider how a caregiver can protect children from becoming targets of humiliation. Please note that there is no answer key for this critical thinking exercise.

Brainstorm ten ways that caregivers can support and guide their children to protect them from stigma and possibly bullying:

1.

2.

3.

4.

5.

6.

7.

8.

9.

10.

References

Gilbert, P. (1997). The evolution of social attractiveness and its role in shame, humiliation, guilt and ther-apy. *British Journal of Medical Psychology*, 70(2), 113–147.

Hart-Johnson, A., & Johnson, G. (2022). Caregivers' family relations assessment and communica-tion strategies. *Science Publishing Group*, 11(5), 157–168. https://www.sciencepublishinggroup.com/article/10.11648/j.pbs.20221105.12.

The Mind Shift Foundation. (n.d.) *We're here to promote self-worth, wellbeing, and positive mental health.* Retrieved from https://mindshift.org.au.

Pattison, S. (2000). *Shame: Theory, therapy, theology.* Cambridge University Press.

The Answer Key for Section 14.0, Activity 53

1. True
2. False: Inferiority, Hopelessness, and Disempowerment
3. True
4. True
5. True: The story about *The Wise Chicken* and the turtle illustrates how unrealistic ideas shape perceptions. In the story, the turtle's perceptions of inferiority are an example of internal shame and unrealistic logic.

Silver Linings

MODULE FOCUS

- Section 15.0. Rays of Hope. Explore reasons for optimism and hope.
- Section 15.1. Learned Hopefulness. Explore ways to reframe hopelessness into hopefulness.
- Section 15.2. Embracing Vulnerability as a Strength. Learn how vulnerability is considered a strength.
- Section 15.3. Help Children to Write Their Stories. Develop ways to teach children to reframe their stories using the lens of strength and resilience.

Resources

Read Guidebook: Hart-Johnson and Johnson (2025) | Chapter 15, "Elpida: Hope and Resilience"

Introduction

Hope

In this workbook, we provided information, analysis, and a framework to form a well-rounded overview of the topic: parental incarceration. We also integrated knowledge drawn from other subject matter experts: child advocates, criminologists, scientists, neurologists, bibliotherapists, health and human services professionals, and others who specialize in topic areas of:

- Family member incarceration
- Child development
- Communication

Taken together, this context provided the framework to create a powerful tool chest of helpful aids to build the user's understanding and mastery on topics relevant to parental incarceration.

Many of the helpful tools that we recognized and integrated have been around far longer than the issue of mass incarceration. While the problem of mass incarceration in the United States proliferated around the 1970s, there are protective factors that can stave off harmful effects. Current research informs us that strategies to bolster resilience and foster self-care can go a long way in strengthening the family system. Caregivers can engage in their own self-help and self-care toward holistic well-being. Children can develop coping strategies and ways to self-regulate even in the most difficult situations and circumstances. There is truly hope founded upon empirical research that children can and do survive the incarceration crisis. This module is all about building hope and fostering an environment for building resilience.

Section 15.0. Rays of Hope

Section Focus | Case Example

HOPE

Let your hopes, not your hurts, shape your future.
—Robert H. Schuller

Section Objectives

☐ Gain knowledge about the concept: assumptive world
☐ Understand the linkage between the assumptive world and attachments
☐ Critically reflect on the concept, silver linings

Overview

"The assumptive world concept refers to the assumptions or beliefs that ground, secure, stabilize, and orient people."
—Beder, 2004–2005, p.255

ASSUMPTIVE WORLD

The *assumptive world* is a term that relates to how humans develop belief systems that ground them in predictability, make them feel secure, and provide them with life orientation. In other words, these ideals are the core beliefs about how life is lived and the way that life should be. When faced with trauma, loss, disappointment, and death, those beliefs are challenged, if not shattered to their core.

Everyone holds ideals about how life should be. However, profound life events can disrupt the assumptive world of affected individuals. As it turns out, humans relish predictability from the time of infancy well into adulthood. We still look for consistency in our days to ground us and give us hope, but life also can be an ongoing continuous chain of events, some of which we have little or no control. Our ideas and ideals are shaped by our belief systems, values, and expectations aligned by worldviews.

Coherence in our lives depends upon the belief that life can be meaningful, worthwhile relationships can be maintained, and that we as individuals will develop a sense of purpose and place in the world. We achieve this through maintaining connectedness and relationships with family, friends, co-workers, even neighbors. These are the anchors that steady our lives.

Our ideals set the expectations for a person's life course. For instance, some parents hold high ideals for their children. They may expect their children to grow up, go to college, graduate, and live "a normal life." However, radical interruptions to these life ideals may impose shifts in a person's beliefs and outlook towards the future. Unanticipated events—accidents, death, disabilities, and family-member incarceration—can negatively change a person's worldview. When this type of shift occurs, people tend to question their faith, existence, and even reconsider their foundational beliefs about the world and how it works. Some people find themselves asking, "What's it all about?" *These rhetorical questions align with a person's assumptive world.*

In other words, adverse events that shift a person's outlook on life may lead to cynicism and pessimistic outlooks (Anderson et al., 2013) and a change in a person's belief about their assumptive world. Consequently, people may become angry because of unforeseen circumstances disrupting their lives. Such events include incarceration of a significant loved one. These circumstances may cause people to lose hope and give up on having a bright or even a predictable future.

Looking for the positive aspects of negative situations might require a bit of reflection. *Silver linings* are considered the ability to find something good from the bad. This concept means taking active steps to reclaim a person's values and belief system or form new outlooks. Sometimes, finding a silver lining might mean recognizing that something negative happened, but some good also occurred. Digging deep to find strength as a caregiver also helps children develop frameworks for building fortitude, grit, and optimism.

Foundational Learning

Assumptive world and attachments. To understand the profound effects when one's assumptive world is challenged, *attachment theory* comes into play. Bowlby indicated that based on the attachment framework, separation from a loved one brings on fear, distress, and separation anxiety. Recall that babies form attachments to their mothers and when their bond is disrupted, they may develop disorganized, avoidant, or insecure attachments (review Module 2). Beder (2005) reminds readers that loss occurring later in life reminds us of these early relationships formed as a child. He suggests that violations against one's assumptive world emotionally takes us back to earlier maternal loss or exposure to parents' attachment styles (*see Section 2.3*). This may determine how a person recovers from an existential crisis. For example, a person with secure bonds as a child may rationalize that loss is inevitable and that while it hurts to lose familiarity with persons, places, and things, there is hope for recovery and regaining one's footing. A person experiencing recurring abandonment may feel as though life has once again radically shifted towards uncertainty, unfulfilled relationships, a vulnerable state, and unfinished business. If the loss is a significant person, this state of grieving or separation-based suffering is sometimes remedied through creating ongoing bonds with the absent person (symbolically or ritually).

The absence of coping using, perhaps, meaning-making rituals and other practices may leave cynicism, anger, and frustration resulting from the randomness and senseless losses occurring in one's life. Questions align with a victimized posture, asking, "Why me?" Often this question leads to more unfulfilled answers. Bad things do happen to good people, and it is not always explained how life can be predictable one moment and randomly disrupted the next. However, people do find ways to emerge from despair by acknowledging the loss. As Worden (2018) reminds (see Module 2), managing the grieving process of loss requires figuring out how life has changed, accepting the new/altered life state, and figuring out how the absence of the person, place, or thing will now be represented in our lives and to what degree it exists in this new world.

Silver Linings. Finding silver linings in life may require searching for something good that came from challenging situations. This process may require reflection, and it may unfold gradually over time. Here are a few examples of looking beyond the immediate to see the "glass half-full" instead of "half-empty."

- An employee got laid off from their job. However, weeks later, they find a job that pays more, is closer to home, and the worker feels more appreciated by management.
- A son became incarcerated. However, while in prison, he became sober, learned carpentry skills, and is now employed as a carpenter.
- Unfortunate circumstances caused a grandmother to care for her grandchildren. While it was initially a struggle, she now has close bonds with her grandchildren.

The above circumstances align with how a situation may initially seem bad but later was found to have benefits or a bright outcome. Optimism is a mindset on how positively life or circumstances might turn out.

ACTIVITY 57

Silver Linings

Critically reflect upon Section 15.0. Think about the terms, *assumptive world* and *silver linings*. Note what they mean to you. When life presents challenges, sometimes, a person's faith or outlook is tested, or their faith may cause them to feel disempowered. However, people can and do find the positive in their circumstances. Changing one's outlook might require reflection and practice. Consider completing exercise Table 15.0. *Silver Linings Reflections.*

Table 15.0. Silver Linings Reflections

Personal Reflections	*Note your answers*
What are your strengths (e.g., empathy, patience, dedication, forgiveness, nurturing)?	
What have life circumstances taught you about yourself?	
As you ponder the responsibilities of caregivers, what are the steps that caregivers can take to strengthen your role?	
What is the good in the situation concerning the incarceration of a parent? Consider all aspects, and jot down at least one silver lining.	
What is your superpower as a person? (analytical, optimistic, caring, dedicated, focused, etc.)	
Caregivers need to provide structure, routine, stability, and safety. What steps can a caregiver implement right away to lend support to children impacted by parental incarceration?	

Please note that there is no answer key for this critical thinking exercise.

Section 15.1. Learned Hopefulness

Section Focus | Case Example

Glorious Miracles

"There are only two ways to live your life.
One is through nothing is a miracle.
The other is though everything is a miracle."
—Albert Einstein

Section Objectives

☐ Learn about ways to transform thoughts of helplessness to empowerment
☐ Critically reflect on the application of the CESESMA Model of Empowerment to enhance the skills or embrace a change of attitude

Overview

It can feel good to be in control of life circumstances. This feeling of agency may feel light and in-the-flow of life. The opposite may hold true when circumstance leave no room for personal input in decision-making and control over conditions. At times, everyone may feel disempowered, or even helpless.

While an occasional bout with feeling down is normal, prolonged negative thoughts can affect a person's emotional and motivational states (Buzzai et al., 2021). Its best to set some personal ground rules and lean toward optimism.

Optimism has a broad function whereby people learn to believe that there is potential for a positive future. Learning to have hope after experiencing disruptive and challenging situations can take time—but it is possible. Hope is personalized and engenders ideas of what life should be like if endeavors manifest. Anticipation of good, paired with visualization of what it might look like, may usher in beliefs toward positive change and outcomes. This process generally lifts one's spirits.

Taking steps to rebuild hope can include reframing perceptions. Finding hope can entail examining internal strengths and uniqueness. When the world is seen through a lens of strength and possibilities, it generally *feels better*. In other words, taking steps toward self-help and positive change might bolster optimism. *Making meaning* might include accepting the current situation and finding the silver lining, in spite of it all. Consider personal challenges where the silver lining became an awareness of inner strength, grit, and fortitude.

Foundational Learning

Learned helplessness can be counteracted. Consider juxtaposing or transforming the focus on the following common symptoms (Butkowsky & Willows, 1980):

- Lack of motivation |examining ways to set small goals one step at a time to regain focus and motivation.
- Giving up |surround yourself with like-minded supporters; those who encourage you and point out your strengths.
- Low self-esteem |start with your strong points, positive attributes and character, and take steps towards offering yourself daily affirmations on your positive qualities—see the good in you.
- Being passive| using your positive qualities, build upon them through being assertive and learning communication skills that illustrate competence and interpersonal skill
- Easily frustrated| practice self-love, self-compassion, and set realistic goals— remind yourself that no one is perfect
- Refusal to ask for support or help|recognize that you are not alone. Seeking help or support is not a sign of weakness, it illustrates self-awareness and self-care.

Children (and caregivers) can develop empowerment strategies to improve quality of life and optimism. CESESMA is a Nicaraguan charity that supports children and

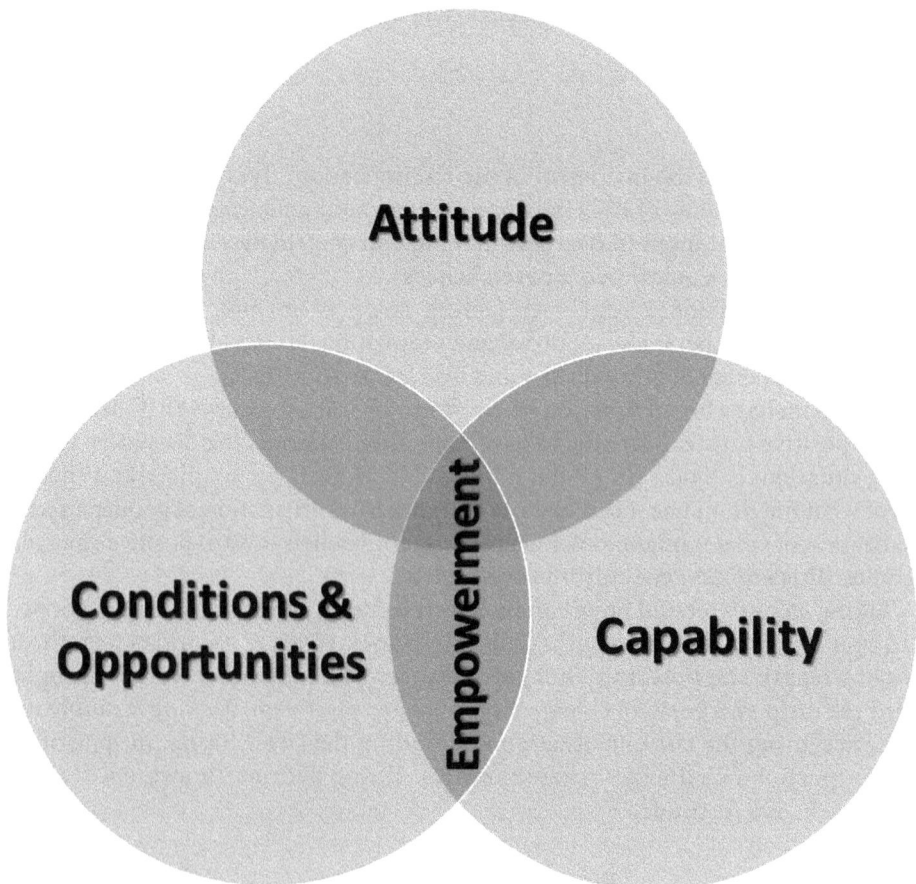

Figure 15.1.0. CESESMA (2010, p. 44) Model of Empowerment | Sheir (2015) Spanish Translation, p.213)

adolescents. The CESESMA Model of Empowerment (Shier, 2015, p.213) considers three significant components (strengths: attitude, capability, and conditions/opportunities). Review the conceptual model in Figure 15.1.0.

ATTITUDE

- Acknowledge personal abilities
- Feel capable of taking actions
- Recognize your human rights
- Be ready to collaborate
- Develop self-esteem
- Be willing to face challenges
- Tell yourself it's okay to lighten up and laugh

CAPABILITY

- Know that you have the ability to do and change things
- Use knowledge, skills, and facts to influence perceptions
- Develop autonomy to think and act for oneself
- Learn from others

CONDITIONS AND OPPORTUNITIES

- Believe in one's ability to do things
- Joining in group activities
- Having parental support

Activity 58

Silver Linings

In this activity, critically reflect upon sections 15.1. *Overview* through *Foundational Learning*. Pay particular attention to the CESESMA (2012) Model of Empowerment. Now, note if you possess the identified strengths. If you do not possess identified attributes (attitude, capability, and opportunities), note how you can enhance the skills or embrace a change of attitude. Next, reflect on your children's strengths using the same approach.

Attitude	*Reflect if you possess this strength (Yes/No)?*	*Briefly note what you can do to enhance this attitude*
Acknowledge personal abilities		
Feel capable of taking actions		
Recognize your human rights		
Be ready to collaborate		
Develop self-esteem		
Willing to face challenges		
Capability		
Have the ability to do and change things		
Use knowledge, skills, and facts		
Develop autonomy to think and act for oneself		
Learn from others		
Conditions and opportunities		
The context favors my ability to do things		
Joining in group activities		
Having parental support		

Please note that there is no answer key for this critical thinking exercise.

Section 15.2. Embracing Vulnerability as a Strength

Section Focus | Case Example

Vulnerability as Strength

"...I believe that vulnerability—the willingness to show up and be seen with no guarantee of outcome—is the only path to more love, belonging, and joy."

—Brene Brown (2015, p. xvii)

Section Objectives

☐ Learn ways to ways to embrace the vulnerability that can lead to empowerment.
☐ Identify positive qualities, uniqueness, vulnerability, and develop a plan forward, embrasing imperfections and uniqueness

Overview

Think of the quote by Brene Brown that dares a person to believe that with vulnerability comes a pathway toward love, joy, and connectedness (Brown, 2015). Perhaps, being vulnerable also dares individuals to take a hard look at themselves to see what is happening during times of perceived weakness. This reflection is made with the intent of understanding the good through imperfections. Everybody is different—our uniqueness is our beauty.

Foundational Learning

The RecoveryView.com (n.d.) indicated that most people believe that vulnerability is the opposite of empowerment. Yet, we can choose to mature in this self-identification journey and embrace vulnerability by illuminating our imperfections as part of our unique character. Vulnerability may expose areas that are opportunities for growth and development. Being vulnerable means being truthful and having a willingness to look at one's' blind spots. There are a few ways to embrace the vulnerability that can lead to empowerment:

- Practice self-love and self-compassion. Tell yourself daily that you love yourself!
- Learn to laugh—stop taking yourself so seriously—everyone makes mistakes
- Refrain from guilt and live in the present—forgive yourself
- Be truthful about yourself and your flaws, knowing you can and will improve
- Commit to taking baby steps toward incremental change

ACTIVITY 59

Silver Linings

In this activity, journal your ideas and thoughts about your positive qualities, uniqueness, vulnerability, and your plan forward. Please note that there is no answer key for this critical thinking exercise.

Reflection:

[Please note your positive qualities, uniqueness, vulnerability, and your plan forward]

Section 15.3. Help Children to Write Their Stories

Section Focus | Case Example

REVISITING BIBLIOTHERAPY

Every book tells a story. Kids need books.

Section Objectives

- ☐ Learn the importance of using children's books for development and establishing close bonds.
- ☐ Gain knowledge about how books can align with bibliotherapy
- ☐ Practice creative writing by helping a child write their life story (using and empowerment and strength-based approach)

Overview

Books are a means of providing a host of insights, opportunities, learning, hope, and possibilities. For children, the magic of reading or listening to a parent read a book can be life changing and influence their visions of a bright future. Moreover, Recob (2008) indicated that bibliotherapy (using books to guide problem-solving, coping with life circumstances, and for emotional healing) entails using books for self-enrichment and healing. She suggests that through this process the reader first learns they are not alone in their circumstances. Second, communication is advanced, where literacy benefits can include gaining new perspectives and even reframing how circumstances are viewed. The act of reading to children can influence parent-child close bonds and togetherness/connectedness.

Foundational Learning

A well-written book that illustrates how a person might overcome life's odds offers hope. Some books illuminate methods of coping through example and storylines. Children who read books about challenging topics recognize they are not alone. According to Amy Recob in her book on Bibliotherapy, *When Kids Need Books: A Guide for Those in Need of Reassurance and Their Teachers, Parents, and Friends*, the following are benefits of *bibliotherapy* (Recob, 2008):

- The reader finds that the book illuminates and discusses a situation that the child is dealing with.
- The reader becomes engaged in the story as they realize how the main character is addressing similar situations
- The reader gains self-confidence in the area discussed

- The reader becomes open to taking remedial steps, to seeking support and guidance in accomplishing a plan of action

Be sure to complete Activity 60. If you have read and completed all of most of the exercises in this workbook: Congratulations!

The next sections, Module 16 through 19, focus on the power of children's storybooks designed to discuss difficult topics such as parental incarceration. Consider acquiring the noted books and work with your child, if they are affected, to provide coping strategies and opportunities to bond.

Activity 60

Silver Linings

For this activity, you will imagine helping a child prepare to write their life story by following a few prompts. Remember the power of inspiration and hope! This can be an engaging exercise between caregiver and child. (Note: If you do not have a child, then use the same prompts to rewrite your own story.) Think about *how you wish life to be*. Consider past, current, and desired future conditions. With these prompts in mind, create a story.

1. How does "the new story" begin?
2. What is the main character overcoming the odds?
3. Who is the main character?
4. What changes take place? (e.g., modified view of life and/or change in assumptive world)
5. What is the outcome?
6. Who is involved?
7. What do the characters learn?
8. What does the story teach readers?
9. What are the strengths of the main character (noting that the main character is the child or yourself).
10. What are the superpowers (positive qualities and uniqueness of the charters)

Using your outline, write the story in sequence, making sure to add content, such as places that stand out. Be sure to draw the positive qualities as well as write about what strengths the characters used to overcome the odds. Try not to get too personal; rather, make it an uplift and fun—yet reflective!

How it works: This exercise requires creativity, reflection, and reframing. By using creativity, the author/writer engages in possibilities and optimism. They are able to draw from their lives, examples of overcoming odds through hope. The realism of facing life challenges yet growing through them provides a framework and reminder that life can be difficult, yet given the personal strength and fortitude, a new and brighter day is possible. This exercise teaches both caregivers and their children that life is filled with cycles of good and challenging experiences. However, there can be good found in all situations, including the mere fact that one lived through the difficulties. This my friends are the *silver linings*.

References

Anderson, J.E., Kay, A.C., & Fitzsimons, G.M. (2013). Finding silver linings: Meaning making as a compensatory response to negative experiences. In K.D. Markman, T. Proulx, & M.J. Lindberg (Eds.), *The Psychology of Meaning*. (pp. 279–295). American Psychological Association. https://doi.org/10.1037/14040-014

Beder, J. (2005). Loss of the assumptive world—How we deal with death and loss. *Omega Journal of Death and Dying*, 50(4), 255–265. Doi 10.2190/GXH6-8VY6-BQ0R-GC04.

Brown, B. (2015). *Rising Strong: The Reckoning. The Rumble. The Revolution*. Random House.

Buzzai, C., Sorrenti, L., Tripiciano, F., Orecchio, S., & Filippello, P. (2021). School alienation and academic achievement: The role of learned helplessness and mastery orientation. *School Psychology*, 36(1), 17–23. https://doi.org/10.1037/spq0000413.

Butkowsky, I.S., & Willows, D.M. (1980). Cognitive-motivational characteristics of children varying in reading ability: Evidence for learned helplessness in poor readers. *Journal of Educational Psychology*, 72(3):408–422. doi:10.1037/0022-0663.72.3.408.

CESESMA. (2012). Normativa de Protección hacia Niñas, Niños y Adolescentes. San Ramón, Nicaragua: CESESMA. (CESESMA Model of Empowerment). Retrieved from http://www.cesesma.org/documentos/CESESMAnormativa_de_proteccion.pdf.

Hart-Johnson, A., & Johnson, G. (2022). Caregivers' family relations assessment and communication strategies. *Science Publishing Group*, 11(5), 157–168. https://www.sciencepublishinggroup.com/article/10.11648/j.pbs.20221105.12.

Recob, A. (2008). *Bibliotherapy: When kids need books*. iUniverse, Inc.

RecoveryView.com. (n.d.). *Empowerment through vulnerability*. Retrieved from https://recoveryview.com/article/empowerment-through-vulnerability.

Shier, H. (2015). Children as researchers in Nicaragua: Children's consultancy to transformative research. *Global Studies of Childhood*, 5(2), 206–219.

Worden, J.W. (2018). *Grief counseling and grief therapy: A handbook for the mental health practitioner*. Springer.

PART III

Storybooks and Bibliotherapy

Using Storybooks as Creative Interventions

In this section of the workbook four (4) children's books have been designed to assist facilitators, helping professionals and parents who care for or work with children who have experienced loss including those with incarcerated parents. These stories follow in a long tradition of using stories to explore deeper meaning of language, settings, culture, emotions, behaviors, and experiences of storybooks characters. Oftentimes, children who are affected by the traumatizing experiences of grief and loss may not be able to articulate associated feelings. In their minds, they may have lost a parent to unforeseen or perhaps unfamiliar and unimaginable circumstances. With such conditions in-play, we hope that our books and resources can be used to help children internalize and externalize their feelings and help children understand that storybook characters also go through difficult emotional situations.

So as possible interventions, storybooks can contribute to positive parent-child bonding and interpersonal skills-building through one-on-one reading time or through group-based reading circles. As previously noted, one of the underpinnings of this training is the philosophy of empowerment, whereby individual strengths are nurtured and perceived vulnerabilities are unmasked as human courage.

System impacted caregivers. When a child's parent goes to prison, most often the non-incarcerated caregiver is placed in the guardian role of attending to the child's emotional, physical, and social well-being. This responsibility can be difficult, especially facing challenges such as navigating the legal-justice system on behalf of the individual who is justice system aligned, while also managing personal, psychological, and social (psychosocial) reactions to the family member's incarceration. Moreover, there may be a sense of hopelessness/helplessness given that the caregiver has little say or control over what occurs related to the sentencing, release, or reentry status, leaving them with feelings of disempowerment. Therefore, it is important to promote personal empowerment.

Justice aligned parents. Parents who experienced or are experiencing incarceration may contend with multiple issues, including feelings of disempowerment. There may also be a change in family "roles" as it pertains to the incarcerated parent's absence from the family system, as identified in the C-FRACS model. For example, confined individuals are separated from family and friends and do not have much control over their current circumstances. Their sense of self-directed actions, self-control, rights, and privileges are all decreased to some extent during incarceration. Therefore, through our training, we strive to help individuals restore their sense of empowerment.

Lastly, for bibliotherapy to be effective, books should match the reader's comprehension and interest (Doll & Doll, 1997). While we suggest the use of our books with children within a specific age range, parents/caregivers must consider the developmental maturity of children as well. Books should be explored to understand the actions, consequences and options the characters in the story experienced. When possible, the reader should be able to step into the role of the character and share their insights and vulnerabilities as they might relate to the child or audience.

Baby Star Finds "Happy"

(For children zero to five years)

MODULE FOCUS

- Read and analyze the children's book, *Baby Star Finds "Happy"*
- Introduce bibliotherapy and reading circle concepts
- Practice reading circle exercises

Resources

Read *Baby Star Finds "Happy"*

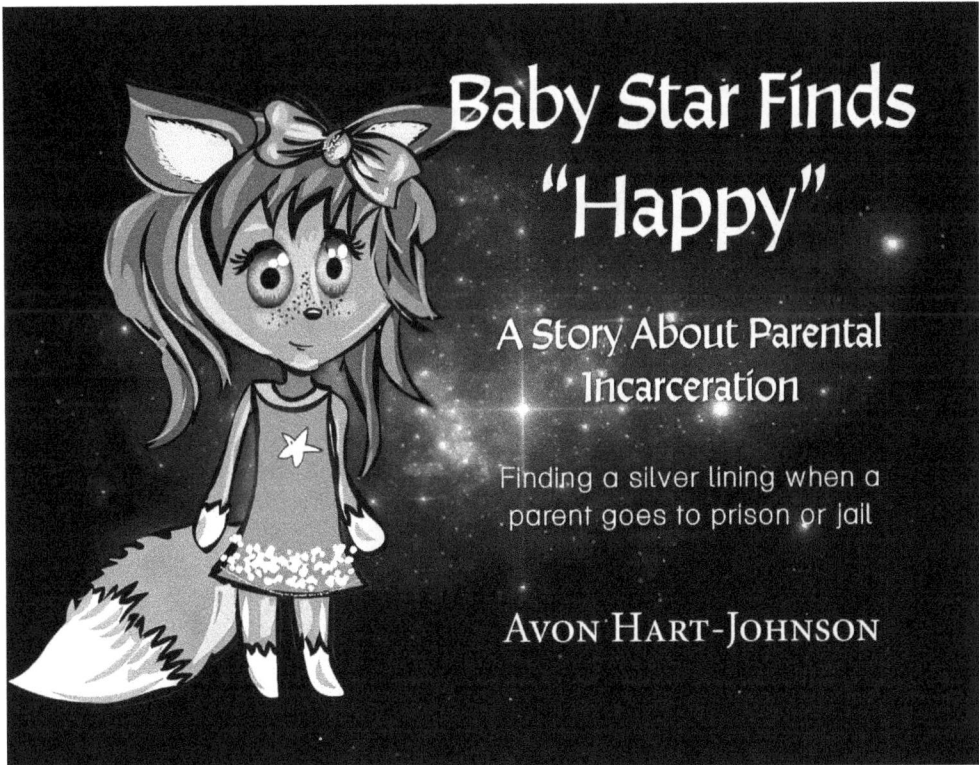

Figure 16.0 Baby Star (illustration by Shaifali Bajad [Fiverr.com].

Additional Resources

Amazon.com:
Hart-Johnson, A. (2021). *Baby Star Finds "Happy."* A Story About Parental Incarceration. Finding a Silver lining when a parent goes to prison or jail. Extant-One Publishing. ISBN 9798775914110.
Review Appendix E, Helping Children Deal with Loss

Introduction

About *Baby Star Finds "Happy,"* by Dr. Avon Hart-Johnson. *Baby Star Finds "Happy"* is a story about a child's journey in embracing friendship, family, and forgiveness when a mother goes to jail. Baby Star learns that sadness is a normal response when someone you love leaves you. She also learns that she is not at fault for her mother's incarceration. *Baby Star Finds "Happy"* can be used as a read-along book for young children even if they are in the early stages of development and do not understand the words. The illustrations help children understand the written words when read aloud. Remember: books can improve literacy/vocabulary and aid in learning new concepts (i.e., persons, places, things, experiences).

Section 16.0. Baby Star: Literacy, Child Development, and Comprehension

Materials

❖ Writing pad or journal

Section Objectives

☐ To increase parents'/caregivers' awareness of the communication options that can be used for children with incarcerated parents.
☐ To increase parents'/caregivers' awareness of developmental stages and emotions experienced by children of incarcerated parents (0 to 5 years).
☐ To help parents identify possible support systems.
☐ To understand concepts related to attachment bonds and building strong interpersonal relationships.
☐ To deepen knowledge about caregiver-child communication and bonding.

Overview

From birth to age 5, children form attachments and develop interpersonal relationships shaped upon trust. Said differently, parents are generally the first people whom children learn to love, and trust, and with whom they create bonds. During early stages of development, children can experience certain emotions without having the developmental skills to express their feelings verbally. Instead, they may display physical reactions (e.g., crying, kicking, and self-soothing behaviors such as rocking or thumb-sucking) when in distress. This behavior may be especially pronounced when a child separates from an incarcerated parent.

During the developmental years of between 19 months and 5 years of age, children begin to develop and master many language skills. Children at this age range may speak between 10 and 50 words. Some understand and use action words (go, stop) or direction words (up, down). Parents and caregivers play an important role in their child's communication skills development. During this time, children learn new words and respond to parental commands. They emulate adults in their play and actions. They also develop trust versus mistrust instincts. Psychologist Eric Erikson believed that if children *do not* build trusting relationships during earlier years with parents or caregivers, they will have challenges forming interpersonal trusting relationships later in life. The incarceration of a parent can be particularly stressful for all family members. Therefore, it is imperative to remember that the child's developmental years are essential to their future well-being and outcomes. Tools such as the storybook, *Baby Star Finds "Happy,"* can help parents/caregivers spend quality time together and enhance bonding through reading.

Foundational Learning: Reading Circle Tips

Before reading this book to children or a group, become familiarized with the story, *Baby Star Finds "Happy."* Read the book twice (alternatively listen to the audio eBook). Read the story once to understand the main context and a second time to understand the essence of the story and characters. Take notes about what stands out in the story. This background information will help provide context to the following discussion points related to the book.

- *Baby Star Finds "Happy"* can be read to infants, too! Scholars confirm that a child's vocabulary rate increases by reading to them even before comprehending the words! Children will hear voice tones, speech patterns, and see your smiles—all contribute to learning and bonding.
- *Baby Star Finds "Happy"* illustrates that children need security. Research confirms that mothers generally provide the foundation of nurturing to help children to develop and build relationships inside and outside of the family.
- Fathers also play an important role in child development, as demonstrated in Daddy Star's role. Fathers also play a key role in their children's lives when they are not living in the household.
- Even infants can feel distressed when separated from the bonds of a parent. When a child is distressed or worried about the incarcerated parent, caregivers can show forms of bonding through hugs (if appropriate) and by keeping these little ones near. You may also reinforce, if fitting, that mom or dad is doing okay, to alleviate their worries.
- When children are 5 years of age and younger, they begin to understand the language, rules, and situations relating to words such as "No!" This foundation may help them to understand the concepts of misbehavior, time-out, and communication about prison and incarceration.

- Research has shown that quality time can include just being near a child when going about daily routines such as cleaning or doing household chores. This type of quality time is shown through Daddy Star's engagement with the children while cooking. Momma Star shows her engagement with the children by building a bed for Happy, the bunny. Such activities can be effective ways to bond—even if the parent is not engaging in a one-on-one activity with the child (Türkoğlu & Uslu, 2019).
- Caregivers (non-incarcerated and incarcerated)should also let children know that they are there for support (even if at a distance). While children may not be able to articulate all of their needs or concerns, caregivers can listen and address their questions as appropriate. Children may not understand the caregiver's answers, but they can feel a parent's love.

Having an incarcerated family member can be stressful. Caregivers are encouraged to assist children and find ways to manage personal stress and emotions. Our research showed that some of the caregivers' emotions (e.g., anger, grief, frustration, worry, anxiety) were sometimes observed in their children's behaviors (Hart-Johnson & Johnson, 2022). We call this a *mirror effect* or *dichotomous emotions*. Caregivers should also be mindful that children experience a wide array of emotions; they should let children know that these assorted feelings are normal. Recall that when Daddy Star told the children of Momma Star's incarceration, he also shed a few tears, a physical reaction indicating that Dad also missed Momma Star. Children need to know that it is okay to feel sad when bad things happen.

16.0.1 Bibliotherapy/Reading

The act of reading to children can help the parent/caregiver strengthen bonds and contribute to children's literacy skills. Researchers maintain that by 18–19 months, a child can speak approximately ten or more words. A child's vocabulary increases from about 100 words up to around 2500 words by age 5 (varying by child and exposure to reading and literacy tools). At age 5, children begin to understand story sequences. An effective way to help children identify with life situations and confront fears is to introduce storybook characters who face similar circumstances (Harris Fries, 2010). Through this vicarious experience (seeing themselves in the characters), the children learn that it is possible to overcome challenges and emerge as victors.

Harris Fries (2010) describes three pillars of bibliotherapy: Safety, Connection, and Action. **Safety** establishes a sense of trust with the reader, where they feel it is safe to explore their emotions. There is no bias or stigmatizing (in the book) that causes judgment. The reader becomes hopeful, and curious. Harris Fries further stated that **connectedness** comes when the reader can relax and settle into the story. There are illustrations of acknowledgment and validation found in stories with bibliotherapeutic principles. As a result, the reader may experience a cathartic release (Shah, 2019). Finally, the reader or the characters in the story move them from a state of helplessness and hopelessness to empowerment. Additionally, the reader creates an **action** plan. Action can be the steps taken to effect change and establish new possibilities.

16.0.2 Family Relations Assessment

Baby Star Finds "Happy" includes themes such as unique family systems; each member can take on different roles, depending upon the circumstances. In our research, and in interviews with caregivers, caregivers needed to know whom they could count on as support in the household when the disruption of family member incarceration occurred. Consider who fills the role(s) of the absent parent due to their incarceration. In the story, *Baby Star Finds "Happy,"* Daddy Star became the primary caregiver while Grandma Star offered her support when Momma Star became imprisoned. This shows a change in the family support system/roles. Caregivers with a similar situation (where someone new comes in to fill the role of the absent person) might explain to a child that mommy/daddy can have helpers to care for them while the parent is away.

A family member's roles and responsibilities can become *ambiguous* when a member goes to jail or prison. For example, sometimes, children are asked to perform additional chores or care for younger siblings. The caregiver should consider whether these chores and new responsibilities are better suited for older children or adults, as they can be overwhelming to the child(ren). Finally, caregivers should remember that kids are kids and try to include some playtime as a routine in their day. Baby Star plays intermittently in the story, conveying that children should be allowed to be children.

16.0.3 Communication

Communication with children is essential when family disruption occurs. While a child's playful behavior may be a sign of positive health, do not underestimate how a playing child could be affected. Therefore, we encourage the parents to deliberately communicate with children, asking them how they are feeling.

Recall Daddy Star's approach to family communication. His approach was truthful and honest when discussing Momma Star with the Star children. Daddy Star used the following communication strategies:

- He selected a time to discuss the absence of Momma Star when all the children were together in their safe and quiet living room.
- He used age-appropriate language which the children understood.
- He did not make promises that he could not keep.

Depending on a child's age, phone calls or letters are options to enhance parent-child communication when a parent is incarcerated. Recall that the Star children talked with Momma Star by phone. Momma Star also took responsibility for being in jail and let Baby Star know that her mom's incarceration was not Baby Star's fault.

CAREGIVER-CHILD COMMUNICATION AND BONDING (BIRTH TO 5 YEARS)

Caregivers/parents can model behavior to help children develop coping skills and create positive social relationships while building solid values. While it can be challenging to communicate when children are infants, children, however, feel love and emotions at an early age, including at birth. Consider the following tips.

° Give the child lots of love and warmth. He/she needs to feel safe and have predictable routines. Even if you are not the biological mother/father, you can be a source of comfort, predictability, love, and caring. Keep in mind that children can feel projected tension, no matter how young they are.

- Maintain routines for bathing, feeding, and playtime; daily routine provides an environment where children feel secure.
- If possible, an in-person visit with the incarcerated parent may allow the child to see the incarcerated parent and reassure the child that the parent is okay (not harmed). Explore if the prison/jail has a family-based program where the parent might bond and read with the child. Family day is an excellent way of enhancing bonding—allowing the parent to hold, feed, and talk to the child (see the storybook, *Jamie's Big Visit*). Also, consider the prison "contact visit" policy.
- The caregiver can share a picture of mom or dad or let the child hear their incarcerated parent's voice by phone or video. This activity may help to maintain contact and bonds.
- As a caregiver, you might remind the child: "Mommy and/or Daddy, Grandma [fill in the role as needed] loves you!"
- Depending on the child's stage of development, you could say: "Mommy and/or Daddy [fill in the role as needed] is away. Don't you worry, I am here for you."
- Of importance, you could remind the child: "I love you, and I am not leaving you."
- Be honest. Children may eventually learn that they have been lied to and even the best intentions can result in complex and fractured relationships.
- Be mindful of the burden of new responsibilities placed on a child. You don't want them to grow up feeling cheated out of childhood. Find the balance between assigning responsibilities and allowing playtime.
- Empower the child to make choices. This pertains mainly to children who are approaching age five. Life can feel hopeless and children may feel at fault and blame themselves for a parent's incarceration. Letting children make some decisions can give them a sense of empowerment. Remember to communicate the child's wishes with the justice-aligned parent.
- As children grow older, they may not wish to visit prison or jail. Be respectful of their choices. Each situation is unique. You as the caregiver will need to work through the best options for visits.
- Consider preschool and elementary school behaviors. Understand that a child's misbehavior in school (i.e., playing, running, talking during structured activities) might be misinterpreted. The school could be their source of relief from an otherwise stressful home environment.

16.0.4 Emotions (Caregivers and Children)

In this story, most of the focus is on Baby Star's emotions, youth, and innocence. She believes she can make anything occur, even keeping her family together when mom goes away (represented by the four-leaf-clover). In contrast, her siblings, Bick and Bell, seem less upset about their mother's incarceration. A caregiver should consider observing all children's reactions.

Specifically, Baby Star's emotions oscillate between happiness and displays of sadness, self-blame, and guilt. However, in contrast, Bick and Bell are seen running and playing and seem not to grasp the reality that their mom has gone, suggesting possible emotional resilience, or nonchalance.

ACTIVITY 61

Baby Star

Reading Activity: Reading Circle Activity for Baby Star Finds "Happy"

Time: 40- to 45-minutes
  (15 minutes, book reading and 25 minutes, discussion, 5 min. summary)
Material: *Baby Star Finds "Happy"* [Audio book if needed]
Goal: Prepare caregivers to use stories to help children cope with life *events*.
Audience: All Readers, especially Parents/Caregivers

Facilitator notes: You may tailor the procedures to a group "reading circle" by direct-ing the questions to the learners in your reading group. For in-person groups, form a semi-circle. Follow procedures 1 through 5, by informing the audience of the content. Next, ask a volunteer to read the hard copy book or use the digital version with audio to play the book. Pose questions to the group for questions identified in Activity 61.1 through 61.2).

Activity Objectives:

- To promote the caregivers' understanding of child development as it relates to separation from a parent who is incarcerated.
- To help caregivers explore options to address difficult topics using the storybook, *Baby Star Finds "Happy."*
- To promote methods of parent/caregiver-child bonding.
- To prepare and read to your child.

Procedures:

1. Prepare for the reading activity and discussion on *Baby Star Finds "Happy."* Finding a silver lining when a parent goes to jail or prison. Note that some of life's most challenging circumstances have teachable moments.

2. Recall how books help children understand complex topics.

3. ICEBREAKER: (Individual or group)Think of the name of one of your favorite childhood books or fairytales. What made the story special? Explain that stories help children believe that they are not alone in their experiences and can overcome challenges.

4. Remember that even if a child is unable to read, pictures in the books help children to figure out what is going on in the story. Pictures help children to visualize things they may not have seen or places they have never been.

5. Remember that when children are from 0 to 5 years of age: Children are like sponges. They absorb and pay attention to what is going on in their environments (even when you think they are not paying attention).

   - Children explore the world through their senses, e.g., sight, hearing, smell, taste, and touch. If they cannot use their senses to connect, it does not exist.
   - Children generally bond with their parents and become attached to their family members during infancy and early childhood.

- Reading is a means to bond with children and to help them to make meaning of their experiences.

PREPARATION

Read the book, *Baby Star Finds "Happy."*

Activity | 61.1. Questions

Activity 61.1, Question 1: Using a journal to record responses, identify ways that Baby Star's family show:

a. Love or family bonds
b. Support
c. Honesty
d. Guilt
e. Senses (sight, sound, smell, taste, and touch)
f. Communication

Activity 61.1, Question 2: Answer the following questions:

a. Why is the four-leaf clover so important to Baby Star?
b. What stands out most about Baby Star's mom? Why?
c. What was the role of Happy in the story?

Activity 61.1, Question 3:

a. Please answer the following question:
  - How would your discussion with your child compare with Momma Star's discussion with Baby Star about being in jail?
b. Please answer the following question:
  - How would your discussion with your child compare with Daddy Star's discussion with the children about mom being in jail?

See Answer Key for Activity 61.1, Questions 1 through 3 after Module 16, Reference list.

Activity | 61.2. Group Activity

Depending on the size of the group, these exercises can be modified using flip charts or virtual chat boxes.

- **Option 1.** Ask a volunteer to record any other emotions the group members personally identify with related to the story.
- **Option 2.** Ask the group to identify how Baby Star feels during stages of the book.
- **Option 3.** Ask for volunteers to engage in a role-play exercise. Ask one participant to pretend they are Daddy Star to explaining Momma Star's absence to Baby Star. Have the other participant pretend to be Baby Star. Ask Daddy Star to explain the mother's incarceration to Baby Star. Write down the audience's thoughts on how they think the discussion went. *Note any takeaways in your journal or record them here.*

Next, ask for a volunteer to role-play Momma Star and explain her absence to Baby Star. Record the steps and discussion points on a flip chart or journal.

There is no answer key for this critical thinking exercise. Facilitators and individuals draw from their own ideas and opinions.

Optional Activity | My Communication Style

ACTIVITY | 61.3

Time: 30 minutes (15 min. per activity)
Materials: Appendix C, Book: *Baby Star Finds "Happy"*
Goal: Choosing the right communication style for difficult conversations
Audience: Caregivers and Parents

You have learned about childhood emotions as it relates to engagement with stories and communication. It is important to reflect upon your notes and determine how this content applies to your family.

Objectives:
- To differentiate between parent/caregiver communication options and identify possible consequences of these choices

PROCEDURE:

This activity will reinforce learning about communication styles. (Optional—use a journal to record notes for section 1.7.)

Question 1. Consider Daddy Star's communication with the children (Direct, Indirect, or Abstain). What style did he use and why?

_____

_____

_____

Question 2. Consider how Baby Star communicated with the family. Record brief notes about her communication here:

_____

_____

_____

Question 3. Record essential components to effective family member communication. Record your thoughts about what happens when communication breaks down. Now, discuss the outcome of abstaining from discussions (e.g., Momma Star was often missing from home).

_____

_____

_____

The Answer Key for 61.3 follows the Module 16 Reference list.

References

Harris Fries, T. (2010.) Bibliotherapy and its potential applications in the foster care environment: Something a child can understand. Retrieved from https://todharrisfries.weebly.com.

Hart-Johnson, A., & Johnson, G. (2022). Caregivers' family relations assessment and communication strategies. *Science Publishing Group*, 11(5), 157–168. https://www.sciencepublishinggroup.com/article/10.11648/j.pbs.20221105.12.

Shah, B. (2019). *The concept of bibliotherapy (book therapy)*. Retrieved from https://booktherapy-by-bijal.medium.com/the-concept-of-book-therapy-165250ee8d6.

Türkoglu, B., & Uslu, M. (2019). The opinions of university graduate working mothers who have 36-60-months-old children about the quality of the time spent with their children: A phenomenological analysis. *International Journal of Progressive Education*, 15(3), 123–143.

Answer Key for Activity 61.1 Question 1

Answers: Learners were asked to use a journal to record responses, identify ways that Baby Star's family show the following characteristics. Suggested answers are below.

a. Love or family bonds: They openly express love towards each other. Baby Star shows love to her family and "Happy." Love is demonstrated through communication, togetherness, and through direct communication.

b. Support: The family supports one another during crisis.

c. Honesty: Using direct communication, Daddy Star is truthful with the children. Momma Star is truthful with Baby Star.

d. Guilt: Baby Star feels guilty because she did not find the lucky four-leaf clover. She believes that the clover has magic power to keep her family together. Momma Star may have felt guilty for becoming incarcerated, as evidenced by her apologies to Baby Star.

e. Senses (sight, sound, smell, taste, and touch): The book is filled with examples of sensory elements. For example Baby Star loves the feel of her brothers hair. The smell and taste of cooked food is a key feature of the book. The sound of the phone ringing when Momma Star calls is a key element of happiness and anticipation in the story.

f. Communication: Communication is demonstrated in many ways, including direct and honest communication between Daddy Star and the children. Momma Star and Baby Star have a honest discussion on the phone, illustrating how to get through difficult conversations.

Answer Key for Activity 61.1. Question 2

a. Why is the four-leaf clover so important to Baby Star? The clover represents hopes and dreams for an intact family.

b. What stands out most about Baby Star's mom? Why? While this answer is specific to everyone's point of view, it is clear that Baby Star's mom is creative, nurturing, and she loves the family. She is also humble enough to apologize. She takes time to explain to Baby Star using age-appropriate language that she made a mistake and she then apologizes.

c. What was the role of Happy in the story? Happy represents the symbolism of love and bonding. Happy also represents unconditional love. He represents hopes and provides Baby Star with comfort and the ability to give and receive hugs—something that she dearly wishes she could do with her mother.

Additional Insights: The clover also represents luck and Baby Star's intuition. Through her wishes, she is suggesting that something is going on in the family that needs to be addressed long before the mom goes to jail. Baby Star's mom shows some signs of being in and out of the family; disappearing at times. Happy represents emotional support for Baby Star and illustrates the power of childhood fantasy.

Answer Key for Activity 61.1. Question 3

The answers to these questions are situation. Each individual may answer the questions based on their perspectives.

   a. Please answer the following question:
   * How would your discussion with your child compare with Momma Star's discussion with Baby Star about being in jail?
   b. Please answer the following question:
   * How would your discussion with your child compare with Daddy Star's discussion with the children about mom being in jail?

Answer Key for Activity 61.2. Group Activity

There is no answer key for this critical thinking group activity. Facilitators should draw from the reading material and highlight key points to engage learners in discussion.

Answer Key for Activity 61.3.

Question 1. Direct. Daddy Star used direct communication.

Examples: He took ownership of his feelings. He listened to his family, children, and others. He told the truth to his children, using words they understood.

Question 2. Indirect. Baby Star used indirect communication.

Examples: She didn't speak up for herself until she found the clover. She felt ashamed and guilty. On one hand, she thought she held power, but on the other hand, she felt as if she had no power.

Question 3. Abstain (held no discussion on the topic). Daddy Star didn't share his concerns at the beginning of the story.

Examples: Daddy Star didn't talk to others about his feelings and how his wife's behavior may have affected him or the children.

Rocko's Guitar

(For children five to seven years)

MODULE FOCUS

- Read and analyze the children's book, *Rocko's Guitar*
- Deepen the understanding of bibliotherapy and reading circle concepts
- Understand and apply knowledge relating to children's emotions and sensory skills
- Practice reading circle exercises

Resources

Read the Book: *Rocko's Guitar*

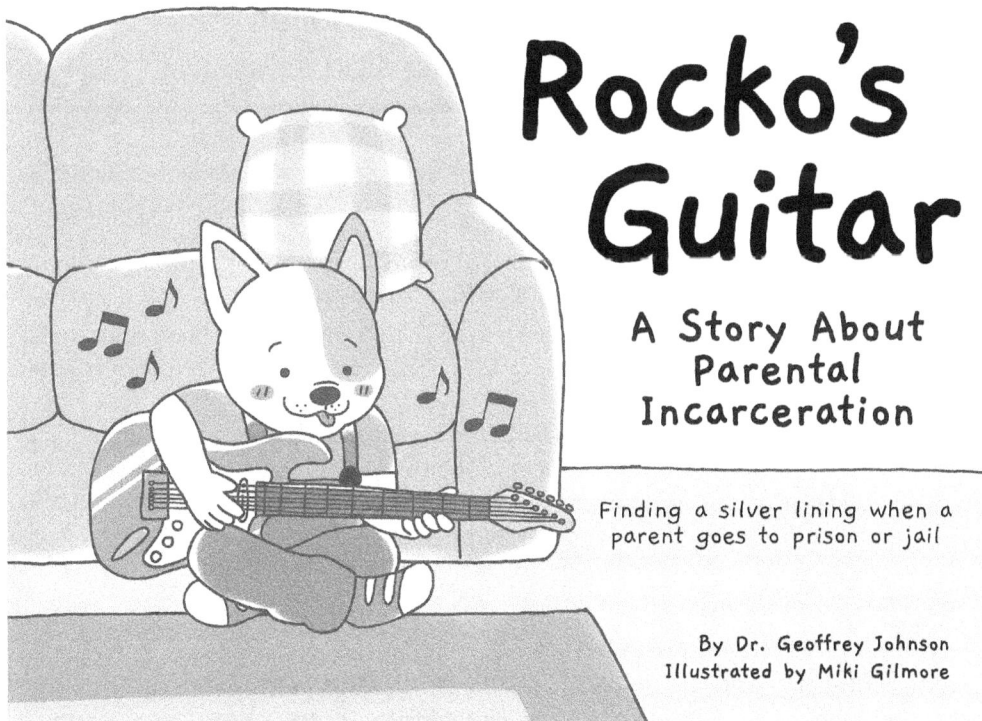

Figure 17.0 Rocko's Guitar (illustration by Miki Gilmore).

Additional Resources

Amazon.com:
Johnson, G. (2021). *Rocko's Guitar*. A Story About Parental Incarceration. Finding a silver lining when a parent goes to prison or jail. Extant-One Publishing. ISBN 9798732160369.
Review Appendix E, Helping Children Deal with Loss

Introduction

About *Rocko's Guitar*, by Dr. Geoffrey Johnson. *Rocko's Guitar* is a story about a young boy who adores his dad, a budding musician. Rocko's bond with his father soared to rocket heights when his dad gives him a cherished guitar for his 6th birthday. However, their relationship must withstand an unexpected separation. Ideally, *Rocko's Guitar* is designed for children ages 5 to 7. The book, *Rocko's Guitar*, can be used as a read-along book for young children even if they are in the early stages of development and do not understand all the words. The illustrations are designed to help children comprehend what is being read to them. Books expand literacy/vocabulary and present concepts (i.e., persons, places, things, experiences).

Section 17.0. Rocko's Guitar:
Literacy, Child Development,
and Comprehension

Materials

❖ Writing pad or journal

Section Objectives

☐ To increase parents'/caregivers' awareness of the communication options that can be used for children of incarcerated parents, using the book, Rocko's Guitar, as a tool.

☐ To increase parents'/caregivers' ability to better understand the developmental stages and emotions experienced by children (5 to 7 yrs.).

☐ To increase parents'/caregivers' self-awareness of emotions, family dynamics, and to consider possible support systems.

Overview

According to Swiss psychologist, Jean Piaget, children between the ages of 5 and 7 are at the preoperational stage of *cognitive development*. This means that they can understand and solve simple logic. They should be able to follow the sequencing of stories as well as begin to recognize problems in the stories and anticipate outcomes. According to Dr. Elaine Taylor-Klaus, children have "magical thinking," [the belief that one's ideas, thoughts, actions, words, or use of symbols can influence the course of events in the material world] (Taylor-Klaus, 2020). When they are around six years old; they also can harbor fears of being harmed, thereby adding possible stress to their young lives. There-fore, caregivers play an essential role in helping children to feel safe. Children at this age also have egocentric thinking, seeing themselves in the center of every situation, includ-ing sometimes blaming themselves when something goes wrong. A child might wrongly accept responsibility for the arrest and/or incarceration of a parent.

At this age, parents/caregivers can communicate with children and expect them to grasp the messaging provided by adults. During this stage of development, children also understand the value associated with performing tasks (e.g., homework, cleaning up their toys). These elements are identified in the story, *Rocko's Guitar.*

Foundational Learning: Reading Circle Tips

Before reading this book to children or a group, familiarize yourself with the story, *Rocko's Guitar.* You may wish to read it twice. (Alternatively, listen to the audio eBook.) Read the story once to understand the main content and a second time to understand the essence of the story and characters. This background information will help to pro-vide context to the following discussion points.

This exercise prepares you to read to your child and for a future discussion about the book and your child's emotions/observations.

- *Rocko's Guitar* illustrates that children need maternal/paternal/caregiver bonds for healthy development. Research confirms that mothers generally provide the foundation of nurturing to help children develop and build relationships inside and outside of the family.[1] At six, a boy's self-image is shaped by his father and/ or male figures in his environment. The feedback received from fathers can be internalized and used as a guide or sounding board for direction.
- Fathers play an essential role in child development, as demonstrated in the story about Rocko. Fathers also play a crucial role in their children's lives even if they are not living in the household.
- Children at the age of six often crave attention from parents and teachers. Obtaining positive and constructive feedback is often critical to the formation of their self-esteem. Rocko's air guitar performances mirror his father's passion for playing guitar and illustrate Rocko's approval-seeking behavior.
- Age six is a remarkable period for the development of cognitive skills, independence, and intellectual and emotional growth. Like Rocko, children at the age of six begin to understand the differences between themselves and others. They also begin to compare and contrast information and experiences gained from parents with those conveyed by peers and teachers at school. Rocko became very confused when his mother's account of events was challenged by the janitor.
- Caregivers should let children know that they are there for support. While children may not be able to articulate all of their needs or concerns, caregivers can listen and address a child's questions as appropriate. Rocko's mother recognized that his questions about his father would not be finished or settled in a single discussion. Rocko's mom promised ongoing communication about his father.

- School counselors and teachers are positioned to provide valuable assistance to children affected by parental incarceration; however, teachers rarely know a child's family/home circumstances. Rocko's teacher asked about his well-being after he missed a day of school. Had she known about Rocko's dad's arrest, she probably would have asked the question privately rather than in front of the entire class.
- Consider whether young children like Rocko should be burdened with maintaining family secrets such as parental incarceration. Consider having age-appropriate discussions and decide how the child should handle the truth.

17.0.1 Bibliotherapy/Reading

The act of reading to children can help the caregiver enhance bonds, as well as contribute to children's literacy skills. Researchers maintain that between 6 and 7 years of age, children use pictures to decode a story and figure out words. They begin to self-correct when making a mistake while reading. They can draw pictures of the family and/or convey their understanding of stories and express how they feel.

Bibliotherapy is guided reading: a technique or strategy that encourages children to discover and relate to the meaning of the text or the story. Reading books can stimulate children's imaginations and expand their understanding. They develop language and listening skills. This process also prepares them to better understand written words. The act of reading improves children's brain functions and increases both vocabulary and comprehension. This process can also empower children to better understand and apply empathy skills.

17.0.2 Family Relations Assessment. Rocko's Guitar

This story includes the theme that family systems and their support networks are unique. Rocko's teacher may also be a means of support for him; however, first, she must be informed about the sensitive subject of parental incarceration. With this information, the teacher could better assess a child's needs for matters such as cognitive development, attention to lessons, behavior, and temperament with adults and peers. If a child expresses extreme anxiety/distress, an educator might recommend psychological or emotional counseling. Additionally, with Rocko's dad's absence, caregivers might consider pairing the child with trusted male role models.

17.0.3 Communication

Communication with children is especially important when family disruptions occur. Rocko's mom was not truthful about his father's absence. Instead, she told Rocko that his dad was on tour overseas. Being dishonest or telling mistruths or partial truths to children can have adverse consequences. Specifically, a child will likely find out the truth through other means or people. Our research disclosed:

- As with Rocko, someone else, e.g., neighbor, family member, may tell children the truth or they may overhear a conversation that reveals inconsistencies in events/testimony.
- As the child grows older, he/she learns more, especially concerning matters involving the family.

- Untruths may result in children having parental/caregiver/adult trust issues.
- Partial truths and lies often lead to amended lies and/or additional falsehoods.

Depending on a child's age, phone calls or letters are options to maintain child-parent communication. Rocko's mom suggested that he write to his father and share events about his life.

Caregiver-Child Communication and Bonding

Caregivers/parents can model behavior to help children develop coping skills and create positive social relationships while also building solid values. Consider the following tips as benefits of reading to children ages 5 through 7:

- Promote social activities for the child to learn to engage in with other children.
- Provide opportunities for the child to develop positive attitudes and coping behaviors. For example, help the child to recognize their accomplishments in school—set examples showing positive behaviors or making the best of a challenging situation. An example might be discussing the value of writing letters to promote communication.
- Encourage the child to discuss his/her emotions and address feelings of being different or having low self-esteem. Share ways to build confidence, such as learning and mastering new skills such as reading, learning new words, excelling in sports or the arts.
- Maintain routines, such as attending school and doing homework so children feel normalcy.
- Acknowledge that children with parents who are incarcerated might be judged as being "different," and stigmatized by peers and, possibly, other adults. Deal with the elephant in the room. Such experiences may be the child's first exposure to shame and, later, stigma. It is vital to help children to understand these feelings. To the extent possible, prepare to address a child's questions. Every situation is different. Stop now and create an action plan.
- Be honest. Children may eventually learn that they have been lied to and even the best intentions can result in complex and fractured relationships later in life.
- Be mindful of the burden of sharing too much information about the arrest and incarceration itself with children. Children need to know that parents are safe and okay, not the details of a parent's alleged crime.
- Empower the child to make choices. Letting children make some decisions can give them a sense of empowerment.
- Be respectful of their choices. As children grow older, they may not wish to visit prison or jail. Each child and family dynamic are unique. You as the caregiver will need to work through specific issues and decide upon the best option for visits and other forms of communication.
- Finally, understand that children's misbehavior in school (i.e., playing, running, talking during structured activities) might be misinterpreted. The school could be their source of relief from an otherwise stressful home environment. Be sure to check in with children to understand what they are feeling.

Bridging the Communication Gap. The following ideas can be considered options to bridge the communication gap between the incarcerated parent and their children. Check with the local jail or prison to verify that these options can be implemented.

- **Consider the value of visits.** Families are unique in their make-up and interpersonal interactions and thoughts about prison/jail visits. As we have learned from our research, not every family member agrees that child visits should take place. You will have to make this decision. Consider reading *Jamie's Big Visit* to help prepare the child for the visit. This book chronicles the visiting process from the pre-visit phase through the actual visit.
- **Write letters.** Children tend to have unconditional love for their parents. While caregivers may have mixed feelings, children generally want to stay connected. Letters are an excellent means of keeping the lines of communication open. Second, writing helps children to express feelings as well as practice their literacy skills.
- **Create a time capsule.** The absence of a parent because of incarceration can be distressing to children. Little ones may face many insecurities along with feelings of separation and abandonment.[2] The incarceration of a family member can be upsetting for the entire household. At times, young children who are vulnerable to experiencing their own complex emotions may be the least informed. Events and milestones experienced without the incarcerated parent may bring about sadness. Consider the time-capsule exercise. The time capsule is a method of collecting keepsakes related to significant milestones that symbolize the event. This process is aligned with the ritual of sharing and preserving memories of moments to be shared with the parent when they return home. The item can also be discussed on the phone with the incarcerated parent (see Appendix E for ideas).

17.0.4 Emotions (Caregivers and Children)

Rocko's mom appears to have been the primary breadwinner in the household; however, she needs financial assistance to make up for lost income when Rocko's dad goes to prison. Rocko's mom is emotionally overwhelmed and uncertain how to discuss issues with Rocko. Meanwhile, Rocko's Mom has personal difficulty coping with Rocko's dad's absence.

Rocko has also never experienced life without his father. He has difficulty coping with his father's absence (as noted in his misbehavior in school).

Note: When a parent is incarcerated, it might seem easier to tell a partial truth or a lie rather than to have a truthful conversation with the child. In Rocko's story, the mom said that Dad was in Europe. However, this untruth was later uncovered. Rocko was left frustrated and confused. A teachable moment occurred when Rocko learned that he had a new support network (i.e., teacher and janitor). While circumstances in the story are challenging for Rocko, the silver lining is that he is loved and supported by all the characters in the story. See Appendix C for examples of discussions with children and their consequences.

ACTIVITY 62

Rocko's Guitar

Reading Activity: Reading Circle Activity for Rocko's Guitar

Time: 40- to 45 minutes
(15 minutes, book reading and 25 minutes, discussion, 5 min. summary)
Material: Rocko's Guitar [Audio book if needed]
Goal: Prepare caregivers to use stories to help children cope with life events.
Audience: All Readers, especially Parents/Caregivers

Facilitator notes: You may tailor the procedures to a group "reading circle" by directing the questions to the learners in your reading group. For in-person groups, form a semi-circle. Follow procedures 1 through 3, by informing and engaging the audience in the content. In step 5, ask a volunteer to read the hard copy book or use the digital version with audio to play the book. Pose questions to the group for questions identified in Activity 62.1 through 62.2).

Objectives:

☐ To promote caregivers' understanding of child development as it relates to separation from a parent who is incarcerated.
☐ To raise awareness of caregivers options that address complex topics, using Rocko's Guitar storybook.
☐ To promote methods of parent/caregiver-child bonding.

PROCEDURES:

Recall your favorite place to visit, especially during childhood. Now, journal about the experience using two or more of the five senses to describe the memory: sight, smell, taste, touch, hearing.

Note that books can be used to help children understand complex topics. Even if a child can't read, pictures in the books help children to figure out what is going on in the story. Pictures help children to visualize things they may not have seen or places they have never been.

- Prepare for reading/reviewing the story, *Rocko's Guitar*, finding a silver lining when a parent goes to jail or prison.
- Let's prepare for discussion. Remember, that when children are 5 to 7 years of age, they:
  1. Explore the world through their senses, e.g., sight, smell, taste, touch, and hearing. [refer back to how the ICE Breaker helped us better understand the concepts.]
  2. Disruptions in the household (e.g., parental incarceration) can leave a child with feelings of isolation and trust issues, especially if falsehoods or secrecy accompany the parent's absence. Children may also feel that the situation is their fault.
  3. Reading is a means to bond with children and to help them to find meaning in new situations and their experiences.

Steps:

Preparation

Read the book, *Rocko's Guitar*

Activity 62.1 Questions

If you have already read this book, please browse your notes and re-read the book as a refresher.

Activity 62.1, Question 1

Using a journal to record responses, identify ways that Rocko's family show:

- ° Love or family bonds
- ° Support
- ° Honesty
- ° Guilt
- ° Senses (sight, hearing, smell, taste, and touch)

Activity 62.1, Question 2

- • How do they communicate?

Activity 62.1, Question 3

Record responses regarding one or more of the following questions:

1. Why is the gift of a guitar so important to Rocko?
2. What stands out most about Rocko's mom? Why?
3. What was the janitor's role in the story?
4. How would your discussion with your child compare with Rocko's mom?
5. Why is the teacher's role important?
6. Now, record any other emotions that you can identify with in the story.
7. Record or write down how Rocko feels during different stages of the book.
8. As a role-play exercise, request volunteers to play Rocko's mom talking to Rocko. Ask another to play Rocko. Have the volunteer (Rocko's mom) to explain Dad's absence to Rocko. Facilitator: Record how the volunteers feel during the discussion and record main points when speaking with Rocko for audience group discussion.

Activity | 62.2 Optional

Time: 15- to 20 minutes
Material: *Rocko's Guitar* [Audio book if needed]
Goal: Hold a discussion with children; create an element of bonding.
Audience: Caregivers and their children

PROCEDURE:

Questions 62.2

1. Review the questions below. Use these questions as a discussion starter with your child or a group of children. Ask the children,

- Why is the gift of a guitar so important to Rocko?
- What stands out most about Rocko's mom? Why?
- What was the janitor's role in the story?
- How would your discussion with your child compare with Rocko's mom?
- Why is the teacher's role important?

2. Ask your child/children these questions to generate a book discussion. Remember, the idea is to enhance communication and bonding. This special attention can be very engaging and meaningful.

3. Ask the child/children who they most identify with in the book and why.

4. Finish the activity on a happy note by asking the children what makes them most happy. This helps the children to return to a state of calm rather than leaving them with thoughts about incarceration.

Note: Talking to children at this young age requires sensitivity; it may be challenging. However, in our research, we found that most parents believe they were better positioned to understand their child's needs than others outside of the family. Using storybook characters as examples, children can learn that they are not alone, the incarceration is not their fault, and that it is okay to return to being a child (e.g., playing and engaging in activities).

Optional Activities: Mending Fences

Activity | 62.3

Time: 30- to 35-minutes
Material: *Rocko's Guitar* [Audio book can be used if needed]
Goal: *Reinforce how caregivers can use stories to help children to cope with life events.*
Audience: Parents/Caregivers and Justice-Aligned Parents

Objectives:

☐ To promote caregivers' understanding of child development as it relates to separation from an incarcerated parent.
☐ To help caregivers identify options to address difficult topics, using the storybook, *Rocko's Guitar.*
☐ To understand and apply methods of parent/caregiver-child bonding.

Procedures:

1. You are going to engage in an activity called "Mending Fences." Consider what the term means to you and record responses on a flipchart (for groups) or in your journal (individual).

2. Mending fences has to do with repairing relationships damaged by disagreement, misunderstandings, or telling untruths.

3. Now, consider who in *Rocko's Guitar* needs to mend fences. List the characters by name and identify the *triggering event*. For example, the triggering event could be the cause of a fragmented relationship, a breakup, or a disagreement. As a group, discuss who needs to mend fences and why. Individuals, consider this exercise using your journal to record ideas.

The Answer Key for Activity 62.3 follows Module 17 Reference list.

References

Hart-Johnson, A. & Johnson, G. (2022). Caregivers' family relations assessment and communication strategies. *Science Publishing Group*, 11(5), 157–168. https://www.sciencepublishinggroup.com/article/10.11648/j.pbs.20221105.12.

Taylor-Klaus. E. (2020). *The essential guide to raising complex kids with ADHD, anxiety, and more: What parents and teachers really need to know to empower complicated kids with confidence and calm.* Fair Winds Press.

Answer Key for Activity 62.1

Activity 62.1, Question 1: Learners were asked to journal to record responses, identify ways that Rocko's family show the following. Here are a few examples of responses.

- ° **Love or family bonds:** Rocko's mom shows unwavering love and support as a caregiver and supporter. She helps Rocko learn ways to remain connected to his dad. She also models how to apologize and get through difficult discussions.
- ° **Support:** Rocko's teacher and Mr. Buddy learn about Rocko's circumstances and provide support. They offer to be role models and help him get through the difficulties of family member incarceration.
- ° **Honesty:** Rocko's family have worked through the challenges of being honest. On one hand his mom was a bit dishonest, but recovered through apologies. Mr. Buddy, on the other hand was very honest and perhaps disclosed information to Rocko that was not his responsibility to share.
- ° **Guilt:** It is likely that all parties felt guilty for various reasons. Rocko may have felt he was to blame for his dad's incarceration. Rocko's mom likely felt guilty for not sharing the truth about the dad, and Mr. Buddy may have felt guilty for oversharing.
- ° **Senses** (sight, hearing, smell, taste, and touch): The story highlights music (sound), the smell of food, the hugs, the graphics bring to life the characters in the story using colorful scenes.

Note: In Rocko's story, the absence of the smell of breakfast cooking in the home during certain parts of the story was significant. It indicated a loss of routine in the household (i.e., the smell of breakfast reminded Rocko of eating with Dad).

Suggested Answer for Activity 62.1, Question 2

- How do they communicate? Indirect and direct communication was used. See variations in communication listed in Appendix C.

Suggested Answers for Activity 62.1, Question 3

1. **Why is the gift of a guitar so important to Rocko?** This was the last gift that Rocko's dad gave him. It also symbolized the father-son connection, likes, and similarities relating to music. The guitar also represented father-son bonds.

2. **What stands out most about Rocko's mom?** Why? Rocko's mom is caring and supportive. She is a hard worker and clearly understands her responsibility of being a mother, provider, and a role model. She loves Rocko and honors the mantra of not talking bad about Rocko's father.

3. **What was the janitor's role in the story?** The janitor highlights how children

find out information regarding the family through third parties. He also represents potential family support.

4. How would your discussion with your child compare with Rocko's mom? This answer is situational.

5. Why is the teacher's role important? The teacher represents educators who are attuned and understanding of young children who face parental incarceration.

6. Now, record any other emotions that you can identify with in the story. This answer is situational.

7. Record or write down how Rocko feels during different stages of the book. This answer is subject to personal interpretation.

8. As a role-play exercise, request volunteers to play Rocko's mom talking to Rocko. Ask another to play Rocko. Have the volunteer (Rocko's mom) to explain Dad's absence to Rocko. Facilitator: Record how the volunteers feel related to the discussion and record main points when speaking about Rocko and his mom. Their answers are likely to be personal and situational, and subject to interpretation.

Answer Key for Questions 62.2

1. Note the answers to these questions directed to children can be drawn from the answer key for 62.1 above.

- Why is the gift of a guitar so important to Rocko?
- What stands out most about Rocko's mom? Why?
- What was the janitor's role in the story?
- How would your discussion with your child compare with Rocko's mom?
- Why is the teacher's role important?

The remainder of the questions are individual and may vary based on children's ideas.

Answer Key for 62.3 Activity

- Rocko has mended fences with his mother, Mr. Buddy, and his teacher.
- Mr. Buddy may need to mend fences with Rocko's Dad, Mom, and Rocko.

MODULE 18

Truth and the Big Dinner

(For children seven to ten years)

MODULE FOCUS

- Read and analyze the children's book, *Truth and the Big Dinner*
- Deepen an understanding related to bibliotherapy and reading circle concepts
- Practice reading circle skillsets and exercises

Resources

Read the Book: *Truth and the Big Dinner*
Amazon.com:
Hedrington-Jones, R.A. (2021). *Truth and The Big Dinner*. A Story About Parental Incarceration. Finding a
    Silver lining when a parent goes to prison or jail. Extant-One Publishing. ISBN 9780996741026
Review Appendix E, Helping Children Deal with Loss

Introduction

Truth and the Big Dinner, by Dr. Renata Hedrington-Jones. *Truth and the Big Dinner* is a story about a little girl named "Truth," who is learning about her self-identity and the importance of self-image. For Truth, the big dinner is a day that she can show off her new hairdo and her affectionate relationship with her mom. She loves her big family. However, they all have concealed the big secret: Truth's mommy is not coming home for the big dinner because she is incarcerated. The book, *Truth and the Big Dinner* can be used as a read-along book for young children in this age group of 7 to 10, or they can read the story themselves.

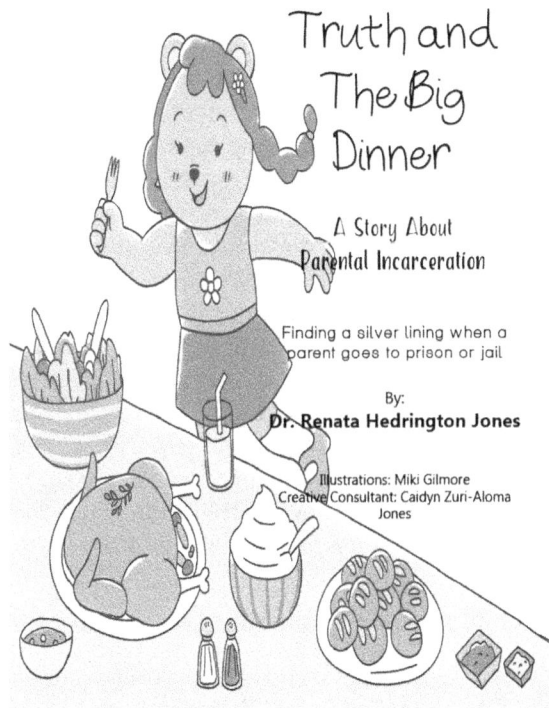

Figure 18.0 Truth (illustration by Miki Gilmore).

293

Section 18.0. Truth and the Big Dinner: Literacy, Child Development, and Comprehension

Materials

❖ Writing pad or Journal

Section Objectives

☐ To increase parents'/caregivers' awareness of the communication options that can be used for children of incarcerated parents, using the book, *Truth and the Big Dinner*, as a tool.

☐ To increase parents'/caregivers' ability to better understand the developmental stages and emotions experienced by children (5 to 7 yrs.).

☐ To increase parents'/caregivers' self-awareness of emotions, family dynamics, and to consider possible support systems.

Overview

At ages 7 through 10, children can conceptualize and process information related to stories. They are curious and begin to think through situations logically. They even begin problem-solving. Caregivers, parents, and justice-aligned individuals should interact and communicate with children with honesty (Themes brought out in *Truth and the Big Dinner*). Children can learn how to solve problems through modeling the behaviors of the parents/caregivers.

In *Truth and the Big Dinner*, the author advises that working through the dilemmas surrounding telling the truth may be painful; however, it can improve the lives of children, the caregiver, and the justice-aligned parent. Telling the truth might also help children cope with future conflicts and challenges.

When a parent is incarcerated, adults and family members may resort to "hiding the truth" from children, or instead, provide "false" information and responses to questions children ask about the absent parent. Based on our knowledge and research, hiding the truth is often done because the parent may not have the right tools to initiate discussions, or they may not feel comfortable sharing the truth. However, our research also revealed that it is better to share age-appropriate truth than to tell a lie.

Foundational Learning: Reading Circle Tips

Before reading this book to children or a group, familiarize yourself with the story, *Truth and The Big Dinner*. You may wish to read it twice (Alternatively, listen to the audio eBook). Read the story, first, to understand the main context and a second time to understand the essence of the story and characters. This background information will help to provide context to the following discussion points.

This exercise prepares you to read to your child and for a future discussion about the book and your child's emotions/observations.

- *Truth and The Big Dinner* illustrates the value of family support in addressing a child's needs. Research confirms that mothers generally provide the foundation of nurturing to help children to develop and to build relationships inside and outside of the family.[1]
- As children grow and develop, it is essential that family members are supportive and model ways to help children cope with life's conflicts and challenges.
- Research has shown that quality time can include just being near a child when going about daily routines such as cleaning or doing household chores. This type of quality time is shown when Truth and her cousins sit and play while her aunts prepare food and set the dinner table. Engagement with children in a variety of situations is important and can be effective ways to (model and) bond—even if the parent is not engaging in a one-on-one activity with the child (Türkoğlu & Uslu, 2019).
- Caregivers should also let children know that they are there for support. While children may not be able to articulate all their needs or concerns, caregivers can listen and address their questions as appropriate. In this regard, children may not understand the caregiver's answers, but they can feel a parent's concerns and love. Therefore, caregivers should try to provide a secure, safe, and trusting environment.

18.0.1 Bibliotherapy/Reading

The act of reading to children can help the caregiver enhance bonds as well as contribute to children's literacy skills. Reading or being read to can serve as a source for modeling behaviors to help children learn how to understand and build positive interpersonal relationships. These models can also help children develop communication and conversation skills. Pre-adolescent children generally have a vocabulary of 10,000 words or more.

Children can benefit both from reading *Truth and the Big Dinner*, as well as having the story read with them and discussed by a parent. By the time a child reaches 7 years of age, they can identify words, sentences, begin to create rhymes, express ideas through writing, and they can identify and spell frequently used words. Children at the developmental stage of age seven to ten recognize sequence and can begin to predict what will occur next in stories. They tend to read and reread specific stories and insert their versions or renditions of events. Children may also use a book's illustrations as visual cues to understand the dynamics of story characters and events. In this regard, *Truth and the Big Dinner* provides child-friendly illustrations to help children learn about family system dynamics when a parent is removed from the family unit via incarceration.

Reading can shape social skills and contribute to the healthy development of self-esteem. This can be especially true when the character of a story is shown to overcome their challenges.

WAYS TO HELP CHILDREN BUILD SELF-ESTEEM AND SELF-IMAGE:

- Allow room for imperfection or failure.
- Love children unconditionally. Tell them and remind them of their strength, beauty, and positive characteristics.

- Encourage them to develop new skills (contributes to self-efficacy).
- Reassure them through the growth process of developing new skills and forming their identities.
- Congratulate the child on their milestone accomplishments.
- Create a "safe space" for discussions, especially for topics dealing with parental incarceration. Be the place of truth. Allow the child to vent and share how they are feeling. Practice having this discussion in your mind or with someone you trust!
- Do not solve the problem for the child. Help the child to develop problem-solving skills with your guidance.

18.0.2 Family Relations Assessment

Truth and The Big Dinner includes themes that show family systems are unique and that family members can take on different roles depending upon the circumstances. For example, Auntie Lou Lou became the primary caregiver for Truth, while Auntie Alice and Auntie Ellen offered Truth support when her mother became imprisoned. Caregivers with similar family dynamics might explain to a child that mommy/daddy has helpers to support and care for them.

This book also provides tips on navigating family relationships and working through challenging discussions like parental incarceration with children. Although Truth's family is not perfect, they offer her a network of enduring love and support. In this regard, apologies can be an important component to mending fences when needed. [See Mending Fences Activities]

Notes: Truth's self-image and self-identity are repeated themes in the story. Truth places importance on looking as beautiful as the other children in the family, even her aunts. Maternal incarceration could exacerbate feelings of stigma and shame and devalue Truth's self-perception and self-image. Addressing Truth's concerns with sensitivity, love, and support may be vital to establishing her self-worth and self-image, being a pre-adolescent female.

18.0.3 Communication

When family disruption occurs, using direct communication (honest, focused, and direct language) with children is essential. Truth's aunts were not truthful with her concerning her mother's incarceration. The aunts used the following communications:

- The family abstained from using direct communication.
- They waited until they had no other choice but to reveal that Truth's mother was not coming to dinner. This illustrates the difficulties that families often face when discussing parental incarceration. The story offers a means to overcome such shortcomings by providing a safe, loving, and supportive environment to discuss sensitive topics and be truthful.
- Age-appropriate language was used to discuss Truth's mother's absence. The aunts did not provide details about the crime but instead spoke to Truth to address concerns about the mom's well-being.
- The story provides a glimpse into several family-member characters and the Big

Dinner. The story illustrates that children should be reminded that life can pose challenges, but family member support can make things bearable.

- Truth asked questions that girls between the ages of 7 to 10 tend to be curious about. Through honesty, the family was better prepared to address Truth's questions.

Caregiver-Child Communication and Bonding

- With proper support, children in this age range (7 to 10) with a justice-aligned parent can avoid the risk for developmental regression (returning back to prior childhood behaviors that have been mastered, such as bedwetting, thumb-sucking, and other forms of self-soothing), poor self-concept, traumatic stress, and impaired ability to deal with future trauma (Travis, McBride, & Solomon, 2005).[2]
- Recall that Truth has concerns or may question her self-image. To address apprehensions, reinforce notions that children are loved and possess their own special/unique beauty. Consider particular ways to help the child build positive self-perceptions and images.
- A child in this stage of development should have acquired basic reading skills. *Truth and the Big Dinner* can be read with the child assisting, or the caregiver and child can take turns reading to one another. If the child avoids reading aloud, do not force it, but consider letting him or her comment on the story or possibly turn pages of the book. In other words, do not force the engagement. It is crucial to establish positive interaction when reading so that the activity does not become a burdensome task that the child wants to avoid.
- Reading a book to children can be a bonding experience. Children might have unaddressed questions about their incarcerated parents. Encourage questions from the child. This may provide insights into their feelings.
- Regardless of the child's development, the use of age-appropriate language during discussions should be based on honesty. Caregivers should attempt to model behavior based on integrity and truth.

18.0.4 Emotions

Truth and the Big Dinner takes readers on the journey of a fragile time in a youth's preparation for and attendance at a big family dinner and her anticipation to spend time with her mother. The author reminds us that telling children the truth about difficult/complicated topics such as parental incarceration "may require bravery and courage." Truth, the story's central character, was not told about her mother's whereabouts or that her mother would not be attending the big family dinner. The family's intentions to protect Truth by not sharing these details resulted in her being so emotionally upset that Truth cried in front of her family after being told about her mother's imprisonment. This single moment could have ruined the big dinner, except for the love and support of Truth's family unit.

ACTIVITY 63

Truth and the Big Dinner

Reading Activity: Reading Circle Activity for *Truth and the Big Dinner*

Time: 40- to 45-minutes
   (15-minute Book reading and 25 minutes discussion, 5-minute summary)
Material: *Truth and the Big Dinner* [Audio book can be used if needed]
Goal: Prepare caregivers to use stories to help children cope with life events
Audience: All Readers, especially Parents/Caregivers

Facilitator notes: You may tailor the procedures to a group "reading circle" by directing the questions to the learners in your reading group. For in-person groups, form a semi-circle. Follow procedures 1 through 2, by informing and engaging the audience in the content. In the *preparation* step, ask a volunteer to read the hardback book or use the digital version with audio. Pose questions to the group for Question 63.1 and 63.2, and optional activities.

Objectives:

☐ To increase caregivers' understanding of child development as it relates to separation from an incarcerated parent.
☐ To understand and assess communications options to address difficult topics using the storybook, Truth and the Big Dinner.
☐ To understand and practice methods of parent/caregiver-child bonding.
☐ To learn about the value of family during challenging times.

Procedures:

1. Icebreaker: Please think about your favorite meal when you were a child. What made the meal special? Who attended dinner?
2. Now you are going to engage in a reading circle activity related to *Truth and the Big Dinner*, finding a silver lining when a parent goes to jail or prison.

Remember, books can be used to help children understand complex topics, e.g., *making difficult decisions/choices*. Reinforce that even if a child cannot read, pictures in the books can help them to figure out what is going on in the story. Illustrations help children to visualize things they may not have seen.

Let's prepare for the discussion. Remember that when children are at the age of 7 to 10 years:

a. They begin to use comprehension skills.
b. Their logic is often based on personal experience.
c. They read and converse about books and life experiences.
d. They begin to understand concepts like cause and effect and consequences for actions taken in stories and life.
e. Peer influences become a vital component of their socialization.

Now is an excellent time to review *Truth and the Big Dinner* notes or reread the book to become familiar.

PREPARATION

Read the book, *Rocko's Guitar*

ACTIVITY 63.1

If you have already read this book, please browse your notes and re-read the book as a refresher.

Activity 63.1, Question 1:

Using a journal to record responses, identify ways that Rocko's family show:

Please consider the following and record responses (or journals), the ways that Truth's family demonstrate:

- Love or family bonds
- Support
- Honesty
- Guilt
- Consequences
- Communication

Activity 63.2

Please answer one or more of the following questions,

1. How did Aunty Lou Lou communicate with the family?
2. What does the Big Dinner represent in Truth's family?
3. What is the role of the aunties and grandmothers in the story?
4. How is Truth's image of herself and self-worth linked to the story of her mom's incarceration?
5. What is the significance of the "Tree" in between the houses?
6. What would have happened if no one ever told Truth about her mother's situation?

Note: The tree symbolizes a family tree.

See Answer Key for Activities 63.1 and 63.2 are found after the Module 18, References list.

ACTIVITY | 63.3 OPTIONAL FAMILY MATTERS

Time: 20 minutes
Material: *Truth and the Big Dinner* [Audio book if needed]
Goal: Prepare caregivers to use reflection as a tool to better understand children's emotions.
Audience: All Readers, especially Parents/Caregivers

READING CIRCLE OPTIONAL ACTIVITIES:

Note answers on a flipchart for groups and in a journal for individual reflections.

- Please reflect and record your answers. What are other emotions you can identify within the story, *Truth and the Big Dinner*?
- Please reflect and record your answers. What emotions does Truth display in various points of the story?
- As a role-play exercise, pretend you are Auntie Lou Lou. Explain Mom's absence to Truth. Please reflect and record your answers in your journal noting the page number.

Note: Children between the age of 7 and 10 years are curious about family matters. A caregiver might recognize that children at this age are genuinely pre-adolescents. They ask questions and they begin to figure out missing pieces to the puzzle. Recall that when the family started talking about consequences, Truth demanded to know what consequences had to do with her mother. Children at this age can handle age-appropriate truth. They may not need to know the details of their parent's alleged crimes, but caregivers should consider the potential damage of telling children partial truths and lies rather than the truth. Working through the dilemmas of telling the truth and not keeping secrets might improve the lives of children, the caregiver, and the justice-aligned parent.

Truth and the Big Dinner illustrates the importance of family support. This support is especially important when children are growing and developing their self-image. This children's book also emphasizes the importance of conversations and discussions. At times, children are described as being out of sight and in another room, playing. However, this book describes how even though Truth played with her cousins, she still worried about her mom's whereabouts.

The children also overheard the adult's conversations and were affected. Caregivers are reminded that children can play and worry at the same time. Be prepared to address their questions and issues if they come up.

There is no answer key for this critical reflection exercise.

ACTIVITY | 63.4 WHO'S GOT MY BACK?

Time: 20- to 30-minutes
Material: *Truth and the Big Dinner* [Audio book can be used if needed]
Journal or note pad
Goal: *Reinforce the importance of family support systems.*
Audience: Parents/Caregivers and Justice- Aligned Parents

Objectives:

☐ To reinforce the importance of caregivers' support systems during stressful events.
☐ To help caregivers understand and explore options of seeking advice and resources when addressing difficult topics with children.
☐ To promote methods of parent/caregiver-child bonding through communication.

Procedures:

1. Now you are going to engage in an activity called "Who's Got My Back?"

2. Think of examples of what the phrase, "Who's got my back" really means? Jot that down in your journal.

3. The term refers to those who look out for us when we are not feeling as though we can accomplish life tasks by ourselves or when we are stressed or overwhelmed.

4. Make note that sometimes people who are outside of our family circle and networks such as helping professionals and trusted individuals can be a means of support. Friends have held that position as *having your back*. Sometimes, people who barely know you, *have your back*!

5. Think about Truth's mother. What support could she draw from the mother? How could she request this support?

Hint: the mother could provide verbal reassurance, encouraging words, and remind Truth that the circumstances is not her fault.

References

Hart-Johnson, A. & Johnson, G. (2022). Caregivers' family relations assessment and communication strategies. *Science Publishing Group*, 11(5), 157–168. https://www.sciencepublishinggroup.com/article/10.11648/j.pbs.20221105.12.

Türkoglu, B., & Uslu, M. (2019). The opinions of university graduate working mothers who have 36–60-months-old children about the quality of the time spent with their children: A phenomenological analysis. *International Journal of Progressive Education*, 15(3), 123–143.

Answer Key for Activity 63.1

Learners were asked to use a journal to record responses, identify ways that Truth's family demonstrated:

- **Love or family bonds:** There were family gatherings, fellowship, and they showed connectedness. They valued rich family tradition of cooking and pot luck dinners. They also illustrated the family bonds through coming together during non-holidays.
- **Support:** Each of the adults in the story illustrated support in a number of ways, including holding family meetings and supporting Truth. They told Truth that she was beautiful and reminded her of her strengths.
- **Honesty:** The story illustrates being slightly dishonest through omission of facts. Then the family became more open and honest with Truth.
- **Guilt:** In different aspects of the story, everyone likely felt guilty about not being forthcoming with the truth. One of the children may have felt guilty because they teased Truth about her mother's absence.
- **Consequences:** After the family meeting, the family members discussed the importance of truth-telling and the consequences.
- Communication

Answer Key for Activity 63.2

1. How did Aunty Lou Lou communicate with the family? Aunty Lou Lou used both abstention (abstained from telling Truth where her mom was, initially). Then she used direct communication when she sat Truth down and told her the truth at the family dinner.

2. What does the Big Dinner represent in Truth's family? The Big Dinner represents family tradition, bonding, culture, and the idea of: It takes a village to raise a child.

3. What is the role of the aunties and grandmothers in the story? There are many Aunties and relatives to support Truth. They represent the extended family network as support.

4. How is Truth's image of herself and self-worth linked to the story of her mom's incarceration? The answer is open and subject to learner discussion and interpretation. It is up to learners to ponder this answer using what they have learned about communication.

5. What is the significance of the "Tree" in between the houses? The tree represents the strong family tree and support network.

6. What would have happened if no one ever told Truth about her mother's situation? The answer is open and subject to learner discussion and interpretation.

It is up to learners to ponder this answer using what they have learned about communication. Hint: Recall what happened in *Rocko's Guitar* when Mr. Buddy shared the truth with Rocko.

Answer Key for Activity | 63.3 Optional Family Matters

The answers to 64.3 are situational and subject to learner's interpretations. Facilitators, read the section module to become familiarized with the content, to guide the discussion.

Answer Key for Activity |63.4 Optional Family Matters

The answers to 64.4 are situational and subject to learner's interpretations. Facilitators, read the section module to become familiarized with the content, to guide the discussion.

Jamie's Big Visit

(For children ten years and under)

MODULE FOCUS

☐ Read and analyze the children's book, *Jamie's Big Visit*
☐ Deepen an understanding of bibliotherapy and reading circle concepts
☐ Practice reading circle exercises

Resources

Read the Book: *Jamie's Big Visit*

Figure 19.0 Jamie (illustration by Andy Hong).

Additional Resources

Hart-Johnson, A. (2017). *Jamie's Big Visit.* Grownup Timeout. Prison Visits and a Parent's Incarceration. Extant-One Publishing. ISBN 9798702126258.
Review Appendix E, Helping Children Deal with Loss

Introduction

About Jamie's Big Visit, by Dr. Avon Hart-Johnson. *Jamie's Big Visit* is a story about a child in elementary school whose father has left him to experience grownup time-out (incarceration). This story chronicles Jamie's experiences before, during, and after his prison visit. This guide helps a parent or caregiver to explain and alleviate the possible fear associated with a child's first prison visit. This book, *Jamie's Big Visit*, can be used as a read-along book for young children in the age group of 10 and under, or they can read the story themselves.

Section 19.0. Jamie's Big Visit: Literacy, Child Development, and Comprehension

---

Materials

❖ Writing pad or journal

Section Objectives

☐ To increase parents'/caregivers' awareness of the communication options that can be used for children of incarcerated parents using the book, Jamie's Big Visit, as a tool
☐ To learn how to prepare children for their first visit with an incarcerated parent
☐ To raise awareness about parents '/caregivers' family dynamics and need for support resources

Overview

Visiting a prison or a jail can be an unfamiliar and challenging, yet an exciting experience for children. Equipment, furniture, and even people may seem unusually big (i.e., big key chains, large doors that are also loud, and the building itself may be huge). Additionally, the rules and conditions of a prison visit might be quite different from non-custodial environments (for example, restrictions might apply, such as assigned seating, command and control oversight, and limited movement). However, there are a few parallels that parents can draw upon to prepare the child for this experience and explain the nature of the prison visiting environments. One similarity is comparing the metal detectors to the screenings and security checks at airports. Remember, no two prisons/jails are identical. Standard security features include limits on bringing in personal belongings and restrictions on physical contact. *Jamie's Big Visit* attempts to address some of these scenarios through age-appropriate humor, language, and illustrations.

At this age, parents'/caregivers can communicate with children and expect them to grasp the conversations with adults.

Foundational Learning: Reading Circle Tips

Before reading this book to children or a group, familiarize yourself with the story, *Jamie's Big Visit*. You may wish to read it twice (Alternatively, listen to the audio eBook). Read the story, first, to understand the main context and a second time to understand the essence of the story and characters. This background information will help to provide context to the following discussion points.

This exercise prepares you to read to your child and for a future discussion about the book and your child's emotions/observations.

Jamie's Big Visit illustrates children's need for structured and routine activities. These activities help children to establish feelings of normalcy. Simple engagement such as having breakfast or dinner together may bring about predictability and help children to feel their lives are normalizing.

The world seems big and prisons may seem even bigger and frightening to children. There are many themes in the story, *Jamie's Big Visit*. These themes illustrate how intimidating a large prison might be for a child. Embracing the size and comparing the prison to non-threatening environments may help prepare the child by setting expectations for the visit. However, do not minimize that large structures with barbed wire can be scary. Therefore, children should be prepared for visits. Remember,

- Children will probably ask questions about the safety and well-being of the incarcerated parent. Try to prepare for questions using age-appropriate responses. The incarcerated parent may have suggestions and guidance on topics as well.
- Some children will ask about the physical restrictions of hugging a mom or dad during a visit. Be prepared to explain concepts such as restrictions and prison rules.
- School counselors and teachers are positioned to provide valuable assistance to children affected by parental incarceration; however, teachers rarely know a child's family/home circumstances.
- All children and circumstances involving parental incarceration are unique. Consider whether young children like Jamie should be burdened with maintaining family secrets such as parental incarceration. Caregivers should assess the benefits of having age-appropriate, truthful discussions with their children.

Note: *Jamie's Big Visit* helps parents to understand that while the complexities of a family member's incarceration can be stressful, children's emotional needs should also be considered. Please consider Appendix B, Do's and Don'ts.

19.0.1 Bibliotherapy/Reading

Ideally, a caregiver/ parent can use this book as a read-along to encourage a child's development and awareness. Children can also draw pictures conveying their understanding of stories and express how they feel. Recall that Jamie's mom helped him draw pictures to share with his dad. These pictures became a vital communication link between Jamie and his dad. Using the children's pictures, parents and caregivers can discuss what the child drew and the child's interpretations of *Jamie's Big Visit* and how it relates to their own experiences.

The act of reading to children introduces them to concepts such as numbers, letters, colors, places, events in a fun and safe manner. Children learn listening skills, and reading books assists with vocabulary building, and memory development. As young readers, they might quickly recognize that there is a big, wonderful world all around them, and reading enhances caregiver-child bonds and contributes to children's literacy skills. Recall that Jamie's dad would read stories to him. Jamie loved this time and experience with his father and dreamed about visiting all the places his dad read about. Also, some children under 10 years of age may be able to read some stories on their own.

19.0.2 Family Relations Assessment

Jamie's Big Visit includes themes that family systems are unique and family members can take on different roles, depending upon the circumstances. For example, Jamie's mom recognized that he needed routines similar to experiences of walking in the evenings with Dad. Jamie's mom felt that it was important for Jamie to communicate with his dad via phone calls and letters. Mom also modified her behavior to eat breakfast with Jamie rather than sleeping late.

19.0.3 Communication

Communication with children is especially important when family disruptions occur, such as a family member's imprisonment. Children also need to be prepared for unfamiliar environments such as prison visits.

Finally, Jamie's mother used direct communication and was truthful about Jamie's father's absence. When Jamie's mom discussed his dad's incarceration, she also broadened Jamie's awareness of the world. For instance, she discussed the court's role in determining how long Dad would be away.

As noted, depending on a child's age, phone calls or letters are options to assist child-parent communication. Jamie's mom also suggested that he write to his dad and inform him of events in his life.

Caregiver-Child Communication and Bonding

° Give the child lots of love and warmth. This can be demonstrated through family activities, paying attention to children when they speak, scheduling one-on-one time with them, and attending events related to their growth, development, and recreational engagement.

° As with children in the age mentioned above ranges, maintaining routines such as attending school and performing homework so children feel normalcy is essential. Schools provide a sense of structure and predictability. This can be a source of comfort and help children feel that their lives are not spiraling beyond their control.

° An in-person visit allows the child to see and process the status of the incarcerated parent. Explore if the prison/jail has a family-based program where the parent might bond and read with the child. Family day enhances bonding, allowing the parent possibly to hold, feed, and talk to the child with fewer restrictions.

  ° Also, keep in mind that the child may not wish to visit a prison. Prisons may
    be an imagined scary place to visit. Consider empowering the child to make
    choices. Life can feel hopeless and children may feel angry or indifferent, or
    even at fault, and blame themselves for a parent's incarceration. Letting children
    make some decisions can give them a sense of empowerment.
  ° The drive to the prison can be lengthy. Activities such as listening to music,
    reading, playing video games, or having a discussion about what topics will be
    discussed with the parent might be ways to use the time effectively and reduce
    both anxiety and boredom.

Consider a Visit

The following ideas can be considered as options to bridge the communication gap
between the incarcerated parent and their children. Check with the local jail or prison
to verify that these options can be implemented.

  ° Consider a visit. Visiting a loved one in prison requires planning and
    preparation. A caregiver must determine where the prison is located and
    acquiring a means of transportation to get there. Many prisons are located in
    remote, rural areas away from towns and cities so transportation can be tricky.
    Long trips will require considerations for food and rest stops. Before getting on
    the road, caregivers need to determine the facility's hours of operation, length of
    visits, rules for visits, and acceptable shoes and clothing for adults and children.
    Also, verify the maximum number of persons allowed per visit. As we have
    learned from our research, not every family member may agree that children
    should visit parents in prison. You will have to weigh the pros and cons and
    make this decision. If visits are planned, consider reading Jamie's Big Visit to
    help prepare the child for this experience.
  ° Write letters. While caregivers may have mixed feelings, children generally
    want to stay connected to their parents. Children tend to have unconditional
    love for their incarcerated parents. Letters are a cost-effective means of
    keeping the lines of communication open. Second, writing helps children to
    practice literacy and writing skills.
  ° Set common goals. Children may feel a sense of connectedness by setting common
    goals with their incarcerated parents, such as establishing vocational or academic
    goals. Journaling might bring about important reflections to be shared during a
    phone call and even be used to record goals, milestones, and events.

19.0.4 Emotions (Caregivers and Children)

Both Jamie and Mom felt sadness. Throughout the story, there are times when they
both encounter similar emotions. For example, they both were emotionally stressed
when standing in line for the prison visit. Parents need to be sensitive that children may
pick up on and feel emotions of their parents or caregivers, similar to their own.

Jamie's emotions in many ways mirror his mom's emotions. However, Jamie has
one special gift from his dad that seems to help him cope during challenging and emotional periods—his cherished key chain. This gift from Dad takes on magical power and
symbolic significance.

ACTIVITY 64

Jamie's Big Visit

Reading Activity: Reading Circle Activity for Jamie's Big Visit

---

Time: 40- to 45-minutes
Material: *Jamie's Big Visit* [Audio book can be used if needed]
Goal: Prepare caregivers to use stories to help children cope with life events
Audience: All Readers, especially Parents/Caregivers

Facilitator notes: You may tailor the procedures to a group "reading circle" by directing the questions to the learners in your reading group. For in-person groups, form a semi-circle. Follow procedures 1 through 4, by informing and engaging the audience in the content. In step 6, ask a volunteer to read the hard copy book or use the digital version with audio to play the book. Pose questions to the group for 64.1 and 64.2, and optional activities.

Objectives:

☐ To promote caregivers' understanding of the child's emotions as it relates to separation from an incarcerated parent.

☐ To help caregivers explore options to address difficult topics associated with parental incarceration and assist preparation for children visiting a prison: Storybook, *Jamie's Big Visit*.

☐ To provide caregivers with options to discuss prison or jail visits.

☐ To promote methods of parent/caregiver-child bonding.

Procedures:

1. Icebreaker: Think about what it is like to visit a prison for the first time. What does it bring to mind? How does it feel?

   a. Now, write down that experience using two or more of the five senses to describe the memory: sight, smell, taste, touch, hearing. (Record in your journal). *Example: The sound of the prison doors reminds me of hearing iron beams crashing to the ground. The smell of the waiting room takes me back to my first time visiting a hospital where the smell of bleach was in the air.*

2. Now you are going to engage in a reading activity related to *Jamie's Big Visit*, finding a silver lining when a parent goes to jail or prison.

3. During this process, we will identify how *Jamie's Big Visit* can be used to help children understand complex topics related to incarceration or a prison visit. Pictures help children to visualize things they may not have seen or places they have never been.

4. Prepare for discussion. Remember that when children are under ten years of age and visiting a prison:

   a. Prison environments are often restrictive, and children may have difficulties sitting still for long periods.

   b. Where physical constraints exist, the parents/caregivers can find creative ways to show love, such as through a "wink" or a smile.

   c. Children should be reminded that their parent still loves them even though traditional movement and touching may not be permitted.

PREPARATION

Read the book, *Jamie's Big Visit*

Activity 64.1 Questions

If you have already read this book, please browse your notes and re-read the book as a refresher.

Using your journal, record responses. Identify ways that Jamie's parents show/display:

- ° Love or family bonds
- ° Support
- ° Honesty
- ° Guilt
- ° Senses (sight, hearing, smell, taste, and touch)

Activity 64.2 Questions

Please read and record answers to one or more of the following questions:

- ° Why is the key chain so important to Jamie?
- ° What stands out most about Jamie's mom? Why?
- ° How would your discussion with your child compare with Jamie's mom?
- ° In what ways is the corrections officer an important character in the story? Why?

Optional Activities:

- ° What other emotions can you identify within the story?
- ° How does Jamie feel during different stages of the book?
- ° As a role-play exercise, pretend to be Jamie's mom speaking to Jamie. Explain dad's absence to Jamie. You may journal your responses and make notes about how you felt when performing the exercise.

Note: Talking to young children about prison or jail visits requires sensitivity and it may be challenging. Using *Jamie's Big Visit* and companion stories as examples, children can prepare for prison visits and anxieties can be alleviated.

ACTIVITY: COLOR MY WORLD

ACTIVITY | 64.3

Time: 20 to 25 minutes
Material: *Jamie's Big Visit* [Audio book if needed]
    Appendix D Coloring Activity Sheet (or a blank sheet of paper)
Goal: Engage in parent-child activity regarding their feelings/emotions and ideas
Audience: All Readers, especially Parents/Caregivers

COLOR MY WORLD

You can use a coloring activity (Appendix D Coloring Activity) to guide your children and discuss their illustrations and feelings. Be prepared for a wide range of emotions. Children may not have all the words to address their feelings, but the important thing is, to be honest, and tell them they are safe and loved.

Now, demonstrate how you would ask your children about their feelings. Using the coloring book activity in (Appendix D Coloring Activity), draw a portrait of yourself standing in front of the home. What are you feeling? Now, draw your child/children. What are each of the children doing and how are they feeling? Now, consider how you wish your child/children to feel in the future. Make a separate drawing to illustrate your wishes.

PARENT-CHILD ACTIVITY

Children can be guided by the parent to express their feelings using the above activity, geared toward parent-child engagement. Note: It is not necessary to use the picture/illustration in Appendix D. You may simply draw a self-portrait on a blank sheet of paper or in your journal.

Note: Remember, parenting children is not always easy. Each person has unique skills and strengths and there are generally ample opportunities to improve family relations. Sometimes, a problem can be solved by requesting the support of a family member, friend, or outside resource. While elements of incarceration tend to make situations more complex, it is not impossible to overcome these challenges. Try to find the silver lining in these situations. Some of life's biggest challenges contribute to building resilience, growth, and positive outcomes. Think about these notes, as you engage in this creative activity.

OPTIONAL ACTIVITY: A KID'S FEELINGS

ACTIVITY | 64.4

Time: 20 to 30 minutes (5 minutes, book review and 20–25 minutes, discussion)
Material: *Jamie's Big Visit* [Audio book can be used if needed] and flip chart
Goal: Identify how children are responding to a visit (before and after)
Audience: Parents/Caregivers and Justice-Aligned Parents

Objectives:

☐ To promote caregivers' understanding of a child's emotions before and after a prison/jail visit.
☐ To help caregivers explore options to address difficult topics about jail/prison visits using the storybook, *Jamie's Big Visit*
☐ To plan and prepare a young child for a visit to a jail/prison to see a parent/family member.

Procedures:

1. Prepare to engage in an activity called "A Kid's Feelings."
2. What impressions do you have of jail or prison visits? Record this feedback in the journals.
3. Now, let's pretend to plan a visit for your child (this is a mock exercise). What are the steps required for preparation (visitor list, website review of rules, transportation, attire/clothing, preparing the child for the actual physical visit, the return home, and processing the visit afterward)? Assess whether the child needs to adjust emotionally both before and after the visit. Talk through the ideas about the visit. Use a journal to record answers.
4. Pretend you are Jamie as he is waiting for his dad to return home and he overhears his mom speaking on the phone (p. 9). What are Jamie and his mom feeling as they wait? Is Jamie's mom responsive to these feelings? Why or Why not? Discuss the importance of recognizing nonverbal expressions of concern with children. You may revisit the book to answer these questions.
5. Using a journal for recording answers, point out how Jamie felt in the story, *Jamie's Big Visit*, when making the drive to Grandma's house. How did Jamie feel during the car ride to the prison?

Using the table, describe how Jamie was feeling at each stage of the process Use the book to reference: Page 3–4 (receiving the keychain); Page 15–16 (the discussion); Page 29–30 (the waiting), Page 31 (the metal detector). *Note: the digital book numbering scheme may differ.*

Stage	Page	Jamie's Feelings (You may use the pictures to assist with this task)
Receiving the keychain	Page 3/4	
During the discussion	Page 15/16	
The Waiting	Page 29/30	
The Metal Detector	Page 31/32	

Note: Prison and jail visits can be intimidating to adults and, especially, for young children if they are not prepared. *Jamie's Big Visit* opens the door for dialogue but does not profess to address all the questions that may arise about prison visits. However, this story offers valuable insight to start a discussion with children.

PARENT-CHILD ACTIVITY:

If you are preparing for a prison visit, please consider preparing the child in your planning strategy. Review the exercises and consider how your child might be impacted both positively and negatively. Find ways to think through your unique circumstances.

References

Hart-Johnson, A. & Johnson, G. (2022). Caregivers' family relations assessment and communication strategies. *Science Publishing Group*, 11(5), 157–168. https://www.sciencepublishinggroup.com/article/10.11648/j.pbs.20221105.12.

Answer Key for Activity 64.1

Learners were asked to record in their journal ways that Jamie's parents showed/displayed:

- **Love or family bonds:** Love was apparent between Jamie and his father. Jamie's mom demonstrated love, compassion, empathy, and bonding with Jamie.
- **Support:** Jamie's mom showed support by being a breakfast partner. She helped Jamie to understand prison visits. She also helped Jamie to remain connected with his father.
- **Honesty:** Jamie's mother was honest with Jamie. Jamie's dad was also honest, using age-appropriate language. He was careful not to over-promise such endeavors as when he would be home. Instead he remained hopeful engaging Jamie the idea of keeping in touch using written and phone communication.
- **Guilt:** At some point in the story, everyone probably felt a little guilt.
- **Senses** (sight, hearing, smell, taste, and touch). *Note:* In Jamie's story, senses such as taste and smell (i.e., the smell of breakfast with Dad), touch, and sight (spending time walking, talking, and sitting under the tree) were significant. During Dad's absence, Jamie's mom had to substitute these activities to restore the loss of routine in the household.

Note: In Jamie's story, senses such as taste and smell (i.e., the smell of breakfast with Dad), touch, and sight (spending time walking, talking, and sitting under the tree) were significant. During Dad's absence, Jamie's mom had to substitute these activities to restore the loss of routine in the household.

Answer Key for Activity 64.2

- **Why is the key chain so important to Jamie?** The keychain is a comfort object. It represents the bond between Jamie and his dad.
- **What stands out most about Jamie's mom? Why?** This answer is subject to learner interpretation. However, Jamie's mom is loving and supportive.
- **How would your discussion with your child compare with Jamie's mom?** This answer is subject to learner interpretation.
- **In what ways is the corrections officer an important character in the story?** Why? The corrections officer showed compassion. He also illustrates how to conduct trauma-sensitive responses and engagement with children.

Optional Activities: The answers to the below questions are subject to learner interpretation.

- What other emotions can you identify within the story?
- How does Jamie feel during different stages of the book?
- As a role-play exercise, pretend to be Jamie's mom speaking to Jamie. Explain dad's absence to Jamie.

Note: Talking to young children about prison or jail visits requires sensitivity and it may be challenging. Using Jamie's Big Visit and companion stories as examples, children can prepare for prison visits and anxieties can be alleviated.

Answer Key for Activity | 64.3

There is no answer key for this activity using the Coloring Activity Sheet.

Answer Key for Activity | 64.4

Learners were asked to review the table below, and describe how Jamie was feeling at each stage of the process. The answers are subject to individual interpretation.

Stage	*Page*	*Jamie's Feelings (You may use the pictures to assist with this task)*
Receiving the keychain	Page 3/4	**Hint:** Jamie likely felt valued, cherished and loved.
During the discussion	Page 15/16	**Hint:** During the discussion about incarceration, Jamie may have felt a little nervous followed by relief because he was no longer confused about his dad's well-being.
The Waiting	Page 29/30	Jamie likely felt anxious and stressed during various points of the story, such as waiting in line to go through the metal detectors. He also had to wait to make the visit to the prison. He also had to wait to see his dad on visiting day. Each of these periods may have been coupled with a bit of excitement, stress, and maybe even fear.
The Metal Detector	Page 31/32	Jamie was clearly stressed because he left the key chain in his pockets. He then became relieved when the security guard spoke kindly to him.

Putting It All Together

MODULE FOCUS

- Learn about the research study that undergirds this workbook
- Consider the implications and limitations of the foundational research
- Explore and consider opportunities for policy changes, social justice reform, and dissemination of this work at the macro level

Resources

Appendix A. Caregivers' Family Relations Assessment and Communication Strategies (C-FRACS)

Introduction

Approximately 2.7 million children in the United States have a parent in custody (prison, jail, or detention). One in 5 children with an incarcerated parent is under the age of five. Approximately 40 percent of parents who are incarcerated have a child under 10 years old. When a parent is incarcerated, affected children are not always informed about where the confined parent is. Resultant ambiguity may leave young children confused, thus internalizing the parent's absence as their fault. The non-incarcerated parent or caregiver can play a critical role in communicating with and supporting their affected children. Scholars suggest that creative interventions such as bibliotherapy—stories—can help children identify with their emotions as they work through distress.

While researchers continue to advance the literature on parental incarceration, there is still a limited understanding about how parents or caregivers communicate about this social problem with the affected children. This study addresses this research gap, in part through data collected from eight (8) focus groups and three (3) individual interviews with parents and caregivers (n=22). Data analysis entailed axial, second-order coding, and constant comparison of thematic data. Participatory focus group activities contributed to the initial design of a web-portal digital toolkit (see www.dcprojectconnect.com/publications), case story presentations, resources, and three hardback and digital storybooks for age-appropriate parent-child communication about incarceration.

Section 20.0. C-FRACS

Materials

❖ C-FRACS theoretical model (see Figure A.1)

Section Objectives

☐ To increase the reader's awareness of the impacts of parental incarceration on children
☐ To provide insights regarding the study methodology, sampling, and data analysis
☐ To explore the theoretical model and explain the research study
☐ To share the major themes identified in the research study
☐ To discuss future research opportunities, limitations, and implications

Overview

This workbook was founded upon our primary research with caregivers of children with incarcerated parents. The purpose of our qualitative study, *Caregivers' Family Relations Assessment and Communication Strategies (C-FRACS)*, was to understand parents' and caregivers' communication practices with their children regarding parental incarceration and to determine how they viewed the use of storybooks to help with these discussions.

Foundational Learning: The Theoretical Framework

The study was conducted between October 2018 and December 2019. Using a grounded theory methodology, data collection commenced until theoretical saturation was met (Strauss & Corbin, 1998). Saturation was identified after about the 4th focus group. Emergent questions were identified and added to the initial interview guide. During the second half of the interviews (after theoretical saturation was achieved), we created storybooks based on the identified themes and developed interview questions as a subset of research questions #2 (How, if at all, can storybooks be used to support discussions on parental incarceration?). We then refined the books according to the feedback from the parents. Each of the books was subsequently peer-reviewed by subject matter experts and a child psychologist. The final products were self-published books and a web portal to store digital books and other resources for use by caregivers.

This focus led us to construct two overall research questions:

20.0.1 Research Questions

- Research Question #1*: How do caregivers communicate with children of incarcerated parents about parental incarceration?
- Research Questions #2: How, if at all, can storybooks be used to support discussions on parental incarceration?

We addressed these research questions using an exploratory qualitative research study from which this workbook, our guidebook, and children's books are an outgrowth. Following Institutional Review Board approval, we held eight focus group discussions with 22 caregivers/parents of minor children. The caregivers qualified for the study if their child was under ten years old and had one or more parents who had or were serving time in jail or prison. Approximately 50 percent of children impacted by parental incarceration are in that age group. These are also the critical developmental years where children's environment and family connections influence their emotional, physical, social, and cognitive development.

20.0.2 Theoretical Framework

The theories that underpinned this study were: ambiguous loss (Boss, 1999) and Goffman's (1963) description of stigma. Boss' ambiguous loss theory provides a basis for understanding potential trauma and the emotion parents may identify in their children who may be distressed over the loss, ambiguity, and sudden disappearance of a parent due to incarceration. Goffman advances our understanding of how, if at all, stigma may shape the discussion between parent/caregivers and their children related to parental incarceration.

AMBIGUOUS LOSS

Several theories advance an understanding of how children are affected by parental incarceration. These theories include ambiguous loss, stigma, family systems theory, and maturational theory. *Ambiguous loss*, coined by Pauline Boss (1999), explains that people can be "stuck" in grief because they lack closure. Boss explained that this state of limbo intensifies because of the person's inability to move on. The theory describes two types of ambiguous loss:

- Physically present but psychologically absent
- Psychologically present but physically absent

A person can share the same space yet appear distant and emotionally or cognitively unavailable (physical presence/psychologically absent). An example is a mother preoccupied with worry and who lacks responsiveness to her child. On the other hand, an incarcerated family member may influence the day-to-day conversation, operations, planning, and decision-making, yet live outside the home. This ambiguity brings unsettling feelings. The family may feel tethered to the incarceration and all the conditions of having an incarcerated loved one.

STIGMA

Erving Goffman (1963) indicated that *stigma* is a condition where people are identified as being "less than," "not good enough," "undervalued," and discredited. Examples of stigma include racism, colorism, classism, and other "isms." People with mental health and different abilities (physical impairments) are also at risk for stigma. As mentioned earlier, children and their families may face stigma.

LIMITATIONS

Every research study has its limitations. In this particular study our limitations include a small qualitative sample. While the sample was small, the data was rich and in depth. From the themes and grounded theory framework, we were able to glean content to write journal articles, children's books, a textbook, and this workbook. Additional limitations include having only women who self-identified as female participating in the study. A more representative sample would have been preferred, including other gender identifications. Finally, study could benefit by having a qualitative evaluation of the story's validity and application. We would also like to see the CFRACS grounded theory applied to other similar contexts and findings in this domain of research.

20.0.3 Major Themes

The data from the focus group interviews were robust, rich, and deep. They held many thematic insights, yielding four theoretical constructs included in the mid-level theory, *Caregivers' Family Relations Assessment and Communication Strategies* (C-FRACS):

- Caregivers Assessment of Family Dynamics and Other Support Systems: This is the informal assessment that caregivers conduct to determine the family's well-being and requirements for support.
- Mirrored Emotions between caregiver and child (the official name is *dichotomous emotions*). This theme represents the mirrored emotions experienced between caregiver and children. In other words, if the caregiver was sad, we also found through caregiver reflections that their child was sad, too.
- Gatekeeper Communication Protocol. The caregivers were the communication brokers, deciding when, how, and if the child would communicate with their incarcerated parents. This theme also describes how caregivers shared information about the incarcerated parents with children and others.
- Communication Strategies: The communication strategies entail four main methods: direct, indirect, abstain, and reflections. *See Appendix C for list and an explanation of the theoretical model.*

20.0.4 Other Theories

FAMILY SYSTEMS THEORY

Murray Bowen developed *family systems theory*. This theory illuminates how the incarceration of a family member may impact the entire family system. Bowen indicated that families have interrelated emotional processes.

MATURATIONAL THEORY

Maturational theory conveys that biological systems are responsible for child development. Genetics and biology work together during child development. The benchmarks for development convey general guidance for expected milestone advancement per age group and may serve as indicators of well-being (Gesell & Ilg, 1949).

GESTALT PARENT COACHING MODEL

Melnick (2014) discussed *Gestalt Parent Coaching* (GPC) as a means of "assisting parents to become aware of their patterns and interactional patterns between family members. The coach heightens awareness of family relationships and incorporates this information into coaching sessions" (p.136). Trust and self-awareness are essential characteristics of this coaching model that support the parent's success. The core elements of GPC that pertain to this program include (Melnick, 2014):

- ° Identifying personal strengths aligned with parenting style;
- ° Embracing one's value system;
- ° Advocating in the best interest of the child(ren); and
- ° Establishing stable, safe, predictable, routine parenting and clarifying roles within the family system.

In the process of "finding a silver lining when a parent goes to prison or jail," as our books suggest,[1] our strategy helps confined individuals and caregivers find ways to apply self-empowerment strategies.

Taking care of children can be a phenomenal responsibility. In our research, we identified grandparents, aunts, cousins, mothers, and others (such as fictive kin), who cared for children of incarcerated parents. In some cases, the parents themselves felt they were not emotionally mature to meet the demands and expectations of parenting and communicating with the children.

Our research found that bibliotherapeutic resources, i.e., storybooks used as creative interventions, can assist parent-child communication.

Using a Strength-Based Focus

This workbook considers strength-based approaches, which entail treating all people with unconditional high regard (Rogers, 1978). Ultimately, we desire to ensure that children have positive, healthy, and structured engagement with their caregivers and parents. Therefore, a strength-based focus offers facilitators and steering participants' children to view themselves through a positive lens.

Glossary

Bibliotherapy: The use of reading material or other media to help with problem-solving, promote emotional healing, build self-awareness, and enhance personal well-being.

Carceral System: The network of systems under the auspices of the penal system, including prisons, jails, detention centers, training camps, and other places of confinement used by law enforcement to detain people.

Caregivers: In this text, caregivers are considered parents, guardians of children, fictive kin, and others caring for the child while the parent is justice aligned.

Children: We generally refer to children in this text as any youngster under the age of 18. However, this book is for caregivers with children at the age of ten and younger. Note: children of any age and even adults may use the material for discussions to increase their understanding of life concepts and principles (and to understand grief, separation, and loss)

Facilitators: A person who leads the training and manages the group exercises.

Incarcerated: Refers to the status of being presently held in a prison or other correctional institution. It does not claim guilt or innocence (contrary to words like "convict"), nor does it attach a permanent identity to an often-temporary status (like "prisoner," etc.).

Interventions: Targeted and non-clinical processes and training designed to enhance the well-being of children and their caregivers/parents.

Justice-Aligned: Having had the experience of incarceration, detention, arrest, or confinement in the corrections/carceral system.

System Aligned/Impacted: Having had contact with the justice system or those who have incarcerated loved ones.

Source: Glossary Terms adopted from Underground Scholars Initiative, UC Berkeley, 2400C Bancroft Way, Berkeley CA 94704. Language Guide for Communications About Those Involved in the Carceral System.

C-FRACS

Theoretical Model: C-FRACS

Note: The theoretical model is annotated using alpha-numeric references. For example, [A] represents the process, "Caregivers Assessment of Family Dynamics and Other Support Systems."

In the research study titled Caregivers' Family Relations Assessment and Communication Strategies, Hart-Johnson & Johnson (2022) the research question was posed: How do caregivers communicate with children of incarcerated parents? The data revealed that before children were informed of their incarcerated parent's status and related information, the caregivers first assessed the well-being of the children as illustrated in process [A]. Through this informal analysis, caregivers sought to better understand the health and fitness for children to hear potentially emotional and sensitive topics related to the parents. If a child is physically unwell, it is likely that hearing news about the parent would exacerbate the child's condition. Additionally, the process of family assessment aims to understand how the family is faring to better support the children and themselves. Item [A] is also connected to [a.1] role clarity and [a.2] role ambiguity. When the families experienced an incarceration crisis, they sometimes indicated that there were clear roles developing. For example, mothers may need to find another source of income to make up for the loss of financial resources from the primary breadwinner who is no longer in the home. Children may have clearly defined roles of helping out with household functions and caring for siblings. However, [a.2] represents potential role ambiguity where the family is a bit disorganized in their roles. The confusion around the incarceration status, not knowing who is in or out of the family because of the uncertainty of pending court cases, sentencing, or even the confusion in who is managing what chores in the home represents ambiguity. In some cases, [a.2] represents parentification.

Dichotomous Emotions (mirrored emotions):

Item [B] is related to the assessment and has two sub-components. First, dichotomous or mirrored emotions suggest that caregivers and their children experienced similar reactions to the parental incarceration. For example, the caregiver may have grieved the loss of the incarcerated spouse, while her children felt the same. This assessment extended to self-awareness of personal feelings as well as attunement of the child's feelings. Item [b.1.1] indicated that when caregivers were emotionally ambivalent, it is likely that they were not going to be forthcoming in talking with the incarceration with the child. It may have been because of feeling ill-prepared or unwilling for any given reason(s). Our

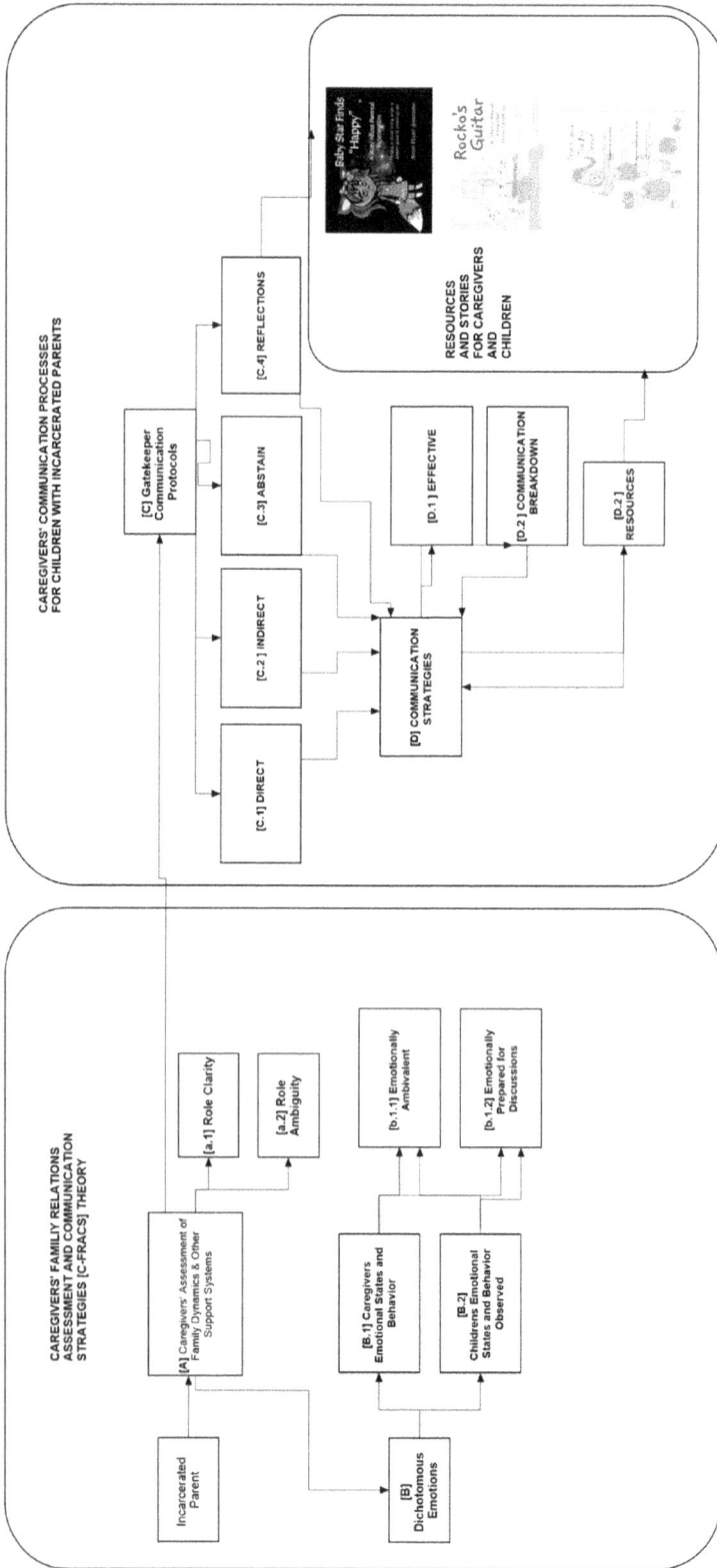

Figure A.1. CFRACS' Theoretical Model.

research participants indicated that their primary goal was to help children cope with possible grief and loss while also managing other conditions related to the parental incarceration. Therefore, they were hesitant at times to further burden the children with the information about their parents. Item [b.1.2] represents parents who felt emotionally prepared to hold a discussion. They were forthcoming and direct with their children.

Gatekeeper Communication Protocols

The second component of the C-FRACS model represents the connection between assessment and communication strategy. The strategy is not static; it is dynamic and may change, depending on the circumstances around the family system. However, this part of the model answers the research question about how caregivers communicate.

The majority of caregivers (i.e., biological parents, aunts, grandmothers, or any guardian of the children) conveyed that they believed that they understood the children's emotions and well-being better than anyone else. Our research revealed that this informal assessment resulted in mostly four outcomes: (c.1) being direct by telling the child the truth; (c.2) being indirect by providing the child partial truths, or (c.3) not sharing information about the parent at all abstain and (c.4) reflection. Direct communication is considered straightforward, direct, clear, and age-appropriate communication. Indirect communication involves passive communication, false narratives, made-up information or mistruths shared with children about their parents (e.g., the parent is in the military, school, hospital instead of jail or prison). Some caregivers decided not to say anything at all, leaving the children to wonder where their parents were (abstention). Finally, many of the caregivers reflected upon their decisions and indicated that if they could do it all over again, they would have used age-appropriate language and told the child(ren) the truth. The informal assessment also appeared to help the caregiver discern if the child was at risk for retraumatized experiences.

Communication Strategies

The final part of the model shows a linkage between communication strategies [D] and their outcomes and a linkage to the bibliotherapeutic resources. In some cases, caregivers believed the communication protocols to be [d.1] effective, meaning the discussion with the child contributed to their overall well-being. In other cases, they admitted that lying or half-truths could and did result in [d.2] communication breakdown. Finally, all of the participants believed that storybooks ([d.3] resources) using bibliotherapy could help to explain parental incarceration, thus addressing Research Question #2.

In all instances, the caregivers' goal was to protect the child against further anticipated stressors, distress, and emotional harm. Caregivers suggested that parental incarceration may disrupt and cause shifts in the family's equilibrium. For example, 4 out of 22 (18%) caregivers/participants indicated that their children changed residence, transferred to different schools, and some integrated into a relative's household, thus disrupting the child's routines.

Participants believed that resources were welcomed (and needed) and that storybooks could be useful to impart sensitive information to children.

Do's and Don'ts of Grief

Children of incarcerated parents may grieve the loss of a parent, no matter how young or old they are.[1] Expressions of grief likely will vary according to their development and maturity. While many researchers suggest that the children are at risk for adverse outcomes when placed in environments fraught with risk, protective measures such as secure attachments, predictability and close familial bonds can mitigate the chances of children developing maladaptive behaviors.

Reading is a wonderful way to connect with children. According to some scholars, books can be used as a communication aid between caregivers and their children to discuss the absence of the incarcerated parent (Nutbrown et al., 2019). In addition to reading to these little ones, consider the resources on https://www.dcprojectconnect.com/publications. Please also consider these Do's and Don'ts as they are applicable to your child, and based on your judgment:

Do's

- If you see signs of withdrawal, distress, deep mourning, or a change in sleeping, eating, and other odd habits in the child, consider seeking professional help.
- Being close by or in the same room might assist with bonding if you are a caregiver and have not established a rapport, built trust, and had a chance to create a secure environment with the child before the incarceration of the parent.
- If the child is old enough to ask you about their parents, as a response, give them age-appropriate information, perhaps: "Mommy/Daddy is not here right now. I am taking care of you until he/she returns. We will speak to Mommy/Daddy by phone soon."
- Help the child return to routine and predictability. For example, pre-school/school activities, walks at the park, reading to the child, and watching children's television shows are activities that you can engage in together to promote bonding.
- If the child is old enough, tell him/her that the incarceration of the parent is not their fault.

Don'ts

- Do not lie or make up information to explain where the absent parent is. This may be devastating if the child finds out differently (see *Truth and The Big Dinner*, by Dr. Renata Hedrington Jones; *Rocko's Guitar*, by Dr. Geoffrey Johnson, and *Baby Star Finds "Happy,"* by Dr. Avon Hart-Johnson).

- Do not talk negatively about the incarcerated parent in front of the child. This can result in conflict and mistrust and be a source of distress for the child.
- Do not allow the child to wonder about the absence and loss of a parent without explanation. Abstention from addressing concerns can be for a child a source of ambiguity and stress. Use age-appropriate words to explain the parent's status. You do not have to explain the crime. If the child has been harmed by the absent incarcerated parent, please consider seeking professional advice.

APPENDIX C

Communication

C-FRACS | Communication Styles

Communication protocol (style)	Description	Possible outcomes
Direct	Parents/Caregivers with this communication style provide children the truth about the incarceration without having to reveal details about the crime, itself. They state the truth clearly and, in an age-appropriate manner. They advocate for their rights as parents and recognize their role in the family. Caregivers recognize their own emotions and understand the power of projecting their emotions on their children. They are respectful of themselves and others.	• They prioritize their communication, noting transparent, respectful, and appropriate thoughts and the needs of children and their families. • They take ownership of their feelings, using "I" words • They listen to family, children, and others • They make good eye contact, feel in control of themselves even if they cannot control their environments or all situations. • They speak in a clear tone, not shouting or whining • They feel a connection to their children and support systems • They seek outside resources when needed
Indirect	Parents/Caregivers with this tendency have developed a pattern of avoiding tough topics such as parental incarceration. These individuals may believe that telling a lie is better than the consequences or impact of the truth. They may feel overly protective of the child. They may believe the truth will hurt. Discussions about incarceration may be avoided and fabricated. Children may be told partial truths.	• Their feelings and rights as parents are felt to be insignificant (feeling hopeless/helpless) • Use partial truth to discuss difficult situations • Fail to communicate because life seems out of their control • Feel resentful towards others (angry) • Feelings are put on the back burner because of parental incarceration • Do not always speak up for themselves • Speak softly or apologetically • Examples: • "People don't care about me ... they have forgotten all about me."

Communication protocol (style)	Description	Possible outcomes
Abstain (not discussing)	Parents/Caregivers with this communication style and tendency may have any of the following behaviors regarding parental incarceration: Abstain from discussing matters about incarceration—pretending that it will simply go away. Rather than speak directly, they mutter to themselves, complain, and use sarcasm They act as though they agree with plans, yet they work to sabotage the efforts through ways that may not be obvious.	• Withdraw from the conversation and social contact with others • "Feels sorry for oneself, claiming I am weak and powerless." • Think that they appear open and agreeable when they are not • Remain stuck, choosing to avoid steps of empowerment • Complain about the incarcerated parent or the non-incarcerated caregivers behind their backs rather than talking it out
Reflection (looking back)	Parents/Caregivers with this communication style and tendency spend time thinking about past practices and conversations and ponder their meaning. These caregivers figure out what went right and what they could do better when discussing parental incarceration with children. They might express concerns but try not to beat themselves up over events and prior discussions. These caregivers seek ways to communicate better. They know that sometimes "burned bridges" can take a long time to rebuild.	• These individuals reach out to support and use tools to help them rebuild their confidence and lives. They reflect how to: • Listen, develop confidence, and understanding age-appropriate language takes time and work. • Spend time developing emotional, spiritual, and family bonds. • Look for programs to support the goals of becoming better support for the family. • Recognize that difficult discussions may need to be well-paced and reflect the maturity/age of the child • Practice showing empathy, listening, and prioritizing other's needs, rather than placing themselves first (for example, inquiries about a child's well-being and progress are of genuine interest). • Find ways to gain the support of family members who advocate for the best interest of the child(ren). • Understand that there are possible "re-do's" and that forgiveness begins with self, first.

Coloring Activity

Ask your child to draw a picture of themselves standing outside the home. How does she/he feel? What will they do once inside? What are their biggest wishes related to their home and family? Use this drawing/ coloring activity as a means of holding a discussion with children, seeking to better understand how they feel about the home setting and family life. You can create your own picture scenario as well.

Helping Children Deal with Loss

Ideas to help children deal with a parent's absence from significant events or milestones, e.g., missed birthdays, kindergarten graduation.

The absence of a parent because of incarceration can be distressing to children. These little ones may face many insecurities along with feelings of separation and abandonment.[1] The incarceration of a family member can be upsetting for the entire household. At times, young children who are vulnerable to experiencing their own complex emotions may be the least informed. The crisis and emotional upheaval that a parent experiences may result in the nonincarcerated parent and caregiver becoming emotionally distraught. The caregiver may be limited in their response to children due to their own distress.

Moreover, the caregiver may lack or have inadequate tools to discuss this sensitive topic. Activity sheets around the discussion of parental incarceration may help. Check out our website and books for a variety of topical material.

For this activity, we explain how creating a time capsule for children who are age 10 and younger may serve as a means to maintain bonds with the absent parent. This is especially important if the child cannot visit the prison to see the parent. This time capsule can be used as a collection of keepsakes that represent significant milestones occurring in the child's life while the parent is incarcerated.

- **Objective:** Use symbolism, keepsakes, and/or journal as a method of maintaining bonds and creating lasting memories between child and parent.
- **Participants:** Caregivers, siblings, teachers, and others can help provide children with materials and ideas. As the child matures, they may discover their own items to retain in the capsule.
- **Materials:** Be sure that the child selects items that are non-perishable and are not dangerous. Also, it is wise to offer the child guidance on what items to store in the box/time capsule. For example, non-flammable and safe items are best. Use your discretion to guide the child.

Steps

Step 1: Select a durable box, plastic container, or chest/basket with a top that can be used to store items as a time capsule. Encourage the child to name the time capsule (e.g., Daddy's time capsule).

Step 2: Encourage the child to fill the time capsule over periods of time by placing keepsakes, drawings, letters, and symbolic objects like a glove, hat,

or something that reminds the child of the absent parent. Mementos such
as key chains, a parent's jewelry, a favorite item like a scarf, or other items of
significance may also be a great idea to place in the container. An old phone
filled with photos or pictures are ideas that might work as well.

Step 3: Maintaining the time capsule is a matter of preference. Milestone dates are
a great time to carry out the ritual of placing an item of significance in the time
capsule. Other occasions may be graduations, birthdays, and other significant
days when the absent parent cannot be present, yet symbolically are thought of.

Step 4: Retaining or gifting the time capsule. Whether the child decides to
retain the memory box or give it to the parent when they return from prison
is up to them. The ideas behind the time capsule are explained below in the
"discussion" section.

Discussion

Children's sense of time is different from that experienced by adults. A time capsule
can be used as a keepsake that represents a timeline of significant and meaningful memories that occur over the time of a parent's incarceration. The symbolism of the significant bonds between the parent and the child is represented by the added content, over
time. This container can also be used to store items that the child wishes they could give
to the incarcerated parent, but the prison/jail does not permit items to be delivered to
the facility. The child can use these items as a point of discussion when she/he speaks to
the dad/mom on the phone or via letter. This ritual may be a means of coping with difficult holidays when the children cannot be with the parent—for example, a ritual of creating an ornament, dated with the year.

Storage

Store the time capsule in a place for safekeeping. Items can be added to the capsule
as time goes on. For example, significant milestones such as a kindergarten diploma can
be placed as a scroll in the container. An undelivered letter, coloring book page, favorite
picture, or other items can also be placed in this keepsake container.

Caregiver Resources

Caregivers' Resources (Self-Care)

The following is a list of resources for self-care, mindfulness, and meditation.

Online Breathing Exercises: Breathe Remix: Free breathing exercise application (app). E-mail sign-up required. "Open": https://o-p-e-n.com/breathe

Relationship Mindfulness: Focuses on strategies to build healthy relationships. https://www.mindful.org/how-to-be-mindful-in-love

Caregiving Mindfulness Education Course: Training for all caregivers. Provides free resources for emotional well-being, informs caregivers about secondary trauma and other unique challenges of caregiving and dealing with loss. https://zencaregiving.org/mindful-caregiving-education-explained

Parent Training and Support Groups: The Family Tree provides trauma-informed practices and interventions. They support parents of children 0 to 18 years old, with a focus on issues related to mental health, violence, substance abuse, domestic violence, and justice aligned issues that children face. https://familytreemd.org/programs/parenting-education

Mindfulness: Mayo Clinic. (2020). Mindfulness exercises. Retrieved from https://www.mayoclinic.org/healthy-lifestyle/consumer-health/in-depth/-mindfulness-exercises/art-20046356

Additional Resources

Emotional Intelligence: https://www.psychologytoday.com/us/basics/emotional-intelligence https://www.mindfulnessmuse.com/emotional-intelligence/anger-inoculation-in-4-steps.

Moving Beyond Anger: https://www.nytimes.com/2002/11/12/health/behavior-beyond-anger-studying-the-subconscious-nature-of-rage.html.

Reducing Anger: https://www.psychologytoday.com/us/blog/urban-survival/201602/new-study-shows-brief-meditation-can-reduce-anger.

Saying I'm Sorry: https://www.healthline.com/health/why-am-i-so-angry

Understanding the Evolution of Self: https://www.psychologytoday.com/us/blog/evolution-the-self/201401/the-anger-thermostat-whats-the-temperature-your-upset.

Getting Support: What to Expect

Privacy, confidentiality, and informed consent: Support organizations must protect confidentiality and offer privacy when discussing client information. Confidentiality is a legal right. Safeguarding an individual's personal information is fundamental and should abide by the codes of conduct as per their professional credentials (e.g., the Ethical Standards for Human Services Professionals) National Organization for Human Services (n.d.). Informed consent entails a person's right to understand the risks, benefits, and details of services and treatment before agreeing to receive the procedure, medications, or therapy.

Participation in planning: Individuals have the right to contribute their insights and options toward their well-being. This means they bring their history and symptoms or needs, and the supporting personnel then proposes a matched set of resources to meet those needs. The methods are not prescriptive but rather collaborative.

Needs assessment: The process of understanding client /constituent history, their unique situations and requirements for restoration of personal well-being is captured in a needs assessment. This is generally a questionnaire about: physical health, mental health, housing and shelter, financial wherewithal, relationships and support, and individualized service planning.

Right to self-determination: Every individual has the right to free choice without coercion or interference. Fundamental to any service provider relationship is the notion that people can engage in their own treatment planning. They can make decisions that align with their personal goals. They can problem-solve with guidance without being directed by a professional, toward what is best for them and their children. They can refuse treatment, therapy, participation, and consent. Helping professionals may offer recommendations and referrals, especially for the impaired or those who cannot choose for themselves.

Chapter Notes

Module 17

1. Morton, J.B., & Williams, D. M. (1998). Mother/child bonding: Incarcerated women struggle to maintain meaningful relationships with their children. *Corrections Today, 7,* 98.
2. Morgan-Mullane, A. (2017). Trauma-focused cognitive behavioral therapy with children of incarcerated parents. *Clinical Social Work Journal, 46*(3), 200–209.

Module 18

1. Morton, J.B., & Williams, D. M. (1998). Mother/child bonding: Incarcerated women struggle to maintain meaningful relationships with their children. *Corrections Today, 7,* 98.
2. Travis, J., McBride, E., & Solomon, A. (2005). *Families left behind: The hidden costs of incarceration and reentry.* Urban Institute Justice Policy Center.

Module 20

1. See *Baby Star Finds "Happy," Truth and the Big Dinner, Rocko's Guitar,* and *Jamie's Big Visit.*

Appendix B

1. Kids Health. (2005–2019). The Paediatric Society of New Zealand and Starship Foundation 2005–2019. Retrieved from https://www.kidshealth.org.nz/bereavement-reactions-age-group.

Appendix E

1. Morgan-Mullane, A. (2017). Trauma-focused cognitive behavioral therapy with children of incarcerated parents. *Clinical Social Work Journal, 46*(3), 200–209.

References

Anderson, J.E., Kay, A.C., & Fitzsimons, G.M. (2013). Finding silver linings: Meaning making as a compensatory response to negative experiences. In K.D. Markman, T. Proulx, & M.J. Lindberg (Eds.), The psychology of meaning (pp. 279–295). American Psychological Association. https://doi.org/10.1037/14040-014.

Arden, J.B. (2010). Rewire your brain: Think your way to a better life. John Wiley & Sons.

Bailey, B.A. (2021). Conscious discipline: Building resilient classrooms. Oviedo, FL: Loving Guidance.

Briere, J. (1996). Trauma Symptom Checklist for Children (TSCC), Professional Manual. Odessa, FL: Psychological Assessment Resources. Retrieved from http://www4.parinc.com.

Butkowsky, I.S., & Willows, D.M. (1980). Cognitive-motivational characteristics of children varying in reading ability: Evidence for learned helplessness in poor reader. Journal of Education Psychology, 72(3):408–422. doi:10.1037/0022-0663.72.3.408

Center on the Developing Child at Harvard University. (2011). Experiences build the brain. https://www.developingchild.harvard.edu.

Center on the Developing Child at Harvard University. (2015). The science of resilience. (InBrief). www.developingchild.hardvard.edu.

Center on the Developing Child at Harvard University. (2019). Early learning nation. http://earlylearningnation.com/2019/08/the-consequences-of-forced-separation/.

Centers for Disease Control and Prevention. (2021). Risk and Protective Factors| Violence Prevention| Injury Center. Retrieved fromhttps://www.cdc.gov/violenceprevention/youthviolence/riskprotectivefactors.html.

Felitti, V.J., Anda, R.F., Nordenberg, D., et al. (1998). Relationship of childhood abuse and household dysfunction to many of the leading causes of death in adults: the Adverse Childhood Experiences (ACE) Study. American Journal of Preventive Medicine, 14(4): 245–258.

Hart-Johnson, A., Johnson, G., & Hedrington-Jones, R. (2022). "Mommy, I want to talk to my dad": Exploring parental incarceration, bibliotherapy, and storybooks. Open Journal of Social Sciences, 10(11), 391–418.

Hooyman, N.R., & Kramer, B.J. (2006). Living through loss: Interventions across the life span. New York: Columbia University Press.

Mayo Clinic. (2020). Mindfulness exercises. Retrieved from https://www.mayoclinic.org/healthy-lifestyle/consumer-health/in-depth/mindfulness-exercises/art-20046356.

National Organization for Human Services (n.d.) Ethical Standards for Human Services Professionals. https://www.nationalhumanservices.org/.

Nieman, P., & Shea, S. (2004). Effective discipline for children. Pediatrics & Child Health, 9(1), 37–50. Doi. 10.1093/pch/9.1.37.

Palmer, T. (n.d.). Handling the arrest of a family member: Before and after incarceration. https://www.fateh.net/handling-the-arrest-of-a-family-member-before-and-after-incarceration.

Recovery View. (n.d.). https://recoveryview.com/article/empowerment-through-vulnerability/#:~:text=Vulnerability%20is%20a%20human%20trait,to%20receiving%20a%20spiritual%20awakening.

Robert Yuhas & Stuart Goldman Productions (Producers), & Robert Yuhas (Director). (2021). Barack Obama: Finding hope (director's cut). [Video/DVD] Vision Films. Retrieved from https://video.alexanderstreet.com/watch/barack-obama-finding-hope-director-s-cut.

Shocklye, L. (2019). The consequences of forced separation. When traumatized children return to traumatized parents. https://developingchild.harvard.edu/media-coverage/the-consequences-of-forced-separation-when-traumatized-children-return-to-traumatized-parents/.

Strategies for Youth. (n.d.). Our Publications. https://strategiesforyouth.org/our-publications/.

Index

www.ingramcontent.com/pod-product-compliance
Lightning Source LLC
Chambersburg PA
CBHW050836300326
41935CB00043B/1760